INTRODUCTION TO TELEVISION PRODUCTION

KEN FIELDING

ARIZONA STATE UNIVERSITY

Longman
New York & London

Introduction to Television Production

Longman, 95 Church Street, White Plains, N.Y. 10601

Associated companies:
Longman Group Ltd., London
Longman Cheshire Pty., Melbourne
Longman Paul Pty., Auckland
Copp Clark Pitman, Toronto

Executive editor: Gordon T. R. Anderson
Development editor: Elsa van Bergen, assisted by Jeffrey L. Campbell
Production editor: Ann P. Kearns
Cover design: Kevin C. Kall
Text art: Susan J. Moore, K & S Graphics
Production supervisor: Kathleen M. Ryan

Library of Congress Cataloging-in-Publication Data

Fielding, Ken.
    Introduction to television production / by Ken Fielding.
        p.   cm.
    Includes bibliographical references.
    ISBN 0-8013-0313-3
    1. Television—Production and direction.   I. Title.
PN1992.75F5   1990
791.45′0232—dc20   89-36619
                                              CIP

ABCDEFGHIJ—DO—99 98 97 96 95 94 93 92 91 90

Contents

Preface   *vii*

Chapter 1   The Production Machine   1

The Television System • *Development of Television Production* • *The Power*   3
of Television • *Television's Limitations* • *How the System Works*

Categories of Television Production • *Where Production Takes Place* • *How Television*   7
Is Distributed • *Production Method*

The Television Production Process • *Production People* • *Production Tools* • *Using the*   11
Tools of Television Production • *Television Is a Team Activity*

Controlling the Production Machine   16

Summary   17

Review Questions   18

PART ONE   TOOLS AND TECHNIQUES OF TELEVISION PRODUCTION   19

Chapter 2   Video Cameras   21

What the Camera Does • *Light to Electricity to Light* • *System Limitations* •   21
Other Limitations

How the Video Camera Works • *Optical System* • *The Image Sensor* • *The Viewfinder* •   25
Auxiliary Equipment and Systems

How to Operate the Video Camera • *Camera Operator's Responsibilities* • *The Role of*   43
the Camera Operator

How to Use a Video Camera • *Camera Perspectives* • *Basic Shots* • *Moving Shots* •   53
Composition

Telling the Story with Pictures • *On Assignment*   66

Summary   69

Review Questions   70

Chapter 3   Lighting and Settings   71

Functions of Lighting • *Illumination* • *Illusion of Depth* • *Mood or Setting*   72

Properties of Light • *Quantity* • *Quality* • *Direction*   75

Sources of Light • *Natural Light Sources* • *Artificial Light Sources*   85

Television Lighting Equipment • *Components of Television Lights* • *Types of Television*   87
Lighting Equipment • *Typical Studio Lighting Instruments*

Procedures and Precautions • *Electrical Safety* • *Heat* • *Falls*   91

Lighting Techniques • *Three-Point Lighting* • *Supplemental Lighting*   93

On Assignment   97

Settings • *Functions of a Setting* • *Types of Settings* • *Selecting a Setting*   101

Summary   104

Review Questions   105

Chapter 4   Microphones   106

Sound in a Visual Medium • *Sound to Electricity to Sound* • *System Limitations* •   107
Attitudes • *Separation and Synchronization*

The Sound Gathering System • *Sound Control* • *Sound Gathering* • *Signal*   108
Processing • *Monitoring System*

How to Gather Sound • *Criteria for Selecting Microphones* • *Microphone Placement* •   119
Microphone Cables and Connectors • *Adjusting Audio Levels*

Using Natural Sounds   123

Summary   124

Review Questions   124

Chapter 5   Generators   126

Television Graphics • *The Role of Graphics in Television Production* • *Historical*   128
Perspective • *What Graphics Do* • *Graphics Generators* • *Considerations in*
Creating Graphics

Advanced Video Generator Systems   135

Audio Generators/Synthesizers   136

Monitoring Systems • *Types of Monitoring Systems*   136

Test Signals • *Calibration of the System*   137

Summary   142

Review Questions   143

Chapter 6   Storage and Retrieval Systems   144

Historical Perspective • *Magnetic Recording and Playback* • *Development of Videotape*   144

Using Storage and Retrieval Systems • *Functions of Storage and Retrieval Systems*   146

The Magnetic Recording and Playback Process • *Magnetic Recording and*   148
Playback Equipment • *Storage Process* • *Retrieval Process* • *Operating Modes*
and Procedures

Storage and Retrieval Equipment: Operating Characteristics • *Audio* • *Video* •   156
Operating Principles • *Film and Slides*

On Assignment   161

Summary   163

Review Questions   164

Chapter 7   Mixing, Switching, and Editing   165

The Function of Mixing, Switching, and Editing   166

Mixing • *Components of the Audio Console/Mixer* • *On Assignment* • *Specific*   166
Functions • *Operating the Audio Mixer*

Switching • *Components of the Video Switcher* • *Methods and Procedures* • *Specific* 175
Functions

Editing • *Components of the Videotape Editing System* • *Advanced Systems* • *Methods*   189
and Procedures • *Using the Editing System*

Summary   199

Review Questions   200

PART TWO   PROGRAM ASSEMBLY PROCEDURES   203

Chapter 8   Field and Postproduction   205

The Process • *Systems to Be Used* • *Personnel*   206

On Assignment • *Preproduction* • *Collecting the Tools* • *Location Set-up* •   207
Production • *Postproduction*

Summary   217

Review Questions   218

Chapter 9   Studio Production   219

The Process • *The System* • *Personnel*   219

On Assignment • *Timing Methods* • *Discussion of Procedures*   221

Summary   235

Review Questions   236

PART THREE   PUTTING THE MACHINE TO WORK   **237**

Chapter 10   Production Planning and Producing   239

The Role of the Producer   239

The Process • *Research and Planning* • *Preliminary Questions to Be Answered* •   240
Preparation • *Execution* • *Evaluation*

Summary   251

Review Questions   252

Chapter 11   Directing and Editing   253

The Selection Process • *The Role of the Director or Editor*   253

Directing • *Types of Directing* • *Directing Procedures*   258

Editing • *Editing Procedures* • *Decision Making*   268

Summary   272

Review Questions   273

Chapter 12   Program Evaluation   274

The Elements of Evaluation • *Sources of Feedback* • *Trust Your Instincts* • *Watch the* 275
Work of Others

Some Steps to Getting Better • *Analyze Results* • *Practice Skills* • *Give Yourself a*   277
Second Chance • *Learn the Terminology of Production* • *Experiment* •
Listen and Observe

A Professional Attitude   279

Review Questions   280

Glossary   *281*

Bibliography   *303*

Index   *305*

Preface

Television production has changed dramatically in the last quarter century. Once the domain of broadcast stations and networks, production techniques are now used also in corporate communications, education, health care, and community activities. With two-thirds of the homes in the United States having at least one videocassette recorder (VCR), home video camcorders and editing systems are selling briskly. Production has reached the consumer.

As television production has entered into various areas of society, a number of new texts have been offered for what might be termed the "do-it-yourself" market. These books tend to be very detailed, using a nuts-and-bolts approach to how to work the equipment; many of them never get much beyond the hardware aspects of the production process.

In the colleges and universities that teach television production, the approaches and textbooks still often reflect the techniques of the 1960s, with emphasis on the broadcast station/studio production model or an outdated focus on specific tools of the trade.

The nature of production has changed as markedly as its applications. No longer confined to studios and huge remote television vans, production is now done primarily in the field; single-camera techniques are often the norm, with final assembly of finished tapes accomplished in computerized editing and postproduction facilities. Graphics for these productions, once the product of art departments, are now done primarily with computerized character generators and paintbox systems.

The time is right for a new book. Many schools recognize that there is a significant oversupply of production people for the professional positions available. Curricula are changing, deemphasizing a full-blown production syllabus while at the same time recognizing that a basic understanding of the production process is essential for graduates who may earn degrees in such related areas as journalism, management and sales, advertising and public relations, or instructional media. An introductory production class will continue to be a part of the core curriculum in many institutions that recognize the broad need for such basic understanding.

This book is intended for use in such a course. It takes a professional approach to production; includes both studio and field/postproduction; and introduces the basics and provides a firm foundation for those who will never take another television production class as well as for those who will go on to pursue a career in production.

Many students take the introductory television production course because it is required. Although they may later develop an interest in further production courses, texts that provide great detail and technical information can be overwhelming. This book should be understandable for everyone. Some theory is presented, but the approach is primarily a practical one. The bibliography provides some suggestions for further reading for those students interested in production specialization. For students who go no further, it should provide a handy reference when their chosen specialty brings them into the production setting once again.

Each chapter offers the vocabulary of television production, with both an extensive glossary and on-page marginal highlights reinforcing key terms and concepts. In contrast to some earlier texts, this text recognizes the fact that terminology and equipment differ from facility to facility and project to project.

Because of budget constraints, most schools share the problem of being unable to keep pace with the endless stream of new and improved tools. This book takes that into account and deals with the basic equipment in a way that applies to a broad spectrum of cameras, microphones, and other hardware manufactured over the past 15 or 20 years.

For example, most field cameras require periodic white balancing (to assure that colors are properly rendered under the given lighting conditions). This text deals with the *reason* for white balancing and its *effect,* while leaving the specifics about which button to push to the individual instructor. There are few pictures in this book that were supplied by equipment manufacturers. Much equipment in use today will be outdated soon; few students will see any of it unless they enter the industry immediately upon graduation. Readers will, however, find generous illustrations of what the equipment does and how it is used.

The book assumes that the material presented will be amplified and augmented with production laboratory work and lecture-discussion. The chapters could be assigned in different sequences to fit most any introductory course outline. Fundamental concepts in this text should provide a good starting point for in-class discussion and demonstration. The concepts and techniques presented will be most fully understood, of course, if they are put to use in carefully supervised beginning production assignments.

One of the top priorities in production classes is to offer the students a hands-on experience as soon as possible. Students are naturally excited about operating the equipment; the sooner that process can begin, the sooner the course can move on to the more important area of using the equipment for identified purposes. The complexity of much of the equipment and the procedures needed to use it mean that a lot of information must be assimilated to reach a threshold at which hands-on use can begin. The material is organized with the intention of facilitating that process.

The structure of this text should provide a convenient and flexible base upon which to develop a course outline. Rather than requiring the basic material to be delivered through lecture, it allows the instructor to *expand* upon the material and to enhance the acquisition of knowledge through personal experience tailored specifically to the facilities and projects of the course setting.

Throughout the book, emphasis is placed on the use of TV production tools and processes *as a means to an end,* not as an end in themselves. While this book is primarily intended to introduce college students to television production and the hardware associated with it, it makes a clear distinction between "operating" equipment and "using" equipment. Anyone involved in production must understand the operational aspect. But until clear goals are defined and careful planning applied to a project, the operation of production facilities is little more than idle entertainment, similar to pinball machines or video games. The later chapters introduce the basic concepts of production planning, producing, directing, and editing.

The critical nature of internal communication among the members of a production team is thoroughly explored. Personal experience has demonstrated time and again how ineffective some people in the communications business are at communicating with one another. There is repeated reference to the team concept of production in this book. While single-camera production has increased the opportunity for individuals to have greater control of the production process, it still is true that most productions require the efforts and cooperation of several people. To that end, it is essential that production students understand from the outset that coordination and direction of the efforts of others is an integral part of the television production machine. That concept is a thread that runs throughout the chapters.

ACKNOWLEDGMENTS

Many people helped with the development of this book. I would like to extend my appreciation to all named below specifically. But I would also like to thank all of my former co-workers and students who shared their skills and ideas with me during the past 24 years. Experience certainly is the best teacher in the television production field, and I have been fortunate to share that experience with many highly talented and dedicated people.

Two people deserve special thanks for the encouragement to initiate this project and their support during its development: Gordon T.R. Anderson, executive editor at Longman, and Dr. Douglas Anderson, director of the Walter Cronkite School of Journalism and Telecommunication at Arizona State University.

Numerous people participated in the production of this book. My thanks to Professor Frank Hoy and Nick Van Nice for their help with the photography, to Marian Buckley and Keith Campbell for their work on the manuscript, and especially to Jim Dove for all his help in the production laboratory.

Thanks to Charles Allen and the staff at KAET-TV, Anne Ragsdale and the staff at KECI-TV, and Dave Wilson and the staff at the University of Montana Telecommunications Center.

Thanks also to Thomas Bonifield, Gus Chambers, Gregg Hayes, Michelle Henry, Claudia Johnson, Deke Joralman, Mike Kar, and Kimberly Maus for working with me to create the photographs.

CHAPTER 1

The Production Machine

You experience the world around you through impressions gathered with the five senses: sight, hearing, smell, taste, and touch. Your body reacts to the physical phenomena occurring in your sphere of recognition and produces sensations that are transmitted to your brain where they can be interpreted and used to form an impression of your environment. Just as your senses contribute to your experience, television presents sights and sounds for your consideration.

The distribution system delivers images and sounds from source to TV set.

You are probably most familiar with the **television distribution system**, as diagrammed in Figure 1.1. It actually delivers the sights and sounds to your home, school, or office. Sometimes they arrive over conventional local broadcast channels; sometimes on videotape, cable, or from far out in space via satellite. There are few places in the world not served by some element of the distribution system.

The sights and sounds you receive are prepared for distribution through the process of **production**, which captures or creates them and then assembles them into a new sequence. A complex array of electronic tools — starting with the camera — and communication systems operated by skilled production personnel gathers pictures and sounds to illustrate ideas, record events, tell stories, and profile personalities.

The distribution system can:

transport images of reality across space so that you can witness events that are happening almost anywhere in the world;

create and deliver unique and unreal visual images and sounds: television production in the hands of a creative and imaginative person can create fantastic new worlds;

preserve those impressions and images over time: through television and the magic of videotape, you can experience sights and sounds created seconds, hours, or years earlier.

1

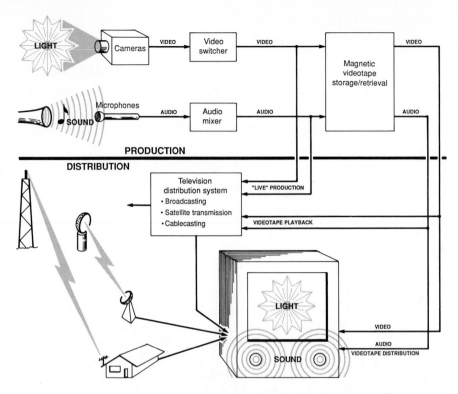

Figure 1.1. A basic television production and distribution system. The television system converts light and sound into electronic signals, processes those signals, and reconverts them to light and sound at the television receiver.

*The equipment, systems, and personnel of the **production machine** assembles pictures and sounds into a program.*

All the tools and systems, together with the personnel needed to run them, can be thought of as forming a complex "**production machine.**" The production machine assembles images and sounds, known as **production elements**, into a product, a television presentation in a form useable by the distribution system.

__Producers__ determine the message to be communicated.

Those who determine how this machine will be used are called television producers. The **producer** determines what ideas, events, stories, and personalities will be the subject matter. To do so, a producer not only must know how the production machine works but also must understand the message to be communicated and the needs of the intended audience.

You will no doubt have the opportunity to produce some programs as part of your training. This book will teach you how to function in the basic production positions; the elementary steps for producing a program are covered in part 3. Understanding the production process and the demands of the jobs of various production personnel is an important aspect of becoming a producer. Note that although running the production machine is a necessary prerequisite to producing good programs, not even the most skillful production can transform a poorly conceived or prepared idea into an effective presentation.

THE TELEVISION SYSTEM

Development of Television Production

A workable television production and distribution system was introduced barely 50 years ago. In its short history, the system has changed dramatically due to profound technological improvements in the equipment and increased sophistication and skill of the people who use that equipment.

Early television was basically a transportation device. It could move pictures and sounds of events over geographic distances. Edward R. Murrow demonstrated the power of television to compress distance when he showed viewers the skyline of Manhattan and the Golden Gate Bridge simultaneously in the early 1950s. Millions of viewers on earth watched Neil Armstrong take the first step onto the surface of the moon in the late 1960s. In the 1990s satellites allow events from anywhere in the world to be transmitted worldwide instantly.

*With **magnetic videotape**, images and sounds can be stored, retrieved, or used in different ways.*

Development of **magnetic videotape recording** in the late 1950s transformed television into a time machine through its ability to capture and store images and sounds. Further development of videotape editing systems in the 1960s allowed the manipulation of those stored images and sounds to create new sequences that could be replayed at a later time. Figure 1.2 shows a typical videotape machine used in the 1960s. The later development of equipment that could play videotape in **slow motion** allowed television to give viewers a new insight into many activities. The **instant replay** revolutionized television coverage of sports events.

The Power of Television

Clearly, the ability to transport pictures and sounds through time and space makes television an extremely powerful communication medium. As you begin to learn how to use the production elements of the medium, it's important that you appreciate the distinction between how television works and what it does. Just as the ability to operate an automobile is of little value without maps and a clear idea of your destination, so those who operate the production machine must have a sharply defined goal before starting up the machine. Furthermore, those who operate the system must have a profound respect for the impact that television can have on those who view its output.

Just think of your own experience. Try to imagine how different your life would be in the absence of television. Think of all the places you have seen, the events you have attended, the people you have met, the artistic expression you have enjoyed, all through television. For most people, television has provided numerous unforgettable impressions.

Figure 1.2. This large and complex videotape machine is typical of the equipment used by broadcast television stations in the 1960s to capture, store, and replay images and sounds on magnetic videotape.

Television's Limitations

While high-resolution TV is being developed, images conveyed by television are generally coarse reproductions.

The television system is not without major shortcomings. By its very nature, television distorts the sights and sounds that it captures. By comparison with what the eye sees, television images are rather crude, requiring considerable interpretation by the viewer. Another potential for distortion is in the viewing environment, including adjustment of the equipment used to reproduce the pictures and sounds, which is generally under the control of the user, not the producer.

In the 1980s, development work on a **high definition television system** (HDTV) made possible an improved system with better image clarity and a greater sense of depth. It will probably be some time before this degree of resolution will be widely available, however; it will take even longer for the necessary equipment to filter down to the school setting. Therefore, this book will concentrate on the television system that you have enjoyed as a consumer and are likely to work with as a student.

*Television **distorts reality** as it intermediates between event and viewer and manipulates impact.*

Television **distorts reality** because it can convey only sights and sounds. The sensory possibilities are quite limited. Skillful use of television production techniques, combining the pictures and sounds in unusual and compelling ways, helps offset some of the shortcomings of the television system. This book will introduce you to many of the basic techniques that contribute to effective communication through the limited resources of the system.

In spite of its limitations, television at its best can produce an overall experience that is superior to actually being at the scene. Many sports fans would argue that watching a game on television is better than being there because it allows them to see the game from many different perspectives, to see replays of exciting action, or to learn more about the background of the players or the contest through the comments of the announcers.

You would probably concede that the view on television is much better. But what about the smells, the feel of the arena, the electricity of excitement that often surges through the crowd? Occasionally television conveys a sense of being there. For example, the American Broadcasting Company's coverage of the United States hockey team's memorable victory over the Soviet Union for the 1980 Olympic Gold Medal was truly thrilling for the viewer. But such excitement and viewer involvement is rarely the case.

The fact that television transports the images through time and space further distorts their content. Think of the conflicting emotions experienced by viewers in the 1960s sitting comfortably in their homes eating dinner while watching violent scenes of death and destruction from the Vietnam War. Many credit television with turning the tide of public opinion against U.S. involvement in that conflict. Others contend that such programs create a callousness toward violence and that viewers who watch television frequently have difficulty differentiating between real violence and the "make-believe" violence that is so prevalent in much that passes for entertainment on American television.

Television gives viewers a distorted view in another way as well; you see few mistakes on television. Productions run smoothly, thanks to the fact that little that you see is produced live. And stories usually come to nice, neat conclusions; the anchor person puts the news story in perspective for us; the murder is solved and the bad guy is punished in less than an hour. Programs that might make you uncomfortable are regularly broken up by cheery and funny commercials that take you away from reality. And with the proliferation of distribution systems, you can always change the channel or put in a different tape to move on to something less threatening.

How the System Works

Television uses electronics to capture, create, store, and distribute pictures and sounds, as you saw in Figure 1.1. In television production, the pictures are referred to as **video** and the sounds as **audio**. Light and sound are converted into electronic signals (variations in voltage, current flows, positive and negative charges) that can be processed and manipulated by the system. Eventually, the electronic video and audio signals are delivered to a television **receiver** where they are reconverted to light and sound so that they can be picked up by your eyes and ears. In Figure 1.1 you saw how the total system works.

Video is the image part of an electronic signal; audio the sound.

The visual images that are reproduced are not exact but the brain has an amazing ability to fill in the missing information and derive the correct impression from the cues provided by the system.

Motion in Television

Persistence of vision is one of our natural abilities and is vital to creating moving video images. The television system actually creates still pictures of a scene being viewed. It produces one electronic still image every 1/30 of a second. When a series of these still images is viewed in rapid succession, the retina retains one image long enough so it overlaps the next and the human brain perceives the minor changes in the image from one to another as continuous motion.

Contrast and Color

The television system at its best is able to reproduce only a small fraction of the variations in contrast and color that the human eye is able to detect. However, it does provide sufficient information so that the brain takes over and fills in most of the missing details.

Television Sound

The system converts sounds into electrical signals that can be processed and eventually reproduced with a speaker that re-creates the original sound. The audio portion of the system is more refined than is the video. Audio signals that are handled properly can reproduce most of the range of frequencies audible to a healthy human ear. Much potential exists, however, for distortion and degradation through misadjustment or incorrect operation of the electronic system. Fortunately, just as with the shortcomings of the video image, listeners have the ability to form impressions from limited sounds.

The human eye and brain assist in the effect of TV through retention, interpolation, and interpretation.

Compensating

Though the television images are rather crude and the sound reproduction is sometimes limited, these shortcomings are not always a handicap. Recognizing the ability of humans to fill in the blanks also represents an opportunity to build upon the viewer's imagination.

As you will learn, many techniques are used to enhance the experience provided to the viewer, to provide additional cues that help make up for the absence of greater detail, and to offset the absence of tastes, smells, and feel. For example, the television screen is a two-dimensional surface. But effective camera angles, careful attention to direction of movement within a scene, and skillful lighting all can be used to create an illusion of depth that gives the viewer a sense of the missing third dimension.

Magnetic Recording

Television video and audio signals can be stored on magnetic tape for later editing, replay, and duplication. This is done by magnetizing particles of metal oxide on a tape. Patterns of positive and negative charges are created on the tape, which can thereafter be used to re-create the electronic signals representing the actual video and audio images.

The electronics of the system are complicated, but don't be intimidated. Although you will need to know some basic technical facts to be prepared to use the equipment effectively, this book does not aim to make you an electrical engineer. The goal of this book, rather, is to teach you what the various television tools do and how they can be used to create effective television programs.

CATEGORIES OF TELEVISION PRODUCTION

Television production can be categorized in several different ways: by where it takes place, by how and when the finished product is distributed, and by the production method or combination of tools used in its creation.

Where Production Takes Place

Studio production offers greater control but limited realism; field production is needed for location coverage and natural settings.

Programs are often put together under controlled conditions in a facility specifically designed and equipped for that purpose. This is known as **studio production**. A typical studio production is shown in Figure 1.3. But for many reasons, some productions cannot be shot in the studio and must be done on location; this is generally referred to as **field production**. Figure 1.4 shows a video camera being used in a field production. Studio production is usually easier because of the control it offers. Obviously, field production presents more problems because of the lack of control, but in the case of breaking news stories or major cultural and sports events, there is no way to bring the production to the studio. In fact, in many instances producers elect to work in the field for added realism and vitality. Most early television was done in studios; as equipment has become more portable and reliable, more and more television production has gone to the location.

Figure 1.3. Studio production of news programs like this one is commonly done by broadcast television stations.

How Television Is Distributed

*Live means continuous, immediate delivery of programming. The **kinescope process** has preserved early live TV.*

Productions can be distributed **live** or they can be **videotaped** for later distribution. To say that a production is done live means it is done in a continuous fashion and the audience is seeing the results at the time they happen. Early television was all live since there was no practical way to record the programs. Today, most news programs, many sports events, and many specials like the Academy Awards show are done live for direct broadcast over conventional broadcast stations, cable systems, or satellite program services. But the great majority of television programs are produced on videotape for later distribution.

Videotaped programs may:

be done **live on tape**. In this case the program is produced as if it were live, but is stored on videotape for future distribution. This practice was common in the late 1950s and early 1960s when videotape recording first became available. This approach is still used by some programs, like talk and game shows, because the programs retain the vitality of live production while offering flexibility in both time and method of distribution.

Figure 1.4. Television production personnel, like this camera operator, routinely engage in field production to gather images and sounds on location.

FILMING TELEVISION

Before the development of videotape, some television programs were captured on motion picture film. This was done by a specially equipped film camera using very sensitive film that picked up the optical image from a television screen. The accompanying television sound was reproduced on an optical sound track at the same time. The resulting film record of the television show was called a **kinescope**.

The technical quality of these films was poor. The television image they captured lacked contrast and detail, and the high-speed film necessary to work with such a dim light source produced a very grainy picture.

Though technically weak, this process did preserve some classic performances and productions from the early days of television — dramatic productions from *Playhouse 90*, the antics of Jackie Gleason and *The Honeymooners*, and the investigative journalism of Edward R. Murrow, for example.

*Today, video tape is usually **edited in postproduction** for later distribution.*

or, by far the most common method, go through **postproduction/editing**. Productions are done scene by scene on videotape and then assembled into their final form on a master videotape, edited in a facility known as a postproduction/editing room. This technique provides the greatest control over the nature and quality of the final program and also flexibility of distribution. It is much more time consuming and generally more expensive.

Production Method

Single-camera work, common in the field, can be shot from various angles and edited.

Productions can also be categorized as either **single camera** or **multicamera**. Single-camera productions, obviously, are done with just one camera. If the program is being produced live — a breaking news event, for example — then this single camera must move around the scene in one continuous **shot** to show you what is happening and the camera operator must decide what is important instantly. If the program is being videotaped, then the single camera can take several different shots of the action from a variety of angles, and a videotape editor or producer can assemble the most appropriate shots in the sequence desired. This single-camera-to-videotape style is widely used in both studio and field productions for everything from news stories to commercials to drama.

*A **director** in a control room orchestrates multicamera work.*

When a scene is being covered by several cameras shooting from different angles, the method is called multicamera production. The decision as to which view you will see is usually made spontaneously by a **television director**, who works from a **control room** where all camera outputs are visible and equipment is available to select any of them at any given moment. Fig-

Figure 1.5. The television studio control room during production of a typical small-market news broadcast.

ure 1.5 shows a television control room during a studio production. Most live events will be multicamera productions when possible. A typical professional football game would be covered by at least four to six cameras located around the stadium. Taped programs like game and talk shows are usually done with multicamera set-ups, as are dramatic productions like the daytime soap operas. The ultimate control over production is provided when multiple cameras cover the scene and each camera is recorded on videotape for later editing or, as with a sports event, where the tape can be "replayed" to give the viewer another look at the action from a different angle.

THE TELEVISION PRODUCTION PROCESS

Production People

Television production is a process performed by people with very specialized skills. Some are managers, like the producer whose role was outlined earlier in this chapter. Others perform specific tasks such as operating a piece of equipment or developing ideas for a discrete portion of a program.

Television production personnel frequently learn the basic skills through courses like the one you are taking now. Most then go on to work in some limited production job, assisting more experienced production people. As their experience grows, they take on additional responsibilities and usually find opportunities to broaden their creative involvement with projects. The ultimate goal for many is the producer's job, where they can use the process as a means to express their own ideas or to help others communicate through television.

Production Tools

Production tools can be grouped into four basic categories:

1. Pickup devices
2. Generators
3. Storage and retrieval systems
4. Mixing and assembly systems

Pickup devices convert naturally occurring scenes and sounds into electronic signals that can later reproduce pictures and sounds. The video camera and microphone, like the ones seen in Figure 1.6, are the most common pickup devices. Most of the images and sounds in television programs were

Figure 1.6. A field production team uses a video camera and a microphone to gather images and sounds during an interview.

Capturing   **captured** by one of these devices. Chapter 2 covers the operation and use of cameras, and chapter 4 discusses microphones.

Generators are specialized pieces of equipment designed to produce an electronic signal that can be integrated into the television system directly, bypassing the need to use a pickup device to convert pictures and sounds. *Creating*   Not only can they **create** replicas of real pictures and sounds more easily, in some cases, than a pickup device can record live scenes and sounds; they can also create images and sounds that exist only in the imagination of the user. A **character generator**, like the one shown in Figure 1.7, is an example of such a video tool. It works much like a word processor, creating graphics from a keyboard for direct use in television production. Similarly, **audio generators** and **synthesizers** can create electronic signals for a vast array of sounds and music. These tools will be explained more thoroughly in chapter 5.

Storing and retrieving   **Storage and Retrieval** is done primarily by magnetic recording in television production. Both video and audio signals can be recorded and then replayed using this system. Figure 1.8 shows a videotape machine commonly used in the 1980s. Various other **storage systems** such as 16-millimeter motion picture film, 35-millimeter slides, records and compact discs can be processed with appropriate equipment to retrieve and convert the images and sounds that they contain to electronic television signals.

Videotape has become a major tool during the production process as

Figure 1.7. A character generator being used to create a graphic title.

Figure 1.8. A cassette being loaded into a video tape recorder/player.

well as the primary means of storage and distribution of programs. Chapter 6 deals with the role of videotape in the production process.

Manipulating   **Mixing and assembly systems** allow television producers to **manipulate** the signals from all the various video and audio sources. The images and sounds are arranged into the sequence and proportions desired, blended, and combined into some new form. **Video switchers, special effects systems, audio mixers,** and **editing systems** are all tools used to accomplish this task. The system shown in Figure 1.9 features all these tools. Chapter 7 details these systems, and part 2 deals with the process of assembling television programs.

Using the Tools of Television Production

Many of the tools used in television are widely available to professionals and consumers alike. Naturally, most professionals have access to very sophisticated tools that increase the options available. But it's the way in which the tools are used, the nature of the visual images and sounds that are captured and created, and the ways they are assembled that define and characterize effective production and separate the professional from the amateur.

As an example, consider shooting an event such as a softball game using

Figure 1.9. A videotape editing system in use during postproduction of a television program.

one camera onto videotape. Amateurs station themselves strategically with the camera and then proceed to take one continuous shot full of **panning** movements that call attention to the camera as it sweeps across the scene, mechanically **zooming** in and out while continually changing the image size. Amateurs don't understand the way a number of different shots from different angles and of differing sizes can be used to *build* a scene.

Ability in application of equipment is what separates amateur from professional.

The **professional** achieves just the opposite effect. By skillfully selecting a variety of angles and image sizes that can later be reassembled in an appropriate order, the professional camera operator creates an effect that lets the viewer see all the critical elements of the scene clearly and at the correct time: close-up shots of the pitcher and batter, reaction shots of the fans and teammates in the dugout, pans and zooms where appropriate to follow the action of the game. Since the professional's camera calls no attention to itself, the viewer is often completely unaware of having seen a series of different shots and, in fact, is left with a single unified impression of the scene.

What, then, is the relevance of the comparison? Both camera operators know how the camera works and how to work the camera. But the professional knows how to *use* the camera in an effective way. He is the master of the tool.

Television Is a Team Activity

*Coordination of the **team** is vital to television production.*

To make the television production process work effectively, you must develop an appreciation for the tools involved. But *people* are equally important to the process. You will need assistance from **a team** of other people to operate equipment when the production machine required for a given program exceeds the operational capacity of one person. Multicamera studio production is a good example. To videotape a simple interview program in the studio usually requires a director, an operator for each camera, a floor director, a lighting person, a technical director, an audio operator, a character generator operator, and a videotape operator.

As the person in charge of a production, not only must you know the tools and how to use them — something you can learn from this book — you also must have the ability to lead and coordinate the activities of all those who are involved in the production. The most capable and successful production people have a keen appreciation for the role others play in making the production machine run smoothly.

The development of single-camera shooting techniques coupled with the use of postproduction/editing systems has resulted in much greater opportunity for an individual to control most aspects of a production, to run the machine solo. You may have the chance to do some projects totally on your own. Nevertheless, you will probably feel the need for input from others, whether in the form of assistance with an equipment problem, consultation on the timing of a particularly critical edit, or just a helping hand in the audio room with a complex sound mix. Television production is still essentially a team enterprise.

CONTROLLING THE PRODUCTION MACHINE

Television production is an activity with great potential to fascinate and beguile. As you begin to develop skill in operating equipment and learn how various tools can be used together to create effects — as you begin to make the production machine run — there is a danger that you will lose sight of the ultimate goal of the process. Richard Breyer and Peter Moller make the point quite well in their book *Making Television Programs*:

> Television equipment has the power to seduce. In some ways it is too easy to make a picture with a television camera (point it into a lighted area) or a dramatic sound with an audio board (push a button) or an interesting transition with a video switcher (pull a lever). The production team that is seduced by the technology can be lulled into the illusion that control of it is not necessary.[1]

Without control, production techniques and special effects take on a life of their own. They are used for their intrinsic value with little regard for the contribution they may make to the overall effectiveness of the program. It is easy to spot programs that have fallen prey to this. When you find yourself noticing the techniques being used rather than the message being delivered, it probably means someone has been seduced by the production tools.

SUMMARY

This chapter has introduced you to the production machine: what it is, and what it does. Keep this overview in mind as succeeding chapters introduce the specifics of how the various components operate and how they can be used in the overall process.

The learning process you have started in this book is in many ways similar to the process that accompanied the early development of the television system. Once a workable system had been designed and built, the first step for its users was to figure out how to operate the equipment. Only then could they begin to use the system to produce programs. Once familiar with the capabilities of the equipment, innovative people began to find new and better ways to use it in communicating with an audience.

As new equipment is developed, the process is repeated. Consider the development of videotape recording and playback capability. Its initial use was strictly as a storage and retrieval system. Then one day in 1963 a sports producer named Tony Verna had an idea. Why not record some of the exciting moments from an Army-Navy football game and play them back for a second look during lulls in the live action.

> I still don't know how a tape machine works. I don't even know how the combustion engine worked on the truck that drove the first instant replay machine to the Army-Navy game. And I don't care. I didn't invent videotape, but I was able to conceive and execute the instant replay. You don't have to invent the electric typewriter to be a great writer.[2]

Verna found a way to use the equipment that opened up a totally new and better way of bringing the action to the viewer at home.

This is not a history book. But there are many insights available to those who know some of the history and development of the production machine. Those who would use the system constructively have much to gain from exposure to the body of knowledge and experience of the past 50 years of television. Of special interest to you will be the profound changes in technology that have characterized the system throughout its history.

Finally, consider the end user of the product: the viewer. Here, too, you will find profound change. The sophistication and expectations of today's television audience are in sharp contrast to those of the people who watched the dim, fuzzy, black-and-white picture of the 1940s — although that audience was no less important than the one you will work for today. This book will talk about today's tools and techniques, but the ultimate goal of all our work is, as it has always been, to show and say something to that audience.

NOTES

1. Richard Breyer and Peter Moller, *Making Television Programs* (White Plains, N. Y.: Longman, 1984), p. 5.
2. Tony Verna, *Live TV: An Inside Look at Directing and Producing* (Boston: Focal Press, 1987), p. 44.

REVIEW QUESTIONS

1. What does the television production process do?
2. What role does the television producer play in the television production process?
3. How did the development of magnetic videotape recording revolutionize television production?
4. In what ways does television distort reality?
5. Diagram and label the process through which television captures and reproduces light and sound.
6. What makes television such a powerful medium?
7. What is persistence of vision?
8. List three ways that television can be categorized. Explain each.
9. List the basic production tool categories and explain the function of each.
10. "Television equipment has the power to seduce." How does this statement relate to your study of television production?

PART ONE

Tools and Techniques of Television Production

CHAPTER 2

Video Cameras

Much of what you know about the world around you is learned through visual impressions obtained with the sense of sight. Through visual media like painting, photography, graphics, motion pictures, and television you can expand your world to include scenes from far beyond your immediate physical environment.

When you view any scene, the lens in your eye focuses the light emitted by or reflected from the objects within that scene onto the portion of the eye called the retina. The retina contains cells that are sensitive to light. Those cells produce nerve impulses, which are sent to the brain where they are evaluated to form a mental image of the scene.

Television extends your vision by displaying selected images on a screen that emits light patterns to which the eye can respond. It captures most of those images through an electronic process that is very similar to the functions of the human eye.

WHAT THE CAMERA DOES

Light to Electricity to Light

The video camera is the primary visual pickup device used in television production. It is used to capture visual images from the world around you, convert those images to electronic signals that can be transported and manipulated through time and space, and eventually reconvert them to new visual images displayed on the television screen. Like the human eye, the video camera is sensitive to light (the electromagnetic energy being emitted by or reflected from the objects in a scene). It translates the **pattern of light** from the scene into an electrical signal which is processed through the camera and used to reproduce a corresponding pattern of light on the television

*The camera captures **patterns of light** as signals to be conveyed or manipulated.*

21

screen. The human eye perceives this television picture as a reproduction of the original visual image.

Visible Motion

Each still picture or frame combines into a series that provides a shot. Shots are combined into a scene.

The television screen displays a rapid sequence of still pictures, each one of which is called a **frame**. The television system produces a frame once every $\frac{1}{30}$ of a second. Since most scenes captured by a video camera involve moving objects, each succeeding frame is slightly different from the one that preceded it. But since few things move fast enough to change drastically in only $\frac{1}{30}$ of a second, these slight differences are not readily apparent. When a subtle change occurs over several frames, the viewer perceives the gradual change in position of the object as motion.

Persistence of Vision

As mentioned in chapter 1, the ability to connect the sequence of still frames into continuous motion is called persistence of vision. The cells in the retina retain the image created by light entering the eye briefly after the light is turned off. Since the television screen is blank only briefly between frames (this is necessary in order for the system to reset for the next frame), and the next frame is very similar to the one that preceded it, the brain interprets the small changes in the position of objects within the images as continuous motion. As you might expect, the more rapidly the frames are taken, the less change there will be from one to the other, and the smoother the motion appears.

Shots

The images captured and reproduced by the video camera are called **shots**. Just as words are the basic units of a spoken language, shots are the basic units in the visual language of television production. A shot is made up of a rapid sequence of still pictures of some portion of an object or locale. Usually several different shots comprise a scene.

System Limitations

The image reproduced does not include all of the optical information present in the actual scene. The television picture is technically inferior to the original. Video cameras have improved dramatically over the past 50 years but, compared with the capacity of the human eye or even the quality of a good 35-millimeter photograph, television pictures are inferior. Three major categories of picture quality illustrate the point.

Contrast Range

The camera has limited ability to identify gradations of brightness within a scene. The healthy human eye can see as many as 100 steps between the brightest and the darkest part of any given scene. The very best video cameras under optimum conditions can reproduce only about 30 steps. So television pictures have limited tone reproduction. The **chip chart** shown in Figure 2.1 is used to adjust the **contrast range** of a color television camera. You should be able to see easily the 11 different tones ranging from white to black.

Figure 2.1. The gray scale, or chip chart, is used to adjust the contrast range of the color video camera.

Color Rendition

*The **additive color system** processes each primary color separately and combines them at the TV receiver.*

The television system uses an **additive color** process. It separates the light reflected from a scene into three primary colors: red, blue, and green. A separate electronic signal is produced for each color, processed through the system, and then added back together at the television screen to re-create the coloring of the original scene. (The back cover of this book shows how these three primary colors can be added together to reproduce all of the other colors.) Minor misadjustments at any point in this complex process can result in color distortion. The technical limitations of the system restrict the possible range of color rendition. The net result is that television color lacks much of the subtlety of the original scene.

Resolution

The video camera has a limited capacity to reproduce fine detail. In television, reproduction detail is measured by the number of lines that can be seen clearly in the final image. The standard resolution of the television system in the United States today is 525 horizontal lines. Most high-quality video cameras can produce much higher resolution, but some of that resolution is ultimately lost in the transmission and reproduction process. A typical home television set probably delivers no more than 250 to 300 lines of resolution to its viewer.

That means that there is a lack of fine detail in the image and that small objects in the scene are poorly defined. Compare the photos in Figure 2.2.

Figure 2.2. The photo at the top resulted from direct exposure of high-quality 35-millimeter black and white film. The photo at the bottom captures the image reproduced from a video camera's shot of the same scene. Notice the lack of fine detail and the general fuzziness of the video camera image.

As previously noted, HDTV offers much greater resolution and much sharper pictures. Technology is fairly advanced in Japan; compatible receivers are required, however, and that will slow its use in this country.

Other Limitations

The television system is limited further by the physical dimensions of the television screen.

Aspect Ratio

*The **ratio of height to width** and the two-dimensional quality of the camera's single eye misrepresent reality.*

The video image is displayed on a two-dimensional screen that is three units high by four units wide. This is called the **aspect ratio**: the ratio of the height of the screen to its width.

When the video camera captures a scene, it contains more of the horizontal information than the vertical information. As Figure 2.3 illustrates, basketball courts fit nicely into this aspect ratio; high-rise buildings do not.

The Third Dimension

The television image has no physical depth since it is displayed on a flat surface and was shot from a single point of view rather than the **binocular view** that you normally have of the world around you; as you know from covering one eye, our two eyes function together to afford a sense of depth. The nature of the television image is a serious limitation to your ability to form an accurate impression of the original scene. Several different production techniques will be introduced in this book to help add an illusion of depth to the two-dimensional television image.

HOW THE VIDEO CAMERA WORKS

*The **camera body** houses the image sensor, internal optical system, and associated electronic systems and supports the lens and viewfinder.*

The video camera has three basic parts contained within or attached to a **camera body** (see Figure 2.4). Each part performs one of the steps in the process of converting light to electrical signals and back to light. The parts of the video camera are:

1. Optical system
2. Image sensor
3. Viewfinder

Optical System

The optical system gathers the light from the scene and focuses it on the camera's image sensor, the light-sensitive component that generates electrical signals (discussed further on page 33). Typically, the optical system will consist of two main parts: an external **lens** that defines the size of the area from which light will be gathered, regulating the amount of light entering the camera and focusing the light onto the surface of the image sensor; and an internal **beam splitter**, which separates the light into its component colors as the first step in deriving the red, blue, and green primary colors used by the

Figure 2.3. The television aspect ratio favors scenes that are wider than they are tall. Unlike still photography, there is no vertical format.

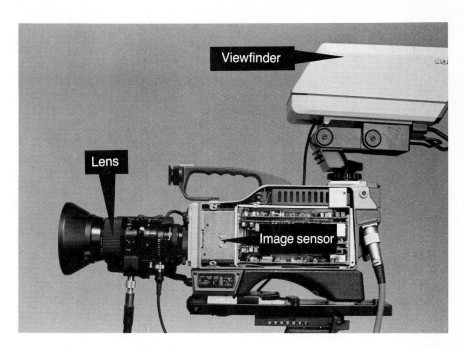

Figure 2.4. Basic parts of the video camera.

*In the **optical system**, the lens controls the area or field of view and the light level to be directed to the **beam splitter**, which interprets color.*

system. (Obviously, black-and-white cameras have no such system but very few black-and-white cameras are now in use. This book deals only with the various types of color video cameras.) In the optical path between these two main parts, the **lens** and the **beam splitter**, most cameras will also incorporate some type of filter, which is used to help regulate the quantity and the quality of the light reaching the image sensor.

The Lens

*Lens views range from **wide angle** to the narrower **telephoto**.*

Light is gathered from the scene around it by the lens. The size of the area from which light is captured is referred to as the **field of view** of the lens. A "**fisheye**" or **wide-angle** lens has a very wide angle of view and therefore gathers light from a large portion of the scene and projects it onto the light-sensitive surface of the image sensor. A **telephoto** lens has a more narrow angle of view and gathers light from a smaller portion of the scene. When this telephoto image fills the surface of the image sensor, the effect is to magnify the objects in the field of view. Wide-angle and telephoto shots of the same scene taken from the same camera location are shown in Figure 2.5.

Focal length, the distance from optical center of lens to point of focus on the front of camera image sensor, defines the field of view.

The field of view of a lens can be expressed in millimeters. This is known as the **focal length** of the lens. It is the distance from the optical center of the lens to the point where the light rays converge to form a focused image as shown in Figure 2.6. A 10-millimeter lens is a wide-angle lens; a 200-millimeter lens is a telephoto.

Figure 2.5. The wide-angle lens, used to take the top photo, gathers light from a large portion of the scene. The telephoto lens, used to take the bottom photo, gathers light from a smaller portion of the scene and thus magnifies the skiers. The telephoto lens also makes the mountains in the background appear to be closer.

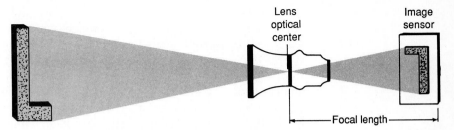

Lens optical center

Image sensor

Focal length

Figure 2.6. The light being reflected from the **L** passes through the lens and is focused on the surface of the image sensor. If the lens were improperly adjusted, the light would not clearly define the image of the **L**. Just as with the lens in your eye, the image created by the video camera lens is actually inverted though your brain subconsciously adjusts for this fact.

*A **zoom lens** has a variable focal length, controlled externally.*

Most modern video cameras are equipped with a variable focal length lens called a **zoom lens**. By physically changing the spacing of the various **optical elements** within the lens (thereby shifting the optical center), the zoom lens can produce a broad range of **fields of view**. Generally, this zoom process is accomplished by means of a lever, crank, or electric motor, which can be controlled by the camera operator.

*The size of **aperture** or lens opening = **f-stop**. This is changed by adjusting the **iris**.*

The lens also controls the quantity of light passing through to the image sensor by means of a mechanical **iris**, or **diaphragm**. Just as the iris in your eye opens and closes to regulate the amount of light reaching the retina of the eye, so the lens iris is used to match the quantity of light to the sensitivity of the image sensor. The opening in the iris is called the **aperture**. The larger the aperture, the more light is allowed to pass through the opening as seen in Figure 2.7.

Figure 2.7. Two iris settings. The larger aperture, on the left, admits more light through the lens. Closing the iris reduces the amount of light passing through the lens.

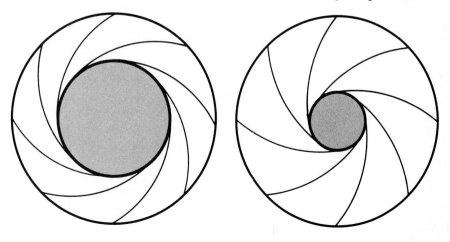

The aperture is changed by mechanically moving the segments in the iris or diaphragm, usually through a ring mounted on the outside of the lens, which can be moved manually or by means of a small electric motor. The size of the opening is expressed mathematically by a system known as **f-stop**. When the aperture is open wide, the equivalent f-stop will be a low number such as 2, 4, or 5.6, and when the aperture is small the number will be something in the range of 11, 16, or 22. The more light available in the scene, the more the iris can be closed to keep within the limits of the image sensor. These changes in iris setting also affect other performance characteristics of the lens that will be discussed later in this chapter.

As the distance between the objects in a scene and the camera changes, the distance between the optical center of the lens and the image sensor must also be changed slightly to maintain focus. This is accomplished by mechanically moving the lens with an external **focus ring** so that the beams of light form a focused image at the desired point, as shown in Figure 2.8.

Depth of field = range of focus.

The focusing characteristics of a lens are described as its **depth of field**. Since the light being reflected back from objects within the scene is coming from various distances and therefore is striking the front surface of the lens at slightly different angles, not all objects can be kept in sharp focus. The greater the range within which objects can be focused, the greater the depth of field. As illustrated by Figure 2.8, wide-angle lenses have greater depth of field than telephoto lenses.

Where depth of field is limited, the camera operator must decide which objects will be sharply focused and which will be blurred and lacking in detail. As you will learn later in this chapter, this characteristic of lenses is not always a limitation and can sometimes be used creatively to enhance the sense of depth in a scene as well as to place special emphasis on an object within a larger scene (see Figure 2.9).

The Filter

To help regulate the quantity and the quality of the light entering the camera, **filters** are used in the optical system. Typically they are mounted internally in the camera body immediately behind the lens, although some cameras may include filters as an external component on the front of the lens.

In situations where there is too much light available and maximum f-stop settings still exceed the needs of the image sensor, **neutral-density filters** can be used to restrict the quantity of light passing through. Extremely bright, sunny days and specialized shots, for instance, of welding or laser beams are examples where neutral-density filters may be needed.

Filters can also be used to help compensate for differences between indoor and outdoor lighting so that the camera properly renders color in any given situation. The process used to adjust the camera for these color differences is called **white balance** and includes the selection of the appropriate filter. That process will be covered more thoroughly later in this chapter, under "How to Operate the Video Camera." The differences between indoor and outdoor lighting will be explained in chapter 3.

Figure 2.8. The upper photo was taken with a wide-angle lens. Because of its greater depth of field, all of the cameras are in focus. The lower photo was taken with a telephoto lens. The shallower depth of field does not allow all three cameras to be sharply focused. The camera operator chose to set the focus on the middle camera so the cameras in the foreground and background are somewhat out of focus.

Figure 2.9. The distance between the snow-covered branches in the foreground and the mountains in the background exceeds the depth of field of this lens. The camera operator must decide where to set the focus.

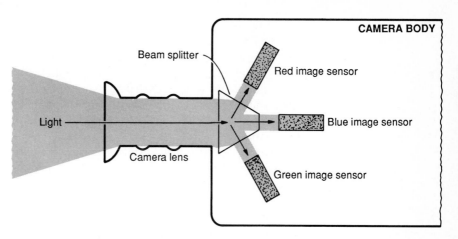

Figure 2.10. In this three-tube camera, the beam splitter is a prism that separates the incoming light into red, blue, and green components and delivers each to the appropriate image sensor.

The Beam Splitter

Incoming light is refracted into its primary color components by a beam splitter, as shown in Figure 2.10. Depending upon the camera type, this might be a **prism**, a **dichroic mirror array**, or a **striped filter**. As mentioned, television uses an additive color system that derives all colors through combinations of red, blue, and green. Therefore, the video signal must include information about the *ratio* of these primary colors in the various elements of a scene. The beam splitter separates the incoming light into these components and delivers each red, blue, and green image to the appropriate pickup device to be **encoded** or converted into a video signal. The independent red, blue, and green video signals can then be recombined or **decoded** at the television screen into a color reproduction of the original scene. The alignment of the beam splitter between the lens and the surface of the image sensor is critical to the accurate rendition of color by the camera and subject to change through rough handling of the camera. One advantage of the **chip camera**, or CCD (charge-coupled device), discussed on page 35 is that the prism is permanently attached and aligned with the surface of the image sensor during manufacture so that no further adjustment is required.

Primary colors are encoded as independent video signals and then combined or decoded at the TV set.

The Image Sensor

A light-sensitive component in the camera produces an electrical signal when exposed to light. Such sensors can be grouped into two categories:

1. Tubes
2. Charge-coupled device (CCD)

Tubes were developed first and various types have been employed in video cameras. They have been constantly refined and improved since the early days of television. **CCDs**, developed in the early 1980s, derive the video signal in a significantly different manner. Both tube sensors and CCDs consist of a light sensitive surface onto which the optical system can project light, and each reacts to the light by producing an electrical signal. In both cases, the surface is segmented or divided like a mosaic pattern. Each segment produces a different electrical signal in response to the intensity of the light falling upon it. The resulting signal fluctuation is an electronic representation of the pattern of varying light intensities being gathered from the scene and projected onto the surface of the image sensor. The electrical variations are processed through the system and reproduced as a similar mosaic pattern on the face of the television screen. Each segment is illuminated on the screen to the same degree that it was originally received on the surface of the image sensor.

Segmented surfaces of *image sensors* *generate the electrical signals that produce the patterns of varying light intensities on-screen.*

Tubes   In tubes, the light-sensitive surface is generally called a **target**. It is covered with photoelectrical material. As light strikes the surface the material produces a positive charge; the brighter the light, the stronger the charge. The tube is then scanned in a systematic fashion from behind by an electron gun that emits negatively charged particles. The gun scans across the target in a series of horizontal passes. The voltage of the scanning beam increases and decreases as necessary to neutralize the positively charged target, creating lines of video information. The voltage fluctuations within each line become the principle ingredient in the video signal, and 525 of these lines make up one complete frame.

The reverse of the scanning process can be used on a television screen to re-create the light pattern that was just derived from scanning the back side of the target. An electron gun in the television screen is synchronized to that of the originating tube and varies its voltage to match that created by the original scene. It emits positively charged particles that cause the phosphorescent material on the back of the television screen to glow, in turn producing an image that corresponds to the image from the target.

One of these tube arrangements is complex in itself. But to create a color television picture, the video camera must produce three separate images; one for each of the primary colors in the system. Individual targets must be exposed by the red, blue, and green light being reflected through the optical system. These red, blue, and green signals are processed through the system and then reproduced by a color television screen made up of clusters of red, blue, and green phosphors, each illuminated to the intensity created by the original light striking the target or targets. The human eye blends these individual dots of color into an image that can be interpreted by the brain. Remember human brains have the capacity to fill in the blanks and to make minor corrections for the shortcomings of the system.

Some video cameras accomplish this color process by using three individual tubes, one for each color. Others use only one tube and employ a striped filter to create separate red, blue, and green patterns on one target. The electronics and power supplies required to do all of this mean that tube-type video cameras are rather large and heavy, though solid-state circuitry dramatically reduced their bulk in the 1970s and 1980s. In the late 1980s, tube-type cameras were still the unit of choice for the best overall video quality.

Charge-coupled Device

CCD, or chip, image sensors produce a video signal that is compatible with the one described above, but they do so in a radically different manner. Instead of a target, the surface of a CCD is covered with thousands of individual cells called **pixels**. When light strikes the surface of the CCD, each pixel is charged in proportion to the intensity of the light. Rather than requiring an electron gun to scan the surface, these charges are stored and then read out line by line to produce a video signal. As you can imagine, this greatly simplifies the electronics of the camera and significantly reduces its overall size. CCDs have the added advantage of being more sensitive to light than tubes so that the cameras can operate in much darker settings.

Regardless of which image sensor is used by the camera you work with, its function is to convert variations in light into the electrical signal that will ultimately yield a reproduction of the original image on the face of the television screen. Unless you have a special interest in the intricacies of the electronics involved, your technical knowledge will probably be focused on understanding the differences in the operating characteristics of the various types of tubes and CCDs so you may use them correctly. Your job is to produce the best pictures possible and to know how to take proper care of the unit to avoid damage.

The Viewfinder

The viewfinder or monitor lets the camera operator see video output.

The part of the camera that allows the operator to see the picture being taken by the video camera is called the **viewfinder**. Generally this will be a small black-and-white **television monitor**, even when the actual signal being produced by the camera is in color. Color viewfinders would be large and complex, making the camera more difficult to operate and maintain. The absence of a color viewfinder can sometimes be a handicap when you find yourself working alone on location and you have doubts about the proper adjustment of the camera's white balance. Many production people carry a separate, battery-operated monitor whenever feasible.

Cameras primarily intended for portable use generally are equipped with a small viewfinder suitable for close-up viewing with one eye, similar to the one in Figure 2.11.

Cameras used in studios or in fixed positions during field production can be fitted with a larger, external viewfinder. These are sometimes built into the camera, and sometimes they are detachable. An example of each is shown in Figure 2.12.

The primary purpose, of course, is to show the operator the **video out-**

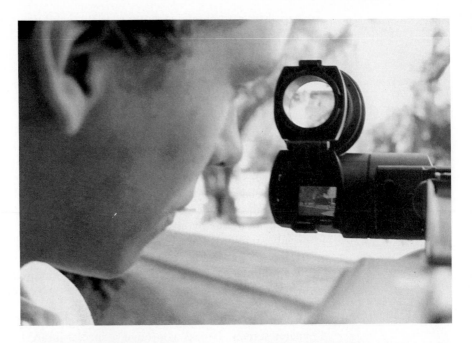

Figure 2.11. The portable video camera has a small viewfinder that can be used with or without the adjustable eyecup. In some shooting situations, it is desirable to keep both eyes open, even when the eyecup is in use.

Figure 2.12. Larger viewfinders are used on most studio cameras. The one at the top is detachable and can be replaced with the smaller one shown in Figure 2.11 when this camera is used in its field configuration. The viewfinder in the lower photo is built into the camera.

SAVE YOUR LIFE!

One skill you should develop as a television camera operator is the ability to keep both eyes open while shooting with a camera equipped with the eye cup style of viewfinder. Doing so allows you to keep track of things going on around you that are outside the field of view of the camera.

This can be especially important when you're on the sidelines at a football game. Many camera operators have been injured because their wide-angle lens didn't reveal how close the players really were to the sideline until it was too late!

The technique is to shift your concentration from one eye to the other. And most camera operators open the non-shooting eye only occasionally, at times when nothing critical is happening in the viewfinder. That's why the football example is so important. The shot is great because the action is coming right toward your camera, you're concentrating on following the movement, and then, WHAM!, the lights go out!

---

put of the camera. Usually there will be some individual brightness and contrast controls that can be used to adjust the viewfinder to the operator's preference without affecting the actual video signal coming from the camera. Some viewfinders include a feature through which the operator may select **return video** to see **playback** of material recorded on videotape during a session or the **outputs from a video switcher** for setting up special effects. More will be said about this in later chapters.

*What the camera sees can be **played back** on the spot.*

Auxiliary Equipment and Systems

Power Sources

The video camera described above requires a source of electricity to power its systems. Studio cameras generally are connected into some larger production system and are powered by the electrical system within the building. Portable cameras generally have a portable **alternating current (AC) power supply** that can be connected to a standard household electrical outlet and a separate **rechargeable battery pack** that allows the camera to be used without the restriction of staying near a conventional electrical outlet. Proper care and scheduling of batteries is crucial to having a reliable power source. Many production organizations go to great lengths to have batteries properly charged after use, assuring that freshly charged units go out with the equipment.

As manufacturers have converted to solid-state electronics, cameras have become much more efficient. Modern color television cameras require only a fraction of the energy needed to power their ancestors.

YOU DIDN'T BRING ANOTHER BATTERY?
(A Personal Account)

We were shooting a story about ground water pollution on the rugged plains of eastern Montana. A rancher whose property adjoined a strip mine believed that the mining operation was contaminating her ground water, killing the grass and poisoning the cattle.

We had toured the mine and talked with company officials during the morning and then packed up and driven 30 miles to hear the rancher's side of the story.

This was a good story, a widow living on land that had been owned by her family for generations, battling the powerful mining company to preserve the land for her children and grandchildren.

The producer wanted footage showing the alleged damage and wanted to conduct an interview with the rancher at a fence on the property boundary so that the ranch and mining operations might be contrasted in the background. We used the rancher's truck to tour the ranch. It was slow going since there were no roads, the ground was rough, and we stopped frequently to shoot. Montana is a big state, and this was a big ranch. We probably covered 15 to 20 miles and took more than an hour before we reached the fence.

Everything was going well. We had gotten to know the rancher well and she was willing to talk openly with us. I hurried to set up the equipment, and we started the interview. As you've probably guessed, less than a minute into the interview, the low-battery warning light came on. Then it hit me: all of the spare batteries were in our car, not in her truck.

We shot until the camera quit. Then I had to tell the producer my predicament. Surprisingly, she was not especially annoyed. We packed up and went back to the ranch house. As it turned out, the producer was not happy with the way the setting looked nor the way the interview was going. She was glad that we had been forced to stop.

After picking up fresh batteries and extra tape, which I had also forgotten, we found a new location that worked well. We got a good story, and I learned a valuable lesson.

Camera Mounts   Most modern portable cameras are small, light, and durable enough to be **hand held** by the operator. This provides great freedom to move the camera into the best position from which to cover the action. But in many situations, some kind of **camera mount** may be desirable. This is especially true where stability of the camera is important or when the weight of the camera would be a burden to the operator. Camera mounts range from simple **tripods** to elaborate **camera cranes** and sophisticated **track dollies**. Some examples are shown in Figure 2.13.

In addition to supporting the camera, most camera mounts include some

Figure 2.13. Two common camera mounts. A studio tripod with detachable wheels and a studio pedestal.

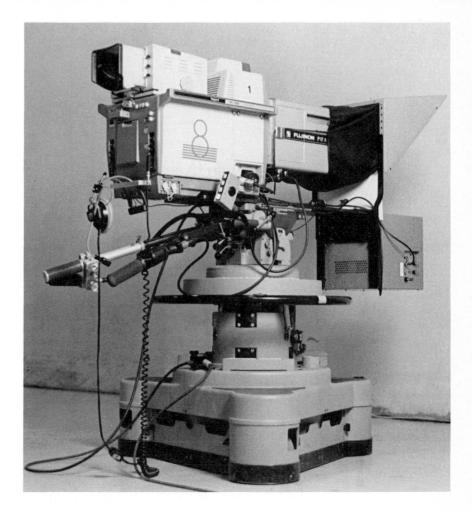

Figure 2.13   *(continued)*

type of **pan-tilt head**, which allows the operator to move the camera smoothly through its horizontal and vertical axis independent of the movement of the mount itself.

Camera Control Units

Color values and intensity can be adjusted by the CCU, or camera control unit.

When multiple cameras are used to cover the same scene, some provision must be made for adjusting them so that the colors and brightness within the scene will appear the same on each camera. This is done by using a **camera control unit (CCU)**, which is a control panel connected to the camera itself by a cable. The CCU allows a person (usually a video engineer) other than the camera operator to compare and adjust each camera, as shown in Figure 2.14. Most studio systems include a **video control position** from which a technician can monitor and adjust the cameras.

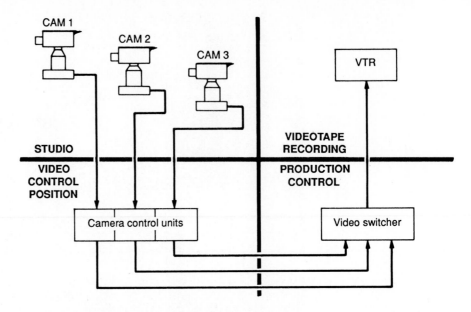

Figure 2.14. In this typical studio installation, the signal of each camera is adjusted with a camera control unit before delivery to the production control area where each can be individually selected for recording.

Sync Generators   When multiple cameras are used together in a production, it is important that they all produce signals that are compatible and can be interchanged. The frames produced by each must occur at the same 30-per-second rate and be synchronized to start and stop simultaneously. If they are not synchronized, when there is a change from one camera to another you might *In a multicamera setup,* see partial frames from each displayed together, disrupting the impression *compatible video is* of continuous motion. Multicamera systems incorporate a **sync generator** *assured by the* **sync** which sends signals to each camera as a reference for synchronization. *generator.*

Intercom Systems   In many production situations, the camera operator will be working as part of a team and will need a means of communicating with other production personnel without leaving the camera. **Intercom systems** are usually incorporated into the camera to allow this communication through the use of **headsets** that include earphones and microphones that can be connected to private circuits between team members. For location work when the cameras are not interconnected into a system by cable, **wireless headsets** that include a small transmitter and battery pack can be used to provide communication among production crew members.

HOW TO OPERATE THE VIDEO CAMERA

Camera Operator's Responsibilities

As a camera operator you will have several responsibilities:

1. Care and protection of the camera
2. Exposure
3. White balance
4. Focus
5. Framing and composition
6. Movement

Each of these will be discussed as it pertains to both field and studio production and single-camera and multicamera work. Keep in mind that these are generalized guidelines and that individual organizations or facilities may deviate from these procedures.

It has already been pointed out that learning to operate the video camera is *not* an end unto itself; it is means to an end. Just as learning to operate a typewriter or word processor will greatly facilitate writing only if you have something to say, so skill as a camera operator becomes productive only when it leads to shots that communicate visual messages effectively. Note the difference between the title of this section and the title of the one beginning on page 53.

Care and Protection of the Camera   When you operate a video camera you are responsible for protecting it from damage and making sure it is operated within the limitations of its design. In doing so you must make sure that:

1. the camera is attached securely to the camera mount being used or is held firmly when being hand held and always placed in a safe spot on the ground or in its case when not in use. This is especially important when working on location in an uncontrolled environment. Studios afford much greater protection for the camera, as it will usually be semipermanently attached to some kind of mount. You must also remember to protect the camera from temperature extremes and moisture.
2. the camera is connected to an *appropriate* power source and is turned on following established procedures. In a studio, this task is often done by a technician, but in field production you will probably be required to do this job.

Be especially careful when working alone on field assignments that you not leave the camera unattended where it can be blown over by the wind, bumped by casual observers, or stolen when you are busy with other production details.

Exposure

Exposure is the amount of light being provided to the image sensor.

Once the camera is set up and ready for operation, it must be adjusted for the proper **exposure**: selecting the appropriate filter and adjusting the iris of the lens as required to provide the proper amount of light to the image sensor. In many situations you may find that there is insufficient light to produce a good image with your camera. Where control of the lighting on the scene is possible, additional lighting units can be used to boost the illumination into the operating range of the camera. When this is not possible, some cameras have a **video boost** feature that increases the voltage going into the image sensor and thus heightens its sensitivity. Boosts may allow you to get the picture, but generally the image will suffer somewhat since it also introduces more "noise" or graininess into the resulting video signal. In most studios, exposure is controlled by a technician using the camera control unit. During field production the camera operator usually does the job. You need to learn the correct procedure for the specific camera you are using in order to obtain the best performance possible.

Inadequate lighting can sometimes be overcome by electronically boosting the image sensor's sensitivity.

White Balance

White balancing: focusing on a white area to set color range being reproduced by a camera.

Once the camera is properly exposed, it must be adjusted for **white balance** to correctly render the colors within the scene to be shot. This is necessary because different light sources have different color qualities; in effect, the light falling upon the scene has a color of its own that will affect the way in which the camera portrays the resulting colors in the scene. This factor will be discussed more thoroughly in chapter 3. As a general rule, your camera will need to be focused upon some white surface illuminated by the light source used so that the electronics can be adjusted to reproduce that surface as white. This may require manual adjustment, or it may be an automatic process that is initiated by a simple switch. White balance is especially critical in multicamera studio production, since all the cameras in use must match when intercut. As with exposure, this is usually done by a technician in a studio situation, but white balancing is normally handled by the camera operator in field production. It is critical here, too, since lighting conditions are often uncontrolled and subject to change from one shot to the next. You must learn and use the recommended white balancing procedure for your camera each time you prepare to work in a new setting.

The procedures covered so far are technical prerequisites to the camera being operational. There will be instances when you will be tempted to rush these steps; perhaps the news story is happening right now and you'll miss it if you delay. Remember, if the camera is not properly exposed and white balanced, the picture you get will probably be unuseable anyway. Learn to do these things efficiently so that they require a minimum amount of time.

Focus

In most production situations, the camera operator is responsible for the proper focusing of the lens. As discussed earlier, this is usually accomplished by rotating a **focus ring** on the lens itself or moving the ring through some electrical or mechanical remote control, as shown in Figure 2.15. This generally depends upon the configuration in which the camera is being used.

In either case, the operator views the image through the camera view-

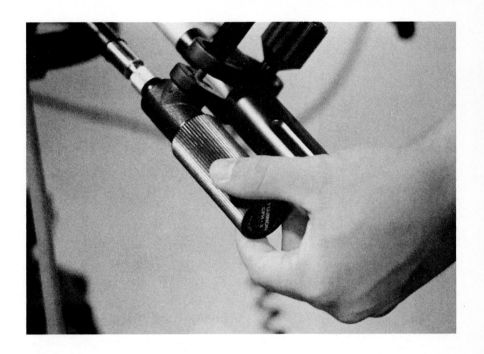

Figure 2.15. The top photo shows the remote control, used to focus the lens in the studio configuration. In the portable configuration, the operator can easily reach the focus ring itself.

finder and adjusts the focus as necessary. Deciding what elements of the picture to focus upon will be discussed as we explore *using* the camera.

Framing and Composition   Obviously, the camera operator also *moves* the camera to bring into view whatever elements of the scene are to be included and selects the size of the image by either repositioning the camera or adjusting the setting of the zoom lens. This is called **framing** and **composition**; see pages 54–66.

Camera Movement   There are several commonly used terms that describe the ways in which the camera can be moved. Sometimes these movements are used to reposition the camera between shots; other times they are used as part of the shot itself to create a specific effect that will include the movement of the camera. As a camera operator, you need to know the terminology for these movements and practice executing them with your camera.

> **Pan** — the horizontal or lateral movement of the camera. A pan is made by rotating the camera on its pan/tilt head around its lateral axis or by rotating the body laterally while holding the camera.

Figure 2.16. Pan.

> **Tilt** — the vertical movement of the camera made by moving the pan/tilt head through its vertical axis or by lowering or lifting the front of the camera vertically while it is supported on your shoulder.

Figure 2.17. Tilt.

Zoom — to smoothly adjust the focal length of the lens and change the field of view making objects appear larger or smaller in the frame. Most often, when the zoom is used as part of a shot, the camera will need to be panned and/or tilted simultaneously.

For example, your camera is taking a shot of a person from head to foot. You want to zoom in to a closer shot of the head and shoulders. But if you zoom in without tilting up, you will get a close-up of the belt buckle, instead (Figure 2.18).

Pedestal — another vertical movement in which the height of the entire camera is changed by raising or lowering some portion of the camera mount. If the camera were being hand held, squatting down from a standing position would give the pedestal effect (Figure 2.19, p. 50).

In each of these camera movements, the camera is operating from a fixed location.

There is another set of movements during which the position of the entire camera changes in relationship to the scene being shot. These are usually done when the camera is on a mount equipped with wheels and is operating on a relatively smooth surface. Similar effects can often be achieved by walking with a hand-held camera, though it takes considerable skill to do smoothly.

Figure 2.18. Zoom. As the camera operator adjusts the focal length of the lens with the thumb control, the image of the bust in the viewfinder becomes larger.

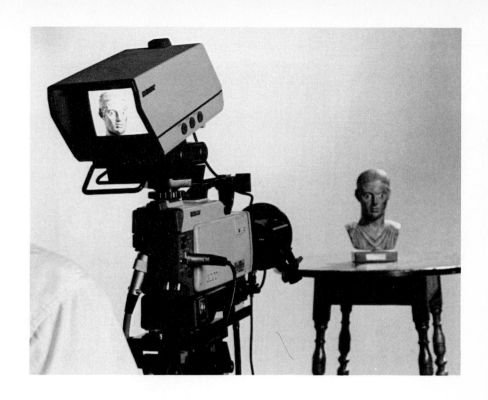

Figure 2.18 *(continued)*

Figure 2.19. Pedestal.

Figure 2.20. Truck.

Truck — a lateral movement with which the entire camera is repositioned along a plane perpendicular to the scene being shot (Fig. 2.20).

Arc — takes the camera on a curving path around an object while maintaining a consistent distance from it (Fig. 2.21).

Dolly — moves the entire camera away from or toward the object in the scene. Produces an effect similar to that of a zoom, as objects appear larger or smaller in the frame. Since the distances between various objects in the scene and the camera are actually changing, the dolly produces a more dramatic change in perspective with regard to foreground and background objects than does a zoom (Fig. 2.22).

These are the basic camera movements used in simple productions. More specialized procedures may be used with elaborate camera mounts such as the **steady-cam body mount**, the **track dolly**, and the **studio crane**. Consult the glossary for descriptions of each.

The Role of the Camera Operator

The role played by the camera operator can be quite diversified. In single-camera field production, the camera operator is often working alone and will make all creative as well as technical decisions. This situation saddles the camera operator with total responsibility for the results but also allows great

Figure 2.21. Arc.

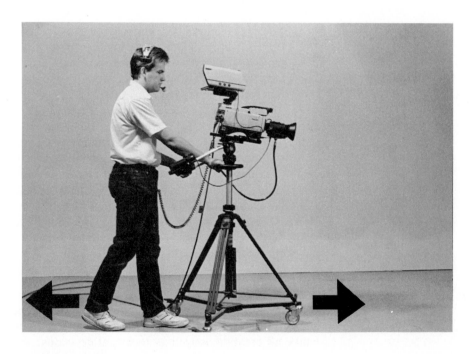

Figure 2.22. Dolly.

freedom and flexibility. Covering a fast-breaking news story with video demands, for example, that the camera operator also be a reporter, making editorial decisions about what shots are important to telling the story effectively.

In multicamera production, the operator will generally be executing the instructions received from a director through an intercom system. The operator's role is to function as part of a production team and to:

1. Frame and compose good shots within the guidelines established for the production.
2. Respond to cues and instructions from the director.
3. Operate the camera safely and efficiently.
4. Remain aware of the overall production while concentrating on a specific assignment.
5. Remain patiently alert and attentive throughout the production process.

Operating a camera is a challenging task. Mastering the technical aspects of adjusting the camera for proper operation is best accomplished through an understanding of correct procedures and experimentation with the camera itself. Experience will teach you much about what to expect from your camera in various shooting situations. Remember, the most creative shots imaginable are useless if not properly exposed, white balanced, and focused.

Framing, composition, and camera movement require skill and judgment. Each improves with experience and practice. It is in these areas that the distinction between operating and using a camera becomes most apparent.

HOW TO USE A VIDEO CAMERA

The camera is used to capture some portion of the visual information available in any given scene or locale. As we have seen, each different view constitutes a **shot** within a scene. Typically, when television is used to show the viewer what is happening, it does so through a combination of different shots shown in sequence to give the audience an overall impression.

Camera Perspectives

Point of view: observer, receiver, or participant.

The camera can take several different **points of view**. These are called **camera perspectives**. Selecting the camera perspective is the first of many subjective decisions that the user of a video camera must make, and the decisions can have a profound effect on the reaction of the viewer. With the exception of some single-camera field production situations such as news coverage, camera perspective is seldom the camera operator's decision since camera perspective has usually been determined in advance by the producer. The commonly used perspectives are called

1. Objective
2. Receptive
3. Subjective

The **objective perspective** is simply the camera assuming the role of an objective observer and watching to see what happens. Surveillance cameras in a supermarket operate from the objective perspective. When television covers an interview or a sporting event, the perspective is usually objective. The camera puts the viewer in the position of someone who is in the room or in the stands, who does not participate and simply watches.

The **receptive perspective** makes the camera a passive participant in what is happening. The activity being covered is happening for the camera and much of the activity will be directed toward the camera. A traditional television newscast places the camera in a receptive position as the newscasters and reporters talk directly to the viewer through the camera. Most instructional and informational kinds of programs are done using the receptive perspective. When the sideline camera at the football game suddenly becomes a means of saying "Hi Mom," it has switched from objective to receptive.

Subjective perspective thrusts the camera into the heart of the action as an active participant. The camera becomes one of the actors in the drama or one of the drivers in the race. Other participants talk to each other as well as to the subjective camera. Naturally, when used wisely, this perspective can create intense involvement for the viewer. Subjective camera has become widely used as the size of video cameras has diminished. For example, coverage of the Winter Olympics in the 1980s included dramatic footage of downhill ski racing from a subjective point of view made possible by high-quality miniature cameras.

These common camera perspectives are routinely mixed together in television productions. Chapter 7 talks more about combining shots from different points of view.

Basic Shots

A progression of shots tells the story of a scene, establishing context and building interest.

Once the perspective is selected, the camera user must decide what angle to shoot from and what portion of the scene to include in the shot. This is known as **framing the shot**. Television production has adopted a number of standardized shots developed by the pioneers of the motion picture industry. While certainly not intended as a restriction, these basic shots provide a starting point for camera users. The most basic shots, which involve no movement of the camera, are:

1. Wide shot (WS)
2. Medium shot (MS)

HOW'D THEY DO THAT?

In the early 1980s, an elaborate camera system was developed for use in covering sports events. The system was called the *stadium camera*. It featured a small video camera that could be suspended by cable, for example, above the playing field of a football stadium. A computer was used to control a mechanical system that could adjust the lengths of the cables in such a way that the camera could have an infinite variety of locations, from high above the field down to directly behind the quarterback as he prepared to snap the ball.

Naturally, this system was complex and expensive, but it provided production people with the flexibility to move the camera at will and to put it into any of the common perspectives. It had the potential to provide unique and dramatic coverage of the game.

The system never caught on, however, either because of its expense and unreliability or because it was difficult to use. I watched only a couple of games in which the stadium cam was used and it seemed to function well. But the shot from this camera was so unusual that it stood out from the rest of the production; it called attention to itself. The change in perspective was so dramatic that it was disturbing to the viewer. I found myself watching and wondering "How'd they do that?" rather than finding that it provided a better view of the game action I was supposed to be following.

Remember, the camera is there to *cover* the action, not to *be* the action!

3. Close-up (CU)
4. Extreme close-up (XCU or ECU)

WS   The **wide shot** provides a wide-angle view of the scene. It gives an overall impression and sets the scene for the viewer. Wide shots are routinely used to establish the setting in which something will happen, as in Figure 2.23.

When you first enter a new environment, you probably do the equivalent of a wide shot by looking around at things in a general way to begin forming an impression of the place.

MS   The **medium shot** brings the viewer in, closer to some element within the scene. Things that may not have been obvious in a wider shot become more apparent. This allows the viewer to begin developing a context for the scene. More details are visible of the principle object of attention and of the immediate environment around it. Medium shots show enough to arouse the viewers' curiosity (Figure 2.24).

CU   **Close-ups** isolate elements within the medium shot and reveal details previously unnoticed, as in Figure 2.25. They answer questions that arose from earlier, wider shots of the scene.

When you entered that new environment, you surveyed the scene,

Figure 2.23. Wide shot.

Figure 2.24. Medium shot.

Figure 2.25. Close-up.

picked out a general area of interest, and moved in for a closer look at what was there.

XCU/ECU   **Extreme close-up** like the one in Figure 2.26 can isolate and emphasize picture elements of particular interest.

Both the close-up and the extreme close-up have filled the screen with a particular element in a scene. In so doing, they have removed the surrounding elements from view and taken the broader context of the scene away. For this reason, conventional technique would probably suggest that a medium or wide shot be provided periodically so that the viewer can keep track of where all the detailed information fits into the large picture. There are no hard and fast rules about how these shots should be used or any particular sequence, and you should feel free to experiment with them in your productions. (Chapter 11 will introduce some basic rules of visual continuity.) Try also to look at the work of others to see how these four basic shots are used.

Moving Shots

Movement is a critical ingredient in most television productions and there are several different ways that movement can be incorporated into a shot.

1.   The elements of the scene can move within a static frame provided by one of the basic camera shots just described.

Figure 2.26. Extreme close-up.

2. The camera can move (pan, tilt, zoom, etc., as outlined earlier) to follow elements within the scene as they move about.
3. The camera can move across static elements within the scene.

Sequence and pace of camera movement establish relationships within a scene.

Each technique has its advantages and disadvantages. Consider the limitations of a static frame showing the action of a basketball game. In order to keep all the players, the baskets, and the ball in the shot, the field of view would have to cover the entire basketball court. That would result in the moving elements all being very small and would make for very dull viewing. But if the camera takes a medium shot and then pans smoothly as the action moves back and forth on the court, everything is bigger in the frame, easy to see and follow. Excessively zooming the lens in and out in combination with panning the rapidly moving players would create a picture that is distracting and difficult to watch.

You see examples and combinations of these movement techniques in most television productions. Camera movements are often used to reveal elements in a scene or to show the juxtaposition of objects in the scene. Zooming the camera in one continuous shot can result in a steady transition through all of the standard basic static shots, starting either with the wide shot and zooming in or the extreme close-up and zooming out.

Knowing when to use each technique is another subjective judgment that production people must make. As a rule of thumb, remember that cam-

---

THE RAILROAD YARD IN ATLANTA

One of the most dramatic and effective camera moves I can recall is in the classic motion picture *Gone with the Wind*. The story is about the Civil War and this particular shot comes at a point in the story where the glory of the rebel cause is fading and the reality of death and destruction has become apparent.

The shot starts on a close-up of Scarlett O'Hara, who is looking for a doctor to assist with the delivery of a baby. Scarlett doesn't know how badly the war is going for the South.

The camera begins to move back, and you see that there are stretchers and wounded soldiers everywhere.

As Scarlett walks through the chaos she becomes more and more distraught. The camera continues to move back and it becomes apparent that this is a railroad switching yard completely swamped with wounded Confederate soldiers.

But the camera continues to pull back. The magnitude of the devastation is slowly revealed over a period of nearly a minute. The shot ends as a tattered Confederate flag flying over the scene comes into view.

The effect achieved by this single camera movement is powerful indeed.

---

era movement tends to call attention to itself when used inappropriately or executed poorly. On the other hand, it can have dramatic results.

Composition

Composition: the arrangement of objects within a shot.

Composition is part of the framing process. It involves the way the various elements within the frame are arranged. This discussion is about basic principles of composition, but it should be emphasized that the judgment necessary to artistically and creatively compose shots is highly subjective.

> **Centering.** When an object is enclosed in a frame such as the television screen, the eye naturally tends to look first at the center of the area enclosed. Objects in the center therefore hold the place of most prominence (Figure 2.27).
>
> **Headroom.** Objects near the edge of the frame tend to seem crowded. This is especially true with the spacing above the person's head. Therefore, allow a bit of extra space above to avoid the appearance that the subject is being squashed by the top of the frame. The photo in Figure 2.28 demonstrates a lack of headroom.
>
> **Rule of thirds.** Divide the television screen into thirds both vertically and horizontally. Place objects of interest at the intersections of the lines marking those divisions (Figure 2.29).
>
> **Eyes in the upper third.** Divide the screen vertically into thirds. Then frame the shot so that the subject's eyes are approximately on the line dividing the upper third from the middle third (Figure 2.30).

Figure 2.27. Centering.

Figure 2.28. Headroom.

Figure 2.29. Rule of thirds.

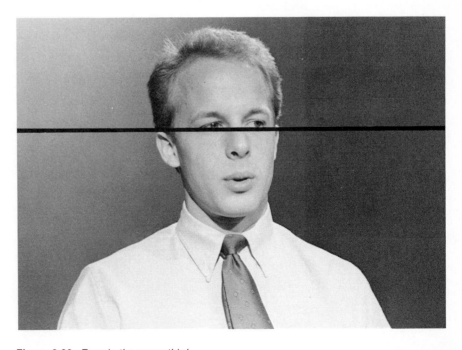

Figure 2.30. Eyes in the upper third.

As you can see in Figure 2.31, the rule of thirds works well until you get to extreme close-ups, when it comes into conflict with the guidelines for headroom. Sacrifice headroom first.

Figure 2.31. Conflict between headroom and eyes in the upper third.

Figure 2.31   *(continued)*

Look space. When the subject is facing toward the edge of the frame, give the person some space to look into (Fig. 2.32).

As you can see, the subject is now facing into the center of the frame, building upon the centering principle and the rule of thirds. If you switch between close-up shots of the two people from the interview setting framed in this way, they each appear to be looking at the other (Fig. 2.33).

Foreground. Objects closer to the camera will normally appear to be larger. Composing shots that include reference objects of known relative sizes in the foreground adds to the sense of depth in a shot (Fig. 2.34, p. 66).

Direction of movement. Movement toward and away from the camera adds to the illusion of depth. It also creates a much more dramatic effect than does lateral movement across the frame (Fig. 2.35, p. 67).

Selective focus. Using the shallow depth of field of longer focal length lenses, you can selectively set the focus to provide pleasing compositions and to shift the center of attention within a given shot, as seen earlier in Figure 2.9.

High or low angle. Positioning the camera above or below an object often changes the background significantly. It also creates an unusual perspective as compared to placing the camera at the same level. For example, placing the camera below a person and looking up at the person gives that person a dominant appearance. Compare the

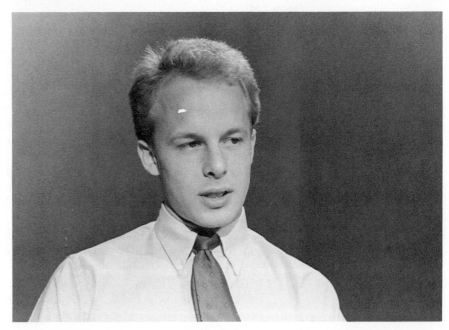

Figure 2.32. Look space.

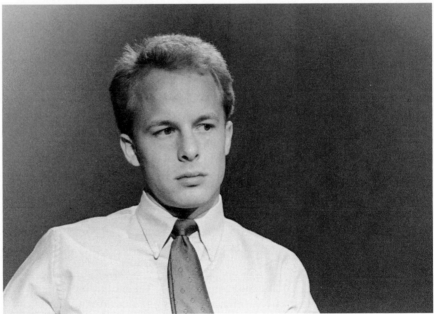

Figure 2.33. Look space makes these two people appear to be looking at each other.

Figure 2.34. Foreground.

impression given by the high and low angle shots of the people in Figure 2.36 (p. 68).

Picture composition is one of the most subjective and elusive aspects of learning camera operation. As soon as you are introduced to a few of the conventional approaches, you must be reminded that these rules are made to be broken. The acid test for any composition is the way it ultimately looks on the television screen and the reaction that it elicits from the viewer. If the reaction is appropriate, then the composition was effective. Skillful camera users are always experimenting with new angles, different fields of view, unusual use of depth of field, or unbalanced and asymmetrical compositions.

TELLING THE STORY WITH PICTURES

To conclude this chapter on the video camera, consider a typical situation that you might face as a camera operator and how you might use the camera to complete your assignment.

On Assignment

The news director of the television station you work for has sent you to shoot video showing the hazards presented by a poorly marked crosswalk on a busy street near a school. There have been several car–pedestrian ac-

Figure 2.35. Direction of movement.

Figure 2.36. Low or high angle.

cidents at the location, the most recent involving a small child. The station management is planning an editorial urging the city to correct the situation, and your video will be used to illustrate the problem.

As you drive to the location, you decide to start with an objective view of the scene during the busy morning rush hour, with heavy traffic and children on their way to school. Wide and medium shots should establish the nature of the problem. You'll get some close-ups of children trying to cross, close-ups of impatient drivers, maybe some sound of skidding tires, children laughing, and other elements to set the scene.

Upon arrival you elect to shoot primarily from the south side of the street, since that will put the school in the background. The sun is low in the sky to your right and you'll need to remember to reset white balance occasionally as it rises higher into the sky. You set up the tripod, power up, adjust the camera's exposure and white balance, check the tape and the audio signal coming from the microphone mounted on top of the camera to pick up natural sound, set the focus on the crosswalk markings in the street, zoom out to a wide shot, and begin to shoot.

The congestion and conflict is obvious. You get the medium shots, some close-ups of kids and drivers; some are nervous, some angry, and others carefree and distracted. Remembering screen direction, you position yourself slightly to the right of the crosswalk so the kids crossing the street are moving from left to right in the frame — and you are mindful to be consistent about that.

Where are the signs and signals marking this crosswalk? You find them and get close-ups. The one for the eastbound drivers, who are facing the sun, would probably be hard to see through the windshield of a car at this time of day. You decide to get a subjective shot from inside your own car to find out. Subjective camera is a good idea. In the car, the shot shows there really is a lot of glare in the windshield. Might as well get a shot from the pedestrian's point of view, too. So you take the camera off the tripod, put it on your shoulder, and, as the reporter grabs the video tape recorder, you walk across with a group of children, tape rolling.

You finish shooting and check the tape by playing it back through the camera viewfinder, using the return video switch. You've got all the necessary elements to bring your viewers to this setting and show them the problem. Back at the station you edit the piece and show it to the writer who will prepare the script for that night's editorial.

SUMMARY

The video camera is the most important piece of video equipment in the television production system. It captures visual images and then converts them to electronic signals that can be transported through time and over distance, to be reconverted later to corresponding visual images. It is a complex electrical unit but the basic operation of the camera is straightforward.

The video camera is used to make shots — individual views of locales and activities — that can be combined to convey an understanding of the setting to the viewer. There are many conventions or guidelines that can assist inexperienced camera operators in using this valuable production tool, and a few of them have been presented in this chapter.

To become a good camera operator, you must master the operating procedures for your camera and develop skill in the basic movement and composition involved in framing images. Learning how to *work* this tool efficiently will allow you to capture images that are technically sound. Learning how to *use* the camera to capture effective pictures will allow you to communicate with the viewer. Ultimately, your skill as a camera user will be judged by the content of your shots and the meaning they express.

REVIEW QUESTIONS

1. Explain how the video camera converts light to electronic signals and back to light.
2. Why do you perceive the television video display as continuous motion?
3. Compare the capabilities of a high-quality video camera to the human eye in the areas of contrast range, color rendition, and resolution.
4. What limitations are imposed by the physical dimensions of the television screen?
5. List the main parts of the video camera and describe the function of each.
6. Compare the performance characteristics of the two categories of image sensors.
7. List the responsibilities of a camera operator.
8. When might video boost be used to obtain proper camera exposure?
9. Why must a color video camera be white balanced?
10. Compare the role of a camera operator in a single-camera field production with that of one in a multicamera studio production.
11. List three commonly used camera perspectives and give an example of how each might be used.
12. List four basic static camera shots and explain the function of each.
13. Describe three ways that movement can be included in a shot.
14. What is composition? Explain some of its basic principles.
15. Explain the distinction between knowing how to *work* a camera and knowing how to *use* it.
16. What is the ultimate test of your skill as a camera operator?

CHAPTER 3

Lighting and Settings

The technical and aesthetic requirements of the camera were explored in the preceding chapter. These are fixed factors, but you can tailor the appearance of the scene being shot to accommodate the needs of the camera. This can often be accomplished through control of the physical setting in which the action happens — both the arrangement of the various visual elements in the scene and the way in which they are lighted. Naturally, in covering news stories and events, this is not always possible or desirable. But to the extent that such control is appropriate, adjusting the lighting and the setting can make your shots look better and enhance the effectiveness of your productions.

Lighting is one of the most important aspects of television production, yet it often does not get the attention it deserves. Good lighting can enhance camera performance and can make a significant contribution to the overall effectiveness of a production. Why doesn't it attract attention? The answer: Good lighting takes careful planning and time to execute. In the rush to get the story on location or the pressure to use valuable studio time for camera rehearsals and taping, lighting often becomes a secondary priority.

In this chapter, you will learn the basic functions and properties of light as they pertain to television production and the various light sources available to you. You also will be introduced to some simple concepts for using lighting to support your initial production efforts.

Entire texts deal with the intricacies of advanced lighting for television. As with many aspects of the television production process, there is no substitute for *experience* with the challenges of lighting. But the material in this chapter will provide a foundation upon which to build an appreciation for the contribution that good lighting can make to the television production process.

What is illuminated is equally important. The locations in which you choose to conduct your productions, whether inside a studio or on location, and the visual setting in which action takes place constitute major factors in determining the audience reaction to your production.

This book will not teach you to design and build sets. It will attempt to impress upon you the importance of the visual setting and suggest various functional and aesthetic factors to consider when choosing a setting for a production.

FUNCTIONS OF LIGHTING

Lighting serves three general functions in basic television production. It serves to:

1. Provide illumination
2. Create the illusion of depth
3. Establish mood or setting

Illumination

Light does the same thing for a video camera that it does for your eye; it provides the illumination that makes seeing possible. Without adequate light coming from a scene, neither camera nor eye is able to perceive the objects within the scene.

The camera can cope with far less contrast ratio than can the human eye.

It is important to note that the camera is not nearly so sensitive as the human eye. It requires much more light and cannot deal with as broad a contrast range as the eye (see chapter 2). Modern cameras are sensitive and able to make good pictures in relatively low light levels, but their sensitivity pales by comparison with the range of the human eye in low light levels.

As mentioned earlier, the image reproduced on the face of the screen lacks some important elements of the original scene as perceived directly by the eye. The image is in two dimensions instead of three; it has a limited contrast range; and it lacks much of the subtlety of color and texture that was part of the real image — but it contains enough visual information for the brain to interpret and fill in the missing information from memory.

Illusion of Depth

In addition to illuminating a scene, good lighting can help create the illusion of depth, the cues that allow the viewer to estimate the form of objects — flat, square, round — and their relationship within the scene as to foreground and background. The most obvious example is lighting objects in the fore-

Effective lighting can overcome the limitations of TV's two dimensions.

ground more brightly than those in the background. Of equal importance is the uneven lighting of surfaces, depending upon where light is falling upon them. That, coupled with the presence of shadows, provides the viewer with critical cues to the three-dimensional nature of the scene being depicted in two dimensions on the television screen. Compare the effect of lighting changes on the scene in Figure 3.1 (p. 74).

WHEN CAMERAS NEEDED *LOTS* OF LIGHT
(A Personal Account)

Early color television cameras required massive amounts of light to make acceptable pictures. The material in the tubes was far less sensitive than that used today, the optical systems were less efficient, and the processing equipment used to boost the signal was more prone to introduce "noise" into the image. All of these factors combined to require very high intensity lighting on scenes to be shot with these cameras.

I recall working in the late 1960s with a studio camera that had four tubes, three called vidicons — relatively low sensitivity devices carried over from the black and white television era — one used for each of the primary color channels. A fourth device, called an image orthicon, was a high-resolution black-and-white tube. The light reflected from a scene had to be split four ways and projected onto these pickup devices. The intent of the design was to superimpose the three color channels on a high-resolution black-and-white channel providing high-quality black-and-white pictures for those in the audience without color receivers (a large percentage of the viewers at the time) as well as to upgrade the resolution of the color signal. While the camera was huge and complex, it did, in defense of the manufacturer, produce quite good pictures.

But lighting for this camera was a formidable task. Huge amounts of light were required; very large wattage lamps were used. The light was so bright that performers became very uncomfortable from the heat and the effect of intense light on their eyes. During long rehearsals and taping sessions, some performers would start to appear as if they were being sunburned. Another problem was that the studio air-conditioning had to deal with all the heat being generated by the lighting. Worst of all, the high studio temperatures would gradually affect the adjustment of the electronics inside the cameras as the performance of some components changed with heating.

As you can tell, when comparing these cameras and lighting requirements with the portable or studio cameras you are using for this course, camera technology has come a long way.

Mood or Setting

Lighting also tells the viewer much about the setting and the mood of the scene. Scenes that are brightly illuminated with all portions of the scene clearly visible connote daytime, of course, but they also suggest an open, straightforward setting in which nothing is being concealed. Compare that with a scene in which only some objects are partially lighted. Nighttime, sure, but also mystery, suspense, or lack of honesty.

An example illustrates the point. Television news broadcasts are almost always brightly lit. Why? Because the purpose of the program is to convey

Figure 3.1. The table lamp is the apparent source of illumination in this living room scene. The light falls off rapidly to deep shadows a few feet from the lamp. By adding set lights on the coffee table and the items behind the couch, depth is added without changing the mood of the scene.

information and to reveal to the viewer information previously unknown. To light a news broadcast with deep shadows and large unlighted areas would convey the wrong impression (see Figure 3.2): news brings information out into the open; it doesn't conceal things in dimly lit rooms.

PROPERTIES OF LIGHT

Three properties of light can be controlled and/or manipulated to serve the three basic lighting functions in the television production process:

1. Quantity
2. Quality
3. Direction

Quantity

Light can be quantified in several ways. You select a bulb for a study lamp based on wattage. The higher the wattage, the more light from the bulb. The common unit of measure that manufacturers use to express the output of their lamps is lux or lumens.

*The intensity of light is measured in **footcandles**, a point of reference.*

In television production, the most common unit of measure is the **footcandle.** Put simply, one footcandle represents the amount of light one foot from a standard candle. The importance of this unit is not its absolute nature but rather its usefulness as a *relative* standard. Television lighting personnel learn the quantity of light measured in footcandles necessary to achieve the results they desire using the equipment available. Then they use a **light meter** (Figure 3.3) that is calibrated in footcandles to determine when they have provided enough illumination to meet those requirements. Figure 3.4 gives you some examples of the quantity of light found in a variety of settings.

As you begin to carry out production projects, you probably will learn how to use the light meter and you also will begin to develop a frame of reference for how brightly lit a scene needs to be and how that translates into footcandles. Light meters are less commonly used in field production because, for most simple assignments, the equipment and control necessary to create the desired footcandle readings simply are unavailable. The process in the field is much more commonly one of adapting to existing conditions through staging and camera adjustment compared with setting the conditions to the values desired, as is possible in a studio.

Measuring Illumination

The quantity of light can be measured by using a light meter in two ways:

1. Incident light readings
2. Reflected light readings

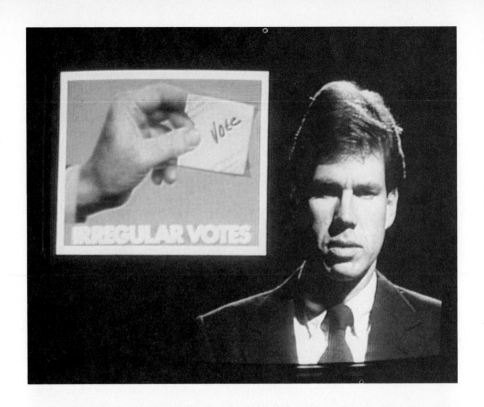

Figure 3.2. Which newscaster do you trust?

Figure 3.3. A typical light meter used in television production. The photoelectric cell produces a weak electrical signal when exposed to light. That signal changes in direct proportion to the quantity of light and can be displayed as a readout in footcandles.

Clear, sunny day	3,000–10,000
Television studio	200
Living room	10–35

Figure 3.4. Typical illumination measured in footcandles.

Incident light is that cast on the subject.

Incident light is light falling on the scene directly from the light source. It is measured by placing the light meter as close as possible to the surface of the object being lighted and aiming the meter directly at the source. The quantity of light measured in this way depends upon several factors:

1. the wattage of the lamp. Just as with your study lamp, the higher the wattage, the greater the amount of light emitted by the television light.
2. the type of lighting instrument being used. The various types will be introduced later in this chapter.

3. the amount of voltage being supplied to the lamp. Anything less than the full rated voltage will reduce the output of the lamp.
4. the distance between the light source and the meter. The farther away, the less light.

Reflected light is redirected by the subject toward the camera.

Reflected light is the amount of light being reflected from the surface of the lighted object. It is measured by placing the light meter near the surface being lighted, but this time the light-sensitive element is pointed toward the object, rather than the light source, and from approximately the same angle that the camera will shoot the scene.

Naturally, the reflected reading in any situation will be considerably less than the incident reading, since it will be affected not only by the amount of incident light falling upon the surface but also the **reflectance** of the material and the relationship between the angle the light is coming from and the position of the meter.

In most cases, lighting directors build the lighting of a scene using incident measurements that they know will result in adequate light being reflected to meet the technical requirements of the camera being used. You should determine the recommended incident light levels for the camera or cameras that you will be using. Many modern cameras are quite sensitive and make good pictures in 50 footcandles of light or less. Conversely, the cameras described previously from the early years of color television required 350 to 500 footcandles of light.

When using field cameras, most operators use the camera itself as a measure of the quantity of light. Rather than determining footcandle readings, the operator uses the camera's **automatic gain control,** or internal metering to adjust the lens iris for the proper amount of light. The lighting is adjusted until the desired quantity is achieved as determined by the camera's exposure settings. In single-camera applications, this technique works very well.

Camera Requirements

Most cameras will operate in a reasonably broad range of light level situations. The critical factor is reaching the minimum level. When too little light is provided, the only alternative is to boost the sensitivity of the pickup device electronically, which, as mentioned in chapter 2, adds to the visual noise or graininess of the picture. Once enough light is falling on the scene to activate the camera at its normal sensitivity setting, the iris within the camera's lens can regulate how much light reaches the image sensor. If the amount of light exceeds the capabilities of the iris, a neutral density filter provided on most cameras can be placed in the optical path to bring the level down into the operating range of the lens and camera combination.

Depth of Field

Lighting affects camera focus and therefore the nature of the message conveyed.

The quantity of light also can be used to take advantage of the depth-of-field characteristics of the lens, discussed in chapter 2. Lower light levels require larger iris openings, which in turn reduce the depth of field. This effect can be useful for placing emphasis on certain portions of a scene, as Figure 3.5 illustrates.

Figure 3.5. Small iris openings made possible by large quantities of light result in greater depth of field. All three cameras are in focus. Less light requires a larger iris opening and a corresponding reduction in the depth of field. Not all the cameras can be in sharp focus.

Contrast Ratio   Quantity of light is dictated by the sensitivity of the camera being used. That does not mean that every element within a scene must be lighted to that level, but those that are to be lighted should be within the operating range of the camera. Other parts of the scene may remain unlit so long as the absence of detail in that portion of the scene is acceptable.

You know that the range of intensity readings, from the highest quantity of light in a scene to the lowest, is called the contrast ratio. Using footcandle readings, if the brightest spot in a scene had a light reading of 200 footcandles and the darkest a reading of 20 footcandles, then the contrast ratio of that scene would be 10 to 1. Contrast ratio in lighting is an important consideration, as you learned in chapter 2, because television cameras are much more limited in their ability to handle high-contrast scenes than is the human eye.

Additive Effect   Later in this chapter you will learn about combining several light sources on a scene. At this point, it's important to understand that several lights falling upon an object from different directions will have an additive effect on the overall incident and reflected light levels. The skillful combining of many light sources on a complex television studio set is learned through extensive study and a lot of experience. The goal here is simply to introduce you to the basics.

Quality

The second property of light, after quantity, to be discussed here is quality. Visible light has a color quality. It can range from red at the lower end of the spectrum to blue at the upper end. The light discussed in this chapter rep-

Light sources give off electromagnetic energy.

resents the visible portion of an **electromagnetic spectrum**, which consists of all forms of electrical and magnetic waves that radiate from a variety of sources like the sun, radioactive ores, electric lamps, and radio transmitters.[1] For example, when you strike a match, a chemical process ignites the materials within the match and, as it burns, it gives off energy in the form of heat and light. The electromagnetic energy released is in the form of waves that oscillate at a frequency that falls into the visible spectrum. Low frequencies represent primarily heat, whereas high frequencies produce the penetrating radiation known as X rays.[2] Your eye sees objects under candlelight conditions as having a slight reddish cast. In fact, the light given off is at the lower end of the visible spectrum; therefore it tends to be in the frequency range that appears red. (Again, your brain interprets the scene and makes a correction for variations in the frequency of the light.)

The light at the upper end of the visible spectrum, for instance, direct sunlight at midday, tends to be blue. But your brain is able to correct what the eye sees since it knows that grass is green, no matter what color it may appear to be because of the color of the light illuminating it. Unfortunately, the video camera has no way to know whether the light illuminating an object is red, white, or blue. If the grass is illuminated by the red light of a candle, the grass will have a reddish cast to it. You may have experienced

---

"SHOW BUSINESS"
(A Personal Account)

The color temperature of location lighting is not always reliable, even when you think it will be. While covering the opening game of a college basketball season I learned that lesson the hard way.

All the lights were on when the technical crew registered and white balanced the cameras about 30 minutes prior to the scheduled air time for the live broadcast. We expected a big audience, since the school was playing for the first time in a brand new arena. The teams were on the floor for pregame warm-ups when we began the telecast, and everything was fine.

But when we came back from a commercial break just before the introduction of the opening line-ups, all the images looked blue; there simply was not enough light to make good pictures. All the arena lights had been shut off so that "follow spots" could be used to spotlight each player as he was introduced; a real show-business opening. I hadn't asked and no one thought to tell me this would happen.

To make matters worse, after the introductions and the arena lights were turned back on, we learned that they were equipped with mercury vapor discharge-type lamps, which take about five minutes to come back up to full intensity and color temperature. Our viewers had to watch the first few minutes of that game with some pretty strange images.

Midday sunlight	5,000–5,400
Television studio	3,200
Living room	2,600–2,900

Figure 3.6. Typical color temperatures in degrees Kelvin.

this phenomenon when you tried to take indoor photographs with outdoor film, and the resulting slides or prints had a reddish brown tint.

Color Temperature

Degrees Kelvin measures the relative color temperature of light.

As with quantity, some unit of measure is necessary to describe and control light quality. The unit is **color temperature.** Television lights are rated on a scale called the *Kelvin scale*, an absolute scale in which 0 degrees Kelvin equals −273 degrees Celsius.[3] Colors you think of as warm have comparatively lower temperature values as outlined in Figure 3.6.[4]

Few television production facilities have the equipment to measure color temperature directly. But most light sources used in television production are *rated* by the Kelvin temperature of the light they produce. In controlled situations, therefore, consistent quality of lighting can be achieved by simply using lights that all are rated for the same color temperature. The most common standard is 3,200 degrees Kelvin.

The color temperature of the light falling on a scene will affect the perceived color of the objects within. (Again, we rely on the brain's ability to correct what we see for how we know it should be, in this case, correcting for the color temperatures of the light that is influencing the rendition of the object.) Video cameras cannot accurately reproduce color unless the lighting provided is of consistent color temperature and the camera has been calibrated to accept whatever lighting is being used as "white" or "neutral" lighting.

White Balance   Video cameras deal with color temperature through a process known as white balancing — a process of adjusting the camera to correctly reproduce colors by giving it a reference that can be interpreted as white under the existing lighting conditions. Once the camera is adjusted to see white as white, then the other colors will also be properly reproduced. This is especially important in single-camera production in the field. The portable lights you use will most likely be rated at 3,200 degrees Kelvin. Sometimes, however, you will want to shoot in direct sunlight; other times, there will be adequate artificial light in the scene and you will shoot without supplemental lighting; in still other cases, you will be confronted with a mixture of light sources with different color temperatures. What do you do?

Methods of   Most cameras deal with this problem in some combination of three ways:
White Balancing

1. Preset indoor/outdoor adjustments that are selectible by the camera operator
2. Provision of a procedure for manually adjusting the camera's white balance to the existing conditions
3. An automatic continuous sensing system that adjusts for various color temperature conditions

You should learn the method your camera uses and how to operate it. The preset approach is simple but provides mixed results, since the preset white balance naturally represents a compromise. Manual systems are the most precise and give the best results but depend on the proficiency of the camera operator to work well. Automatic systems also represent a compromise, and they add to the expense and complexity of the camera.

In the studio, when using multiple cameras under controlled lighting conditions, white balance is no real problem. All the lamps in most studios will be rated for the same Kelvin temperature, usually 3,200 degrees, and the technicians or your instructor will balance all the cameras to render the scene correctly.

*Accurate color reproduction depends on establishing a **white balance** or neutral lighting sensitivity for each camera.*   At this point in your production education the important point for you to understand is the impact that the color temperature of the light illuminating a scene can have on the camera's reproduction of those colors and the necessity for setting the white balance of the camera to compensate for the prevailing conditions. Visualize what can happen when the white balance adjustment is overlooked in the following situation.

You have been using your portable camera to shoot interviews in the television studio. All the lights are rated at 3,200 degrees Kelvin. You have white balanced for that color quality. Your next task is to shoot some additional interviews, outside, in front of the studio building. (Excerpts from these interviews will be later combined into a short tape about the television production curriculum.) When you arrive outside, the students to be interviewed ask that you hurry, because they're already late for class. In your haste, you forget to reset the camera's white balance. When you view the tapes later, you find that the interviews shot outside are tinted blue, since the camera was set to see white under the lower color temperature (redder) studio lights.

Direction

The third property of light mentioned at the beginning of this section is direction. Light sources can be classified as to whether they produce **direct light**, sometimes described as *hard* light, or **diffused light**, often called *soft* light. The most obvious example of this is the difference between a sunny day and an overcast day.

Direct Light

*Light from a **distinct** source produces parallel beams, sharp shadows, contrast.*

When all illumination is coming from a **distinct source**, dense shadows are created in the areas blocked off from that source, and the transition from light to shadow is abrupt.

For example, on a sunny day most of the light comes directly from the sun. When the light strikes the surface of an object it is absorbed and/or reflected back.

Imagine an outdoor sign as seen in Figure 3.7. As you stand before the sign the surface is brightly illuminated and a lot of light is being reflected back at you. In fact, if the surface is a light color you may find it uncomfortable to look directly at the sign for very long. The area behind the sign receives very little light, since the direct light rays from the sun do not fill in this area. The result is a strong shadow or dark area with a clearly defined edge or transition between the light and shadow areas.

Diffused Light

When illumination comes from many different directions — diffused light — the shadows created by the light coming from one angle are washed out by the light coming from other angles. The result is transparent shadows with soft edges.

*When **reflected** and refracted, light has a softer effect.*

To use the sign example again, on an overcast day the rays of light from the sun are diffused by the clouds before they reach the surface. The direct sunlight is broken up and **reflected** in many different directions by the water molecules in the clouds. The result is that less light reaches the surface and some is reflected back out into space. The light that does reach the surface is now coming from all over the sky and the clouds. This diffused light strikes the sign from many different angles and is reflected from the surface in many different directions, as shown in Figure 3.8.

The front of the sign will be well-illuminated and easy to read and it will

Figure 3.7. A bright, sunny day produces direct lighting on the sign. Notice the clearly defined shadows created by the raised letters and the dense shadow of the sign's outline on the ground.

Figure 3.8. An overcast day produces diffused lighting on the sign. The lighting is very flat, with little or no shadow created.

be easier to look at than the sign in Figure 3.7 because it has less total illumination on it. That illumination is coming from many different angles and consequently being reflected in many different directions. It's not all coming back directly to your eye. The area behind the sign will receive slightly less light but the shadow is much less pronounced and the edge much less clearly defined than when the light is direct, again because the light passes the side of the billboard at a number of different angles and the transition from light to shadow is much more gradual.

As you consider the various sources of illumination, you will learn about using direct and diffused light sources to serve the functions of lighting mentioned at the beginning of the chapter: to provide illumination, to create the illusion of depth, and to establish mood.

SOURCES OF LIGHT

Light sources used in television production fall into two categories: natural and artificial.

Natural Light Sources

The preceding section discussed the primary natural light source — the sun. Other sources include the moon, which, as you know, is really a giant reflector of the sun's light; lightning; fire; and other naturally occurring electrical phenomena.

Natural light sources are generally uncontrollable. They can be an excellent means of lighting for television, but the production must be adapted to the lighting conditions rather than the other way around.

The quantity of natural light must fall somewhere within the operating range of the camera used. If insufficient illumination is available, you cannot shoot the scene. If too much is available, as mentioned earlier, neutral density filters can usually be employed to reduce the overall quantity into the operating range of the camera/lens combination.

The color temperature of the light is also generally beyond your control. As you've already learned, however, cameras can be adjusted for white balance to compensate for most situations.

Large, flat, shiny reflectors redirect strong incident light.

There are some actions you *can* take with regard to direction, however. If an overall diffused lighting effect is required for an outdoor scene, you can simply wait for a day when the desired overcast occurs. If you want direct sunlight but need to soften and lighten the resulting shadows, **reflectors** can be used to *diffuse* and *redirect* some of the naturally occurring light into the shadow area, as shown in Figure 3.9. If a silhouette effect is desired with much of the light coming from behind a performer, the production can be staged to position that person with the sun at his or her back.

Artificial Light Sources

Artificial light sources include fixtures and instruments that provide everyday illumination in a given setting, and fixtures and instruments, television

Figure 3.9. The reporter is positioned in direct sunlight. The camera right side of her face (from the camera's point of view) is brightly lighted, while the camera left side has a definite shadow. A piece of white posterboard is used to reflect sunlight onto the camera left side of her face, filling in the shadow and reducing the contrast ratio.

Figure 3.9 (*continued*)

lights, especially intended for use in the production process. Some television lights have been designed primarily for use on location and are portable; some are intended for use primarily in a studio situation. You may have access to either or both for your production projects.

TELEVISION LIGHTING EQUIPMENT

Components of Television Lights

The two most common types of television lights are the spotlight, which provides directional light concentrated in a small area, and floodlights, which provide diffused light over a much larger area. Both types include the same basic components:

1. Lamp
2. Reflector
3. Housing
4. Power supply

Lamp — a filament enclosed in a transparent envelope mounted on a base that can be connected to an electrical source. When the filament is heated by the electrical current flowing through it, light is released.

Reflector — a means of concentrating and directing the light from the lamp.

Housing — a structure upon or within which all other elements can be mounted. Vents for dissipating the heat from the lamp are usually provided and hardware is provided to secure the unit in the desired position.

Power supply — a means of conducting electricity to the lamp. Usually includes a socket, power switch, and cord to connect to an AC outlet or a battery.

Types of Television Lighting Equipment

For your basic television productions you will probably have access to either a portable light kit for single-camera field productions and/or a studio lighting system for multicamera studio productions. Each is discussed briefly.

Portable Light Kits   Light weight, versatile, rugged, and capable of lighting a relatively small scene, portable light kits use existing power at the location. Most basic kits would include:

1. Two or three combination spot/flood lights with simple reflector arrangements equipped with 3,200-degree Kelvin lamps (often called **minilights**)
2. Individual stands or supports that can be adjusted for height

Barn doors, scrims, and umbrellas are among accessories to control the nature and distribution of light.

3. A method such as **barn doors** that can restrict light from reaching portions of the scene that are to be dark
4. A method for diffusing the light, usually either mesh **scrims** that can be placed in front of the lamp or **umbrellas** that can be used to reflect and diffuse the light
5. Power and extension cords
6. Some kind of lightweight carrying case

Placement and use of these units for lighting scenes in a field production are discussed later.

Studio Lighting Systems   Most television studios are designed with the special needs of lighting in mind. They have most or all of these features:

1. Special air conditioning equipment capable of handling the tremendous amounts of heat generated by studio lighting in a quiet and draft free manner
2. A **grid system** made up of pipe or **battens** that is suspended below the ceiling and that provides a place for hanging the various studio lighting instruments
3. A special electrical system, usually consisting of numerous individual circuits, that can power the lighting instruments separately
4. A form of individual control for each circuit, ranging from a simple on/off circuit breaker to elaborate **dimmer systems** with rheostats

for each circuit that allow variations in the voltage supplied to each instrument

5. An array of specialized lighting instruments equipped with clamps for mounting on the grid and an arrangement for aiming and then securing the instrument in the desired position (A separate section on these instruments follows.)

6. A ladder or platform that allows lighting personnel to reach the grid and work with the instruments

Typical Studio Lighting Instruments

As mentioned earlier, most studios will have an assortment of types of spotlights and floodlights.

Fresnel Spotlight   The fresnel spotlight is a multipurpose instrument that features a special lens in addition to a reflector, allowing directional focusing of the light rays from the lamp. Most fresnels include an internal mechanism for adjusting the distance between the lamp/reflector unit and the lens, which allows their output to be "spotted" into a very narrow beam or "flooded" to a fairly broad and more diffuse pattern, as shown in Figure 3.10.

Multipurpose fresnel spots permit highly controlled focusing of light.   **Fresnels** are used to light specific objects, performers, or areas with directional light, which creates clearly defined shadows.

This instrument is the workhorse of television studios because of its versatility. Spotting and flooding a fresnel not only can change the directional nature of the output; it also is a means of raising or lowering the quantity of the output. (A 1,000-watt fresnel on full spot at a distance of 20 feet would provide about 650 footcandles of light in a circle about 1 to 2 feet in diameter. The same unit at full flood would provide about 70 footcandles over a circle approximately 20 to 25 feet in diameter.) For studio use the spotlights are normally equipped with lamps rated at 3,200 degrees Kelvin to provide uniform color temperature.

Barn doors are a common accessory for fresnel spotlights. They further

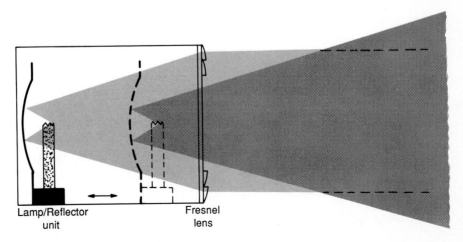

Lamp/Reflector
unit

Fresnel
lens

Figure 3.10. Fresnel spotlight; a cross section

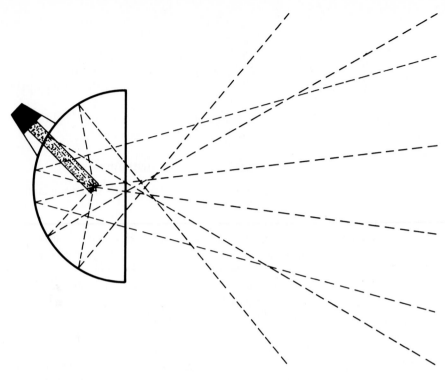

Figure 3.11. Scoop floodlight; a cross section

enhance the ability to control the distribution of the light from the instrument, in effect allowing lighting personnel to shape the pool of light to their needs.

Most fresnel spotlights also have a provision for placing diffusion materials, such as scrims or transparent colored material called **gels**, in front of the lens to further tailor the light output to the specific needs of the production. Scrims alter the directional nature of the light; gels effectively alter the color temperature of the light. Both reduce the quantity of light coming from the instrument.

Scoops

Widely used floods create broad, diffused light.

The most common floodlight used in basic television production is the scoop, illustrated in Figure 3.11. It is a simple instrument in which the housing doubles as the reflector. The lamp is mounted at the center of the reflector, and the resulting output is diffuse while at the same time providing reasonably high quantities of light. As with fresnels, scoops can be equipped with 3,200-degree Kelvin lamps for consistent color temperature.

Scoops are used to provide diffused light over large areas and are noted for creating very soft-edged shadows. They can also be equiped with special frames for scrims and gels, as can fresnels.

Elipsoidal Spotlight

The elipsoidal is a specialized spotlight that provides an even more directional light source than the fresnel spotlight. Elipsoidals are used primarily

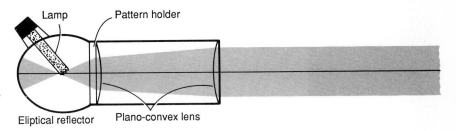

Figure 3.12. Elipsoidal spotlight; a cross section

For precise directional illumination or pattern projection, the elipsoidal spotlight is used.

to project patterns on backgrounds and to light individual set pieces where sharply defined shadows are desired and precise control is necessary.

The elipsoidal (shown in Figure 3.12) is like the fresnel in that both use a reflector/lamp combination, but differs in that it features two plano-convex lenses facing each other, which further focus the light output into roughly parallel beams of light. Elipsoidal spotlights are generally equipped with internal shutters that allow the shaping of the beam, a place for inserting metal patterned cut-outs in the path of the light beam, and a means of adjusting the distance between the reflector/lamp unit and the lenses for focusing.

PROCEDURES AND PRECAUTIONS

Whether using a portable lighting kit or working in a studio setting, you need to know certain basic operating procedures and safety concerns.

Electrical Safety

W/V = A is the formula with which to spotcheck adequacy of power.

Television lights use considerable electrical power. The greater the wattage of the lamp installed in the instrument, the greater the amperage or current flow required. Care must be taken to assure that electrical systems are capable of handling the power demands of the lights, especially when you work on location in old buildings. High amperage generates heat that can represent a fire hazard. It also creates the potential for severe electrical shock.

How do you know whether you have adequate power to meet your needs? You must calculate the load. An easy way to remember the formula is "West VirginiA" — W/V = A, or watts divided by volts equals amps. For example: You're using two 1,000-watt portable lights to shoot a news report in an old building. There's only one electrical outlet available and it is a 110-volt circuit (common household voltage) equipped with a 15-amp fuse. By the formula W/V = A:

$$1,000 \text{ watts}/110 \text{ volts} = 9.09 \text{ amps} \times 2 \text{ lights} = 18.18 \text{ amps}$$

If you connect both lights to the available outlet, the fuse will blow and you've lost the news story. Better to know in advance and find a way to light the scene with one instrument and get the story.

**ANOTHER FIRE HAZARD
(A Personal Account)**

Not only overheated wiring but also lights represent another fire hazard. A popular technique used on location is to focus the light onto a wall or ceiling as a means of diffusing and softening the illumination on a scene. It is called **bounce lighting**.

Beware! I once bought a new set of drapes for a Best Western Motel because a camera crew placed a portable light too close to the corner of the room and became so involved in their production that they didn't notice a problem until the audio operator heard the crackling of the flames.

As mentioned before, most studios have circuits capable of supplying the appropriate amount of power to the instruments in use. When connecting instruments, you must be careful that circuits are not on, lest a short circuit occur, and endanger you as you plug in the instrument.

Heat

Television lights generate a lot of heat. The current flowing through the filament inside the lamp causes it to give off heat as well as light. And while the filament is hot it is extremely fragile. Any jarring of the lamp can drastically shorten the life of the lamp or even cause the filament to break immediately. Good practice is, when the instrument is on, to move it gently while aiming, and to allow it to cool briefly before moving it to a new location. This will greatly extend lamp life.

Be careful when aiming lights, as they will be very hot to the touch and can burn you. Be especially careful with portable lights when they are used in public areas where others are unaware of the risk.

Furthermore, the heat rising from your lights can trigger automatic sprinkler systems, so be careful where you place your portable lights during field production.

Falls

In addition to electrical shock and heat dangers, studio work also involves working on ladders and handling heavy lighting instruments several feet off the floor. Care must be taken to avoid falls and to make sure that instruments attached to the grid are secure. Most studios use the double security of a special twist-lock electrical connector that will support a falling instrument as well as safety chains that prevent accessories and instruments from falling to the studio floor.

LIGHTING TECHNIQUES

Three-Point Lighting

How do you put all this information to use? A basic three-point lighting system is presented here as the foundation upon which to build more elaborate lighting schemes as you gain experience. Keep in mind that the system described is designed to serve the three functions outlined at the beginning of this chapter:

1. To illuminate the scene
2. To create the illusion of depth
3. To create or reinforce the setting or mood

This section concludes with an example of how the basic system can be applied in a typical lighting situation.

*Three-point lighting consists of **key** (spot), **fill** (flood), and **back light** (spot).*

As the name suggests, the three-point lighting system directs light onto a subject or object from three different angles with three separate instruments, as indicated in Figure 3.13.

Key Light   The primary source of illumination on the scene is called the key light. Usually, a spotlight or other directional source, for instance, the sun, does this job.

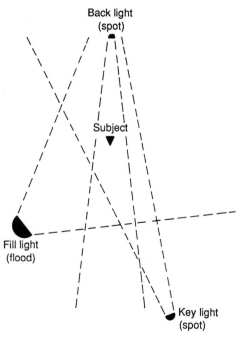

Figure 3.13. Three-point lighting system

If the only purpose was to illuminate the scene, a key light directly above the camera aimed at the subject would suffice. But since it is also desirable to provide the illusion of depth to the image, the light is moved to one side or the other so that it strikes the subject at an angle to create shadows falling away from the light source, providing a clue that the subject is more than simply a flat surface. Compare the results of different key light positions in Figure 3.14.

Fill Light Fill lights are used to fill in and soften the effect of the shadows created by the key light and to provide more diffused light to the scene in general. Fill lights add to the overall quantity of light.

Scoops or other flood lights are generally used for fill lights. In a natural light situation, reflectors with irregular surface texture are used to diffuse and redirect sunlight onto the shadow side of the subject. Notice the effect of adding fill light in Figure 3.15.

Fill light is an important factor in the third lighting function, creating mood. The darker the shadows, that is, the less fill light, the greater the sense of mystery or uncertainty. Fill light is also used to reduce the contrast ratio of a scene to make it match the capabilities of the camera being used.

Back Light As the name suggests, a back light comes from behind the subject. The purpose of the back light is to separate the subject from the background, further enhancing the illusion of depth by emphasizing the distance between the subject and other objects in the scene that are farther away from the camera. Back light has been added in Figure 3.16.

Back light has little or no impact on the overall illumination of the scene. Since it does not occur naturally, when using natural light you can create a back-light effect with reflectors to contribute to mood. Silhouettes can be created on television using back light only, with little or no frontal lighting, as shown in Figure 3.17.

Supplemental Lighting

In addition to the basic three-point lighting, several supplemental lights may be added to a scene to achieve a desired effect.

Background Light is illumination provided to make objects in the background visible as dictated by the mood of the scene, to adjust the overall contrast ratio of the scene, and to enhance the illusion of depth. Variations of background lighting are shown in Figure 3.18 (p. 98) Depending upon the situation, any of the instruments described earlier might be used as background lights.

Set Lights include lighting used to add emphasis, mood, and depth to certain elements within a scene. Spotlights that can be carefully controlled are usually used for set lights. Refer to Figure 3.1 to see the changes as set lights are added.

Figure 3.14. A key light alone provides adequate illumination, but when it is placed directly above and in front of the subject (as in the top photo), the result is a very flat, shadowless image with little depth. Moving the key light to one side (as in the lower photo) creates shadows that add to the illusion of depth.

Figure 3.15. Adding a fill light softens the shadows without totally eliminating them and reduces the contrast ratio between the two sides of the face. It is important that the fill light not create additional shadows. Diffused light sources are generally used for fill lighting.

Figure 3.16. Back light can be added for further modeling. The back light helps separate the subject from the background.

Figure 3.17. The ability of back light to separate the subject from the background is clearly illustrated by this silhouette situation.

How do you apply this system in the real world of television production? Here is an illustration.

ON ASSIGNMENT

Your field assignment is to cover a press conference in the city council chamber. The mayor will be answering questions while seated at a table, as diagrammed in Figure 3.19.

You are the first camera crew to arrive, so you have your pick of camera position and the opportunity to light the scene.

First, you put your camera in a position so that the mayor will be facing almost directly into the camera while talking to reporters. You make sure there is nothing distracting on the wall behind the mayor. Since this is a news event you should not make substantive changes in the setting's appearance, though there is nothing wrong with straightening it up and positioning your camera to take advantage of visually interesting elements that are already there.

You set up your tripod, camera, and recorder. You run a microphone cable to the mayor's table to make sure it will reach from the position you have chosen, and set up your microphone on the table.

Figure 3.18. Backgrounds can often be lighted separately, allowing flexibility in selecting mood and controlling contrast ratio. In staging a scene, you should position performers well away from backgrounds when possible so that each can be lighted independently.

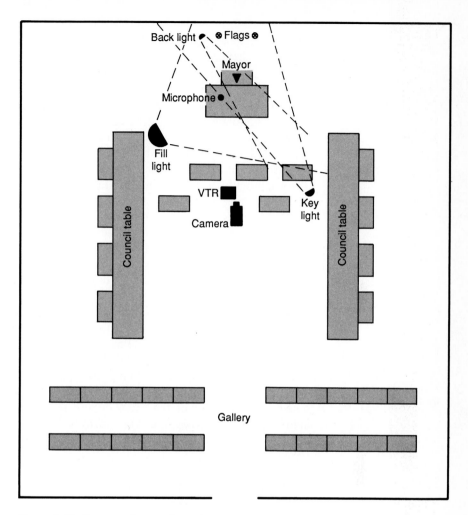

Figure 3.19. Press conference floor plan.

Next, you open your light kit and assemble the lights and stands. One of the instruments in the kit is a miniflood. Two of the instruments are minispots that can be focused. You place one minispot to camera right, the mayor's left. You run a power cord to it, make the connection, turn it on, and focus it on the chair where the mayor will sit. Good, the shadow will fall upon the wall well below and to the left of the camera's field of view. Now, before the key light gets too hot, you adjust the barn doors so that very little of this light is striking the back wall or the top of the desk. You want it to be concentrated on the mayor.

You place the miniflood to camera left, the mayor's right. This is the fill light. You run the power cord. But do you dare plug it into the same outlet that you used for the key light? This is a relatively new building with probably 15- or 20-amp circuits. Let's see. These instruments are all equipped with 500-watt lamps. W/V = A: 500 divided by 110 is roughly 5 amps per light. OK. Let's put two lights in this outlet near the camera, and the last light will be plugged into the outlet behind the table.

To diffuse the light you place a scrim in the front of the flood and then turn it on and aim it in the general direction of the mayor's seat. You allow the fill to cover a large area, including the wall behind the table. In this case, the fill will also provide the background light.

You place the other minispot near the wall behind the mayor to serve as a back light. It can't be directly behind because then the stand would be in the shot, so you place the minispot a few feet to camera left (the opposite side from the key light), plug it in as planned on the back wall, turn it on, and focus it on the area where you expect the back of his honor's head and shoulders to be. Be especially careful to adjust barn doors so that the back light is not in the eyes of the reporters or striking the lens of your camera, which would produce distracting lens flares from light refracted through the lens.

Now you need some help, so you hope the reporter will be back soon. Here she comes. You ask her to sit in the mayor's seat so that you can white balance your camera, check the microphone level, and check your lighting. The reporter holds up a white card directly in front of her face so that it is in the center of the area you have just lighted. You use the white balance procedure for the camera. The room lights are still on so the overall light quality is a mixture of the 3,200-degree Kelvin output from the portable lights and the light from the fluorescent overhead lighting in the room. You must remember that your camera is now white balanced for this mixture. When the reporter puts the card down you zoom in to set your focus on her face and then zoom back to a head and shoulders shot.

Looks good! The light meter in the viewfinder indicates enough illumination. As seen from the camera, the right side of your model's face is more brightly lit than the left. But the fill light brings out sufficient detail in the shadow area. The wall is darker than her face, which provides fairly good separation, and the back light provides a nice rim around the shoulders and the back of the head, further separating the model from the wall. A quick microphone check, and your reporter is done.

You put the camera on stand-by (to save the batteries) and go around to turn off all the lights until they are needed. A quick check of the stands and power cords — are any in a place where they can be bumped or could trip someone? If so, you tape them secure. Now you wait for the mayor and the other camera crews to arrive.

This example illustrates what was discussed at the beginning of this chapter. The procedure described is simple but it took some time. By using this simple approach and allowing enough time to do the job, you will end up with good-looking video. And so will all those other camera crews that show up late and have you to thank for the good lighting!

SETTINGS

Television coverage of personalities and events and presentation of stories and ideas must occur in a setting. That setting is actually defined by the shape of the television screen. But within that screen you must create a visual environment to surround the principle visual element.

The simplest television settings are close-up shots of on-camera performers or inanimate objects surrounded by nothing but a solid blank background. This is called a **limbo** effect; there is no context in the setting other than the fact that it exists within the television frame.

Most television images are gathered from settings that offer a good deal of visual context. They may be shot in real locations or in studio **sets** that create an impression of the real thing. Or they may be shot in abstract surroundings specially created to enhance the visual impression.

Functions of a Setting

Settings have a very practical function; they provide a place for something to happen that is conducive to the needs of a production. **Staging**, the process of moving performers and production equipment within a setting, is discussed in chapter 11.

Whenever feasible, you will want to adapt the physical setting of a scene to meet the needs of the camera, just as with lighting.

You will also seek to find or create a setting that is the most appropriate visual setting in which to deliver the intended message.

*Staging should take advantage of TV's potential as **theater in the round**.*

One word of caution: Often, new television producers make the faulty assumption that television must take place on stage in front of an audience, as happens in the traditional proscenium arch theater. This traditional arrangement means that the audience has only one perspective on the setting. Actually, television is more like **theater in the round**. Cameras and microphones can surround the setting, move through it, look at it from above or below, all to the advantage of the producer. The viewer accepts the fact that the production machines provide many vantage points and perspectives. What would be totally unrealistic or unworkable in real life, becomes completely acceptable within the confines of the television screen.

Types of Settings

Television settings are of two types:

1. Realistic
2. Abstract

Realistic   Much of the material presented on television is from the real world and takes place in real-life settings. In the early days of television, when equipment was not easily portable, great effort was put into creating realistic-looking settings in a television studio. In the 1990s, with highly portable equipment and worldwide live satellite transmission of scenes from locations almost anywhere in the world possible, there is little need for realistic studio sets. Field production takes the viewer to the real setting.

Abstract

Studios are now used primarily to create the second type of setting, abstract. An abstract setting is designed to contribute to the visual impression and to foster the programmatic goals of the production. It need not look like anything real, so long as it supports the functional and aesthetic demands of the production and its topic.

Behind-the-scenes settings have become part of what's communicated.

In the 1980s, the television studio became a widely used and accepted "real" setting. A variety of programs used the behind-the-scenes approach of showing a television studio set from a vantage point that also showed the production equipment and personnel as well as the lighting grid and the studio itself. Many programs are introduced by an on-camera talent who talks to the audience from the production control room or the editing room. Most viewers are so accustomed to this by now that they hardly notice it. To an audience living in a video age, the studio is the logical place for a production to be staged.

The "On Assignment" section of this chapter pointed out that news is one of the exceptions to the usual television technique of tailoring a setting to production needs. In the case of news coverage, television strives to have as little effect as possible on the circumstances of the stories it covers. That clearly includes capturing visual images in their natural settings and avoiding any appearance of staging.

Selecting a Setting

You will probably need to find suitable field locations and to create special studio settings for some of your first productions. In creating or choosing a setting, keep these considerations in mind:

1. Appearance
2. Accessibility
3. Control
4. Visual unity

Appearance

The camera is the true judge of the effectiveness of setting.

The setting should look good on camera. That seems obvious but surprisingly, many production settings contain distracting or inappropriate images. Remember, the camera is the ultimate judge of the setting's appearance. As cautioned in chapter 2, don't rely on your eye to evaluate a setting. Your eye is far more forgiving than the camera will be. Remember also that television production involves seeing things from many different angles, so the setting must be evaluated from the various camera positions that will be used.

Sets are always created but limiting; setting may include the great outdoors.

Many productions require special settings, or **sets**, that can be manufactured or created for a specific purpose. This is always true in studio production work, where a physical environment within which the production can take place will need to be created. Basic field production generally tries to take advantage of existing locations to provide realistic settings. In these situations, however, minor modifications of the location often will be needed to make the setting fit the needs of the production: perhaps nothing more than a rearrangement of furniture.

Set dressing, another aspect of creating a desired appearance, usually involves adding specific items to tailor the existing scene to the production. Large production organizations often have scene shops and art departments that specialize in creating these set dressings.

Some productions may also require properties, or **props**: functional items that are a required part of the scene staging. Common props include telephones, firearms, tableware — things that performers need to play out the action.

Another major factor influencing the setting's appearance is the lighting — naturally existing or lighting that can be created, as discussed earlier in this chapter. Skillful use of lighting to highlight desirable set elements and to hide others, combined with carefully selected camera angles, can make up for a lot of shortcomings in any setting.

Accessibility

Settings need prechecks for availability and feasibility.

Of the two components to the accessibility factor, one is obvious: You must have access to a location and you will probably need permission to use it. Don't ever take this permission for granted; using almost any location will necessitate permission from someone.

The second component deals with the utility of the space chosen. The setting must be workable for the equipment and personnel required to execute the production. For example, there must be adequate space for movement of performers and equipment, adequate power, adequate heating or ventilation, and absence of distracting sounds. You may have found the perfect living room in which to shoot the dramatic scene, but if it's too small to accommodate the cameras, lights, and microphones or if the power is inadequate for the equipment, the setting will simply not work.

Control

Whenever you are working on a production, you will seek to have as much control over every aspect of the process as is possible. The location or setting is especially important in this regard. To achieve the desired results, you really need control of such elements as the lighting, the temperature, the sound, the weather, and the access of nonparticipants. The only way to have complete control, of course, is to work in a studio, but as mentioned earlier, more and more television production is being moved out of the studio. The result: less control! Still, you will always strive for as much control as possible.

Obviously, when covering a breaking news story, you may not have or want control. You will capture what you can as things happen around you. Naturally, your results will depend upon your skill in coping with the absence of control.

Visual Unity   Sets, props, and set dressings are vital to the overall "look" of a production and should receive the same careful planning and preparation that is given to other production considerations.

The selection or creation of a good setting is another area where imagination and preplanning pay off. Effective sets can distinguish your production and enhance the communications process. A consistent look results in a unified impression even though cameras shoot from various angles.

Satellite technology now makes possible the combining of images of two people who are thousands of miles apart, making them appear to be standing side by side in the same room. The discontinuity that you create, however, is your responsibility as a user of the production system. The boundaries of what is possible always seem to exceed the boundaries of what is acceptable or effective. One of your tasks will be to use the system in ways that communicate effectively with the television audience.

SUMMARY

In this chapter you learned about the functions of lighting in television production, the properties of light, and the sources of light. A basic three-point lighting system has been introduced that has many applications that should become apparent during the production projects you will be doing.

This chapter also has introduced the two basic types of settings in which productions are staged. These settings not only have a functional purpose, but they also can make a significant aesthetic contribution to the communications process. You have been introduced to some considerations in selecting a location or creating a setting in which to shoot your productions.

The difference in capability between the video camera and your eye has received special emphasis. Until you have developed considerable experience, never rely on your eye alone to judge settings or television lighting. Always evaluate by looking at the scene through a camera while there is still time to make changes to the lighting or the set arrangement.

Finally, take notice of settings and lighting conditions in everyday situations you encounter. Why do some settings seem more appropriate for the activity they encompass than others? What combination of setting, lighting, and composition is producing the effect you see? And take notice of settings and lighting you see on television. Some of them are very good! And some are not! Based on what you have learned in this chapter, can you determine why?

NOTES

1. Gerald Millerson, *The Techniques of Lighting for Television and Motion Pictures* (New York, N.Y., Hastings House, Publishers, Inc., 1972), p. 12.
2. Ibid., p. 12.

3. Ibid., p. 15.
4. Ibid., p. 16.

REVIEW QUESTIONS

1. List the three general functions of television lighting. Briefly describe each.
2. List three properties of light that can be controlled during the television production process.
3. How is the quantity of illumination in a setting measured?
4. Describe two ways that illumination levels affect camera performance.
5. What is color temperature?
6. How does color temperature affect camera performance?
7. List three methods commonly used to white balance color video cameras.
8. Describe the differences between direct light and diffused light.
9. Why are reflectors sometimes used when working with natural light sources?
10. Briefly describe the two most common types of television lights.
11. List the basic components common to both types of lights and explain their function.
12. Why is the fresnel spotlight considered the workhorse of television studio production?
13. Diagram and label the basic three-point lighting system.
14. Explain the function of each instrument in the three-point lighting system.
15. Why are realistic studio settings less common now than in the early days of television?
16. List three factors to be considered in selecting the setting for a television production.

CHAPTER 4

Microphones

Television can be perceived through only two senses: sight and sound. Yet, sound has often taken a back seat to pictures in television production, having been variously used to supplement, complement, and reinforce the visual message. But if television productions are to realize their full potential, sound must be given equal attention during development of the presentation.

Traditionally, programs dominated by sound have been filled with words. They're known as **talking head shows**, because their content consists of pictures of people talking. Interviews, instructional presentations, coverage of public meetings, speeches, press conferences, all rely almost totally on the spoken language. Most production people find these programs boring to do and, they assume, boring for the audience. Many times that's true, and for that reason great effort has been expended to make these kinds of programs more interesting visually. Sometimes, of course, words are enough: When a president announces the end of a war, a mother expresses grief over the loss of a child, or an athlete celebrates a victory, the words may tell the story best.

Many television production personnel live by the old phrase "a picture is worth a thousand words." They have become so preoccupied with trying to enhance the visual aspects of their work that they have lost sight of the value of sound in communication. The result is often visually compelling programs accompanied by a boring sound component. They're not talking head shows; they're talking picture shows. You should strive to integrate sound and picture, blending natural sounds, music, and sound effects into a cohesive package that takes full advantage of the television system's audio capabilities.

This chapter describes how sound is gathered and introduces the components of the basic audio system. Chapters 6 and 7 then build upon this material and explain how sounds can be manipulated, stored, retrieved, and processed into new forms.

SOUND IN A VISUAL MEDIUM

Sound to Electricity to Sound

Microphones do for sound what cameras do for visual images — they convert sound energy into electrical signals. Those signals can then be processed and manipulated by the television production machine. Eventually they are reproduced as sound again by a speaker, as illustrated in Figure 1.1. As with the video signal, audio signals can be transmitted over great distances, can be stored on magnetic tape to shift time, and can be amplified both in the production process and by the viewer at the receiving end of the process.

System Limitations

Audio technology reproduces a range of frequencies comparable to natural sound.

The capability of the audio system to capture, preserve, and reproduce the quality of the original sound is much greater than the capability of the video system to reproduce pictures. Very sensitive microphones processed with high-grade electronics and reproduced by high-quality speakers can very accurately render the range of **frequencies** of the original sound. The conversion process does introduce some distortion, but it is much less pronounced than the distortion with video.

Perhaps the most significant technical limitation in television audio has been the traditionally poor quality of the speaker used in most consumer-grade television receivers. Fortunately, most manufacturers now offer good-quality audio systems that are capable of reproducing the excellent audio possible with the television system.

Attitudes

Until recently, an equally serious impediment to high-quality audio in television was the lack of concern for quality exhibited by industry production personnel. For years, television producers used the rationale that since most viewers had inferior equipment in their sets, effort to improve the quality of audio was wasted.

Additionally, sound equipment development, especially microphones, lagged behind development of video equipment for many years. To producers infatuated with pictures, the idea of putting a large, unsightly microphone close to a sound source, prominently visible in the picture, was unacceptable. Sound quality suffered to enhance video quality. For the most part, this is no longer true.

In effective productions, sound sometimes is the dominant element in a scene and visual considerations secondary. The development of MTV and the production of music videos in the 1980s illustrate this idea. For years, music had been used in television as a backdrop for video. Theme music accompanied program openings, dramatic scenes often included background music, and occasionally, music was used as the basis for pacing edited visual

Music videos exemplify the powerful merging of sound and sight.

sequences. In **music videos**, the sound has equal importance to the pictures, with video sequences often illustrating the lyrics of the song. Less creative productions sometimes run out of visual ideas and fall back on **lip sync** video, which does nothing more than show the performance of the music. And while this may be effective with some especially talented entertainers, it often provides weak support for the sound.

Separation and Synchronization

Microphones function independent of cameras. The television technical system isolates the audio signal completely from the video signal. They are gathered by separate pickup devices and handled by separate systems during the production process. Ultimately, viewers receive the audio and video signals simultaneously.

Sounds are handled in a linear fashion within the audio system. Unlike video, which consists of a series of still pictures displayed at a rapid rate to simulate motion, the flow of sound is preserved with no elaborate segmentation of the signal. The electrical signal corresponds directly to the original sounds sensed by the microphone. The changing frequencies contained in the electrical signal produced by the microphone correspond to the changing frequencies of the original sounds. The dynamics of the sound are represented by increases and decreases in signal strength. Thus, the ratio of the original dynamics is preserved in the electrical signal. The signal is then converted to sound by a speaker that reproduces the original vibrations and creates **sound waves**.

Sound waves are converted to electricity by microphones; speakers convert electricity to sound waves by vibrating the air.

THE SOUND GATHERING SYSTEM

Sound Control

Sound can be controlled in three primary dimensions during the production process. Careful control of the following dimensions is essential if you are to make the most of sound as a means of communication with your audience:

1. Selection
2. Quantity
3. Quality

Selection You will determine what sounds are captured by the microphone, which sounds are included in the final production, where they are placed, and how they are mixed and blended. The audience will hear only those sounds that you decide are important to the message being communicated.

Quantity You will control how loud sounds will be in relationship to each other and how many different sounds will be present in the final **audio mix**. Rarely, however, will you control the loudness of the final sounds reproduced for the audience, since in most situations the viewing and listening environment is beyond your control.

Quality   You will have considerable control over the tonal quality of the sound. You will determine where and how it is gathered and will often use a variety of **sound sweetening** techniques to enhance the effectiveness of the sound.

Control of these dynamics will be useful only when you have an understanding of how listeners respond to certain sounds. For example, building

*A proper **audio mix** can enhance the illusion of **depth***   on the simple concept that sounds from a source grow louder as the listener gets closer to them, you can create an illusion of depth by **mixing sounds** so that objects on the screen that are supposed to be closer will be louder. **Sound perspective** is created, which helps the audience judge the depth of the television scene.

Sound Gathering

The basic components necessary to capture, process, and reproduce naturally occurring sounds, that is, sound gathering, are:

1. Microphone
2. Signal processing equipment
3. Monitoring

The processes of recording and mixing, and the equipment used, are discussed in chapters 6 and 7.

Microphones   Sounds are created in the real world by vibration. The human vocal chords, the strings on a guitar, the concussion of a gun shot, all cause vibration and create a sound wave that is transmitted through the air. When that sound wave reaches your ear, it causes your eardrum to vibrate in a similar fashion at the same frequency. Nerves then transmit information about how the eardrum is vibrating to your brain where it is interpreted as sound.

A similar process happens in a microphone as seen in Figure 4.1. The sound waves strike the primary component called the **element**. Usually, the element will be either a **ribbon** or a **diaphragm** that moves in response to the sound waves. This mechanical movement is then converted to an electrical signal by the second component of the element, called a **transducer**. The different ways in which the elements accomplish this process delineate the major categories of microphones used in television production:

1. Ribbon microphones
2. Dynamic microphones
3. Condenser microphones

Ribbon microphones capture sound through a thin metal ribbon suspended within a magnetic field. The sound waves cause the ribbon to move

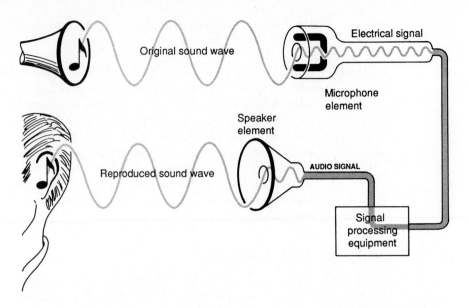

Figure 4.1. The sound wave created by the musical instrument is converted to an electrical signal by the microphone element. That signal is then amplified and processed before being sent to a speaker. There, the electrical signal causes the vibration of a speaker element, which recreates the sound wave captured from the musical instrument.

Ribbon microphones are sensitive but too bulky for general use.

within the field, which in turn creates an electrical signal. The voltage of that signal fluctuates in direct relationship to the frequency of the ribbon's vibration. When this fluctuating electrical signal is applied to the cone of a speaker, a vibration results that re-creates the original sound waves.

Ribbon microphones like the one shown in Figure 4.2 are extremely sensitive and produce excellent sound quality. They are not used extensively in television production because they are bulky, susceptible to wind noise and overloading by loud sounds, and quite fragile.

*Dynamic microphones are durable and resist wind noise, making them ideal for **field** production.*

Dynamic microphones, shown in Figure 4.3, have a diaphragm as the receiving element. The diaphragm is connected to a coil of wire that is surrounded by a magnetic field. When the diaphragm and coil move, an electrical signal is generated in the same fashion as described above for the ribbon microphone.

Dynamic microphones also produce good-quality sound. In addition, the diaphragm is more durable than a ribbon, so dynamic mikes are much more rugged and able to withstand rough handling and loud sounds. Dynamic mikes are especially valuable for field production because of their durability and resistance to wind noise.

Condenser microphones are sensitive, small, and used in all kinds of productions.

Condenser microphones also use a diaphragm as the receiving element. In this case, it is attached to a **capacitor** (a device that stores electrical

Figure 4.2. This Herald M-23a is an example of the classic ribbon microphone design. Newer technology has improved the appearance of ribbon microphones and reduced their size.

charges) with moveable plates. As sound waves move the diaphragm and the plates, the resistance of the capacitor changes in proportion to the frequency of the vibrations, and the voltage supplied to the capacitor by its power supply fluctuates accordingly.

Condenser microphones produce high-quality sound and are generally

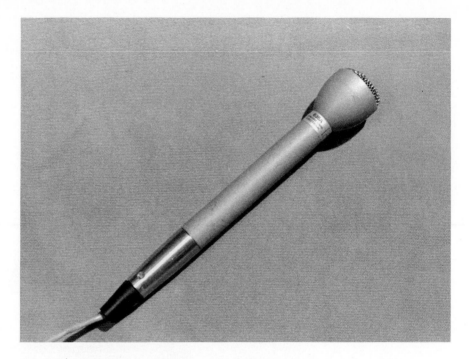

Figure 4.3. The Electro-Voice 635a dynamic microphone is noted for its durability and good performance.

smaller than dynamic or ribbon microphones. That makes them ideal for television use, where appearance — even perhaps the need to conceal the microphone — is a consideration.

Condenser microphones, like the one shown in Figure 4.4, require an external power supply to induce the signal and to **amplify** it to a useable level. Most are equipped with a small battery for this purpose. You will find that keeping a fresh battery in the microphone is one of those small, nagging problems that seem to plague the production process.

Condenser mikes are more fragile than dynamic mikes but are used successfully in both studio and field production. They are somewhat more prone to wind noise because of their greater sensitivity.

Microphone Pickup *Patterns*   A microphone can also be categorized by its **pickup pattern** — the direction in which it is most sensitive. Sounds gathered from within this area will appear close and natural. This quality is known as **presence**, or the quality of being "on mike." On the other hand, when the source is not within the pickup pattern of the microphone, the sound has a hollow and somewhat unnatural quality.

Microphones used in television production commonly have one of these pickup patterns:

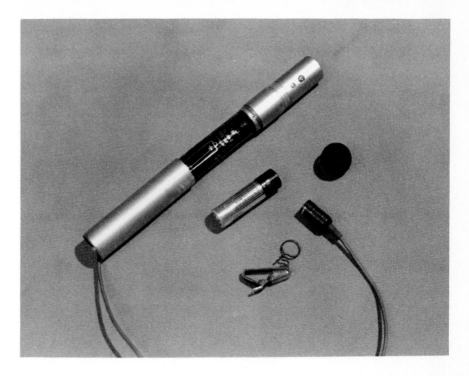

Figure 4.4. The Sony ECM-55b condenser microphone is small and produces excellent sound quality. The battery and power supply are incorporated into the connector.

1. Omnidirectional
2. Unidirectional

*The two basic microphone **pickup patterns: omnidirectional** and **unidirectional**.*

Omnidirectional microphones gather sound in all directions from the receiving element, as illustrated in Figure 4.5. The strength of any naturally occurring sound is proportional to its distance from the receptor, so all microphones are more sensitive to sounds that occur close to the element. The farther away a desired sound source is from the element, the more the microphone will pick up other sounds, reducing the presence of the desired sound.

Unidirectional microphones are more sensitive in one direction, most often directly in front of the receiving element. Generally, a unidirectional mike will be much more sensitive to distant sounds in its pickup pattern, but the pattern will be fairly narrow and the "off mike" quality of sound sources outside the pattern will be more pronounced.

A common unidirectional microphone is referred to as a **cardioid** because the shape of its pickup pattern is like a heart, as shown in Figure 4.6. Some of these microphones (Figure 4.7), have an extremely narrow pickup pattern; they are called **hypercardioid** mikes.

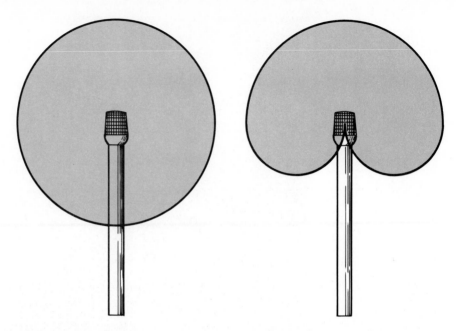

Figure 4.5. Omnidirectional microphone pickup pattern.

Figure 4.6. Cardioid microphone pickup pattern.

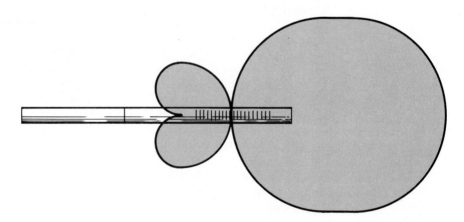

Figure 4.7. Hypercardioid microphone pickup pattern.

Common Television Microphones   There are hundreds of makes and models of microphones with a bewildering assortment of performance characteristics. As you are being introduced to the basics of production, you will probably become familiar with examples of these basic types:

1.   Lavalier microphones

2. Hand microphones
3. Shotgun microphones

Lavalier microphones are small, omnidirectional microphones, like the one in Figure 4.8, used to pick up individual voices. They can be either dynamic or condenser microphones, although as mentioned earlier, condensers are generally smaller and therefore look better. Lavaliers usually are attached to the subject's clothing with a small clip, suspended from a

Figure 4.8. The omnidirectional lavalier microphone should be placed close to the sound source. Newscasters commonly clip the lavalier mike to a tie, blouse collar, or lapel.

cord around the neck, or sometimes even taped to the clothing or to the skin (see the section "Microphone Placement" later in this chapter).

Hand microphones are almost any microphone that can be held by hand to gather sound. In everyday television production, especially news and sports coverage, small, rugged, and dependable microphones like the Electro-Voice 635a, pictured in Figure 4.9, are essential. They are normally omnidirectional dynamic microphones, often equiped with a **wind screen** to protect the element from wind movement. They can be held by a reporter or performer, give good sound quality because they're close to the source, and look acceptable in the shot. Viewers have come to expect the presence of the hand mike and some would argue that it adds to the believability of the presentation, since it contributes a "live" connotation.

Shotgun microphones are typically hypercardioid condenser microphones used on booms and **fishpoles** (an extension arm; see Figure 4.10) in situations where good presence is needed and a narrow pickup pattern is desirable to isolate a sound source in a noisy environment. Shotguns have the added advantage of being sensitive over a great distance and can usually be kept out of the camera shot.

Figure 4.9. News reporters working in the field frequently choose hand microphones. They are easy to use for interviews and stand-ups and can be easily put aside when freedom to move about is required.

Figure 4.10. The shotgun microphone mounted on a fishpole frees the reporter's hands and allows her to move without concern for entangling cables. As she stands and walks toward the camera, the sound person will move along to keep the microphone just out of camera range.

Signal Processing

*A microphone emits a weak electrical signal that must be **amplified**.*

A microphone is useable only when it is part of a larger system that can amplify the relatively weak electrical signal so that it can be recorded or reproduced into sound waves by a monitoring system or speaker (refer to Figure 4.1). Normally, most sound systems include some kind of **gain control** with a metering device that allows its user to regulate the strength of the electrical signal, or audio level. The level is set at a predetermined value and kept there through a variety of manual and automatic gain controls. The monitor or speaker will have a volume control to adjust the loudness of the reproduction, or what you actually hear. Sometimes, a unit called an **equalizer** will also be available to boost or suppress selected frequencies, making possible minor changes ("sound sweetening") in the sound tonal quality.

The initial boosting of the microphone's signal is done by a **preamplifier**, which is usually incorporated into the **audio mixer, audio tape recorder**, or **video tape recorder** into which the microphone is connected. Once the signal is boosted it can be recorded or processed through the system to a speaker.

Audio levels that are too low tend to be susceptible to random system noise that degrades the overall audio quality (the audio will have hum or hiss in the background), and levels that are too high introduce **distortion**, which also degrades the overall audio quality (sounds will be fuzzy and hard to understand).

Audio levels are measured by a device called a **volume unit (VU) meter**, as shown in Figure 4.11, which displays the signal strength on a scale calibrated in both **decibels (dB)** and **percentage of modulation**.

Loud sounds picked up by the microphone will show up as a large deflection of the meter; quieter sounds will result in a proportionately lower reading. Most systems are designed for proper audio levels to be displayed on this scale somewhere between − 10 and 0 decibels or between 25 to 30 and 100 percent of modulation, depending upon which scale you use. Audio signals that are below − 20 decibels or 10 percent are generally too low; those that exceed 0 decibels or 100 percent are too high. How to adjust and maintain proper audio levels is explained below.

Figure 4.11. This volume unit (VU) meter is calibrated in decibels (dB) on the upper scale and percentage of modulation on the lower scale.

Monitoring System

How do you evaluate the nature and quality of the sounds being gathered by a microphone? The VU meter will give you a quantitative indication of signal strength. But to convert that signal into sounds audible to the human ear, you need some kind of **monitoring system**. If the monitoring must be done in the immediate environment of the microphone, it is usually done with **headphones** worn by the audio person. Headphones isolate the reproduced sound from the pickup pattern of the microphone and prevent **audio feedback**, a high-pitched, squealing noise that results from the output of the microphone being looped back into the receiving element. If the audio operator is in a separate room, which is usual in a studio setting, then monitoring can be done with either headphones or speakers.

Headphones prevent feedback when monitoring sound near a microphone.

Don't confuse the audio level with the volume of the monitoring system. The VU meter displays signal strength. When that signal is reconverted to sound by a monitor, it must be amplified or boosted to power the headphone or speaker. When you adjust the monitor volume, you are adjusting the amount of amplification and hence the loudness of the reproduction; you are not changing the electrical signal level.

HOW TO GATHER SOUND

Criteria for Selecting Microphones

Every production situation requires the appropriate microphone.

Doing the job right often depends on selecting the proper tool for the job. That certainly is true with regard to gathering sound with microphones. As you begin work on your first television production projects, you should consider these criteria when selecting a microphone for a given task:

1. Nature of the sound to be gathered
2. Environment in which microphone will be used
3. Visual restrictions
4. Production considerations

Nature of the Sound

What type of microphone is best suited to the sounds to be captured? If the source is a string quartet, use a ribbon microphone, which is very sensitive and will capture the full range of frequencies involved. If it's a rock band, use a dynamic microphone to handle the high volume levels while still giving good **frequency response**.

Environment

If the sound is to be gathered in a studio with good accoustical qualities, an omnidirectional ribbon microphone could do the job. If you are trying to isolate voices in a crowded room, a microphone with a directional cardioid pattern or an extremely directional hypercardioid pattern like a shotgun may be in order.

Visual Restrictions   If the director or the camera operator insists that the microphone not be visible in the shot, a lavalier on a necktie or collar may work. Or perhaps a cardioid on a fishpole is required.

Production   If the script calls for the talent to walk a considerable distance while talking
Considerations   to the camera, a **wireless microphone** with no cable may be the only answer.

As you can see, selecting the microphone will always involve a series of trade-offs. Naturally, the selection process is ultimately limited by the equipment available to you. Learn the operating parameters of the microphones you have and work within them.

Microphone Placement

The microphone must be properly placed if you are to obtain the best performance from it. The microphone should be as close to the sound source as possible. The goal is to place the microphone to take full advantage of its pickup characteristics. Usually that means positioning the mike so the source of the sound is in the center of the pickup pattern.

At the same time, you must try to isolate the microphone from other sounds that could interfere with the desired sound. Wind is an obvious example. If the receiving element is exposed to the wind, the wind-caused movement of the diaphragm or ribbon will create a signal that can obliterate the desired sound. Many microphones have a special foam rubber boot, called a wind screen, that keeps the wind from moving the element without blocking the sound waves.

Placing a Lavalier   For many of your productions, both in the studio and in the field, you will
Microphone   probably select a lavalier microphone. These mikes are actually attached to the person whose voice will be picked up. Several considerations should be observed when using the lavalier:

1. Be courteous while working with the person to be miked. Remember, you are invading someone's personal space when you attach the lavalier. The microphone will change a person's appearance and he or she needs to be involved in deciding where and how it will be attached. On the other hand, you want the best sound possible and must find a microphone position that keeps everyone happy.
2. The lavalier is susceptible to noise from the rustling of clothing. Be careful when concealing the mike under a necktie or collar.
3. Route the cable in a way that relieves the strain of its weight on the attachment point and is visually unobtrusive. This may mean tucking the cable under the subject's belt in back or routing it through the back of a chair and away from the camera. Keep the cable out of the speaker's reach so it will not be held or twisted due to nervousness.

4. Be alert for jewelry that might swing as the subject moves and strike the microphone or the cable. Place the microphone away from jewelry. Be very careful about asking a person to remove jewelry to make room for your microphone, especially if the person is not a paid performer and is participating in the production voluntarily. You need the person's cooperation.

Using a Hand Microphone

*Holding a **hand mike** properly takes training.*

On many occasions you will put a microphone into the hands of a subject. Professional **talent** — performers — reasonably can be expected to know how to use a hand microphone or to follow your instructions. That is probably not true for other people and, therefore, you should not plan to give a hand mike to an untrained person.

The hand microphone, omnidirectional or unidirectional, produces good-quality sound if it is handled properly. Proximity is one of the chief advantages of the hand microphone. Since you've already decided not to worry about seeing the microphone in the shot, it can be held where it will work best.

In a typical interview situation, the hand microphone is held by the reporter, who moves it back and forth between the interviewee and him- or herself. This may seem simple, but inexperienced reporters working hard to pose good questions often forget to move the microphone. Or, an aggressive guest may take the microphone away from the reporter after the first question. It has happened. What do you do? You may stop the interview and explain to the guest that you will hold the microphone. If that's not possible, gently grasp and retrieve the microphone. The audience perceives the person holding the microphone to be in charge of the interview, and to relinquish it to the guest symbolically shifts that control.

Hand microphones can be exposed to rough handling; that's why dynamic microphones are popular in this situation. However, on most models there is a connection between the microphone and the cable near the mike. This can become loose, creating a bad connection. Those who use the microphone should be instructed not to grasp this connection when holding it.

Microphone Stands and Booms

You will probably have access to a variety of microphone stands and **booms** that can be used to put the microphone into the best possible position for sound pickup. Typically, the mike will be clipped or bolted to the support, and then the support can be adjusted to hold the mike in the correct position. Sometimes the microphone support will be visible in a shot; other times it will hold the microphone just out of view of the camera and as close to the sound source as possible.

Frequently you will need to gather sound from a moving source while at the same time keeping the microphone hidden from view. A common piece of equipment for doing this is the fishpole, shown in Figure 4.10. The long shaft with a microphone clipped to one end is held by an audio operator, who moves to keep the microphone in the desired position. If you are assigned this job, remember that rapid movement of the fishpole may create wind noise in the microphone and that you must handle the pole gently so as not to bump it, shocking the element and producing unwanted sound. Typically, you will be wearing headphones so that you can monitor the sound. Also, avoid becoming entangled in the microphone cables.

Microphone Cables and Connectors

A wide variety of microphone connector types are used in television production. One of the biggest problems you will face is making sure that the cables and connectors are compatible with the microphones and the other equipment that you are using. Learn the various connector types and find out where the **microphone adaptors** used to convert from one connector type to another are kept in your facility. As with any other equipment, audio connections must be secure to avoid intermittent or poor-quality sound.

Adjusting Audio Levels

During production, the audio operator controls input, monitors output, and adjusts tonal quality.

Once the microphones have been selected and are in place, the process of gathering sound can begin. As the **audio operator**, you will have several responsibilities during a production, both in the field and in the studio:

1. Adjust the **input gain** of the microphone to obtain the desired level. Normally this is done by adjusting the record level of the appropriate channel of the video tape recorder during field production.

    If the microphone is connected to a sound mixer or audio console, as will typically be the case in studio production, you will adjust the **potentiometer**, or **pot**, for the input channel to which the microphone is connected. In both cases you will make this adjustment by reference to the VU meter to obtain a level that peaks at 100 percent modulation.

2. You will monitor the sound that is being gathered. In field production, most times headphones will be used. In the studio, headphones or a speaker may be used. By monitoring, you are able to make qualitative judgments that are not possible simply by looking at the VU meter. Among these judgments that might require immediate attention would be the presence of the sound, the existence of undesirable background noise, interference and signal noise within the audio system, and tonal factors like popping P's or hissing S's that may be caused by the type or placement of the microphone.

3. If equalization is available, you will adjust the tonal quality of the various inputs to eliminate distracting or annoying frequencies. As an example, you are recording sound in a room where there is a noisy ventilating system fan that produces a low-pitched rumbling sound. By using the equalizer to suppress the low end of the frequency range, you may be able to partially eliminate the rumble

without affecting the quality of the other sounds that may not include those low frequencies.

In a studio production, the audio operator will typically have a number of other responsibilities. These are described in chapters 6 and 7.

USING NATURAL SOUNDS

Microphones are used to capture sounds and convert them into a signal capable of reproducing the sound accurately. To use microphones effectively, you must first know what sounds you want to capture and what sounds you want to eliminate. This selection process starts during the planning of a production and, if done well, makes the actual sound gathering much easier.

Effective use of natural sounds increases reality and drama on the screen.

As television equipment has become more portable and more production has moved on location, the gathering of **natural sound** has become increasingly important. Natural sound is sound that accompanies the activity seen in the video. When the airplane takes off, you hear the take-off sounds — which may be the only sounds or they may be in the background as an audio setting for something else.

Gathering natural sound may seem simple: Just point a microphone where the camera is pointed. Depending upon the setting, however, getting only the sound you want, with the quality you desire, may be quite difficult. There is no microphone equivalent of the zoom lens, which can effectively bring the camera pickup device close to an object by magnifying the image. Microphones must be physically closer to the sound source to achieve the same effect. Using the airplane example, with a wide shot it seems natural that the sound of the engine would be somewhat "off mike." But as the camera zooms in to a medium shot, the sound should have greater presence and that means the microphone must be closer to the source if the audio is to have the same perspective as the video.

Probably the most overused sound source is the human voice. For example, you may have watched television coverage of a dramatic event during which a news anchorperson felt compelled to talk continuously. All the audience really needs is the opportunity to see and hear what is happening.

Verbal descriptions of what is obvious in the pictures may be insulting to the viewer. Rather, use the audio to tell the audience things that cannot be seen and let them hear the naturally occurring sounds that accompany the pictures. When the sounds are especially effective, they can stand alone. In this way, the audience is provided with a richer experience through sights and sounds that reinforce and complement, rather than duplicate, each other.

The talking head is avoided by most production people. But sometimes, when the message is verbal in nature, the most effective approach is a close-up picture of the speaker and clear, direct reproduction of the voice, which allows the viewer to judge sincerity and emotions through facial expressions and nuances in voice.

Words still dominate television news, for example. Reporters traditionally tell stories through written narration and through **sound bites** or **actualities**, prerecorded excerpts of words spoken by newsmakers. Pictures are then gathered to support and illustrate the words. **Natural sound** is used where available and appropriate. Rare is the reporter who gathers pictures and sounds first, edits the visual images and natural sounds to be used, and then supports them with words.

Sound is most effective when it is integrated with the pictures as part of a comprehensive approach to telling the story. Sometimes pictures dominate; sometimes sounds do. The sound must be technically correct and must be consistent with the style of the video. That does not mean that sound and picture should duplicate each other; rather, they should be compatible and complementary.

SUMMARY

This chapter has focused on using microphones to gather sound. You have been introduced to the dimensions of sound that can be manipulated and some of the basic techniques involved in using microphones.

You have learned that sound can be the primary means of communication and that it should not be considered secondary to the visual aspects of the message you are conveying. In your beginning productions you should strive for an integrated and complementary blend of pictures and sounds gathered by cameras and microphones.

Microphones work on the same principle as the human ear. They respond to sound waves with vibration that is converted into a signal that can be processed and interpreted. The microphone gathers sound, but it must be connected to other components that regulate the signal strength and amplify and reproduce the original sound to make it audible to the human ear.

Technical considerations must be met before sound can be an effective means of communication. You have learned the basic steps in using microphones to obtain useable audio signals. From the outset, you must evaluate and select sounds on the basis of how they can contribute to the story you are telling.

Chapter 6 deals with storage and retrieval of the audio signals outlined here. Mixing and combining several sounds as well as combining sounds with various visual elements is discussed in later chapters.

REVIEW QUESTIONS

1. Explain how the television audio system converts sound to electronic signals and back to sound.

2. Why has sound traditionally taken a back seat to video in television production?
3. Discuss the three dimensions of sound control.
4. List the components of a basic sound system and explain the function of each.
5. How are microphones categorized?
6. What is *presence*?
7. Describe three common television microphones.
8. Why are windscreens sometimes needed on microphones?
9. How are audio levels measured?
10. Why are headphones sometimes used to monitor audio signals?
11. What criteria should be used for selecting microphones?
12. What are the responsibilities of the audio operator during the sound-gathering process?
13. What is natural sound?
14. Give examples of television productions dominated by the sound of the human voice.

CHAPTER 5

Generators

Generators produce graphics directly onto the television screen.

There is one group of production tools that, unlike the pickup devices discussed in the preceding chapters, do not need to capture naturally occurring physical phenomena to produce a television signal — they create the signal directly. These tools are called **generators**, since the first physical representation of their output is the image or the sound produced by the monitoring system: a television screen or a speaker.

Generators are used to create a wide array of images and sounds. These tools are the television equivalent of the artist's canvas or the composer's piano; they are an electronic means of creating images. Visual graphics and special sound effects are the most common.

A simple example illustrates the enormous impact that generators can have on production. Making a graphic title can be done mechanically by producing a piece of **flat artwork**, lettering on some card stock or paper, and then shooting the finished work with a television camera to convert the graphic image into a television signal. In the early days of television, that's exactly how it was done. Now, most modern facilities accomplish the same task by using a **character generator**, shown in Figure 5.1, an elaborate word-processing system that can write directly on the television screen. Sophisticated graphics generators can change the type into a limitless array of colors and sizes as well as draw new images, giving the illusion of three dimensions. No piece of artwork is ever created; the keyboard sends an electrical signal that produces the television image. The process used to create the title is faster and easier, and integration of the finished picture into the production is more direct than with earlier systems.

The 1980s produced a revolution in television graphics that parallels the rapid advances made in computer capacity. The potential of modern generators seems to expand almost daily. Aside from the technical limitations of the television system itself, perhaps the only other significant limitation is the imagination of the user.

126

Figure 5.1. A character generator being used to create and store graphic titles.

Generators can also be used to create replicas of images and sounds that occur in the natural world. Often they are used in this way because they are quicker and easier than capturing the actual picture or sound.

These tools also produce video and audio test signals. The signals are used by technicians as standardized references by which to calibrate various processing equipment. You will make use of them to adjust monitoring systems.

Monitoring systems, which have been discussed in preceding chapters, take on new importance with these tools, since they provide the feedback necessary to the user during the actual creation of the pictures and sounds. The graphic artist needs to rely on the color monitor — on its accuracy, for example, in choosing attractive and effective color combinations. The monitor does more than just display a result. It displays options; choices are made based on the way things look or sound on the monitoring system.

These generating tools and techniques are presented together in this chapter because they all produce a television signal directly from the control inputs of an operator. The images and sounds that result occur totally within the television system. Their only tangible form is the display seen or heard on the monitoring system.

Remember, this book is about the basics of production: the discussion of generators is limited to what you need to know in order to work with simple equipment on projects typically assigned in an introductory course. Near the end of this chapter, some more advanced systems are described.

TELEVISION GRAPHICS

The Role of Graphics in Television Production

Graphic symbols have been an important part of visual communication from the time of the cave drawings of prehistoric man. Written language and the development of the printing press and photography have advanced this process. Television, of course, is a relative newcomer to visual communication. But because of its portability and its capacity to display motion while capturing and transporting images through time and space, television is among the most powerful means of communication. Video can display all other visual forms within the technical limitations of the medium itself, and it can transport and proliferate those forms to an extraordinary degree.

Television graphics include printed language displayed on the screen, charts, graphs, drawings, and other artistic renderings. Graphics are sometimes displayed in rapid sequence to create **animation**, in which the viewer perceives apparent motion.

Graphics are commonly used to communicate such information as titles, names, addresses, telephone numbers, scores, or statistics. They are used to convey information that does not lend itself to other visual or aural methods or to communicate concepts not easily visualized. Other times, graphics serve to support messages contained in other aspects of the presentation: to reinforce or emphasize important points. A common example is the use of a name and title graphic in news programs to identify the newsmaker being seen and heard, much as newspapers use captions.

Historical Perspective

In the early days of television, most graphics were the product of an art department. Trained graphic artists produced two-dimensional flat artwork that could be shot by the video camera for later inclusion in television productions. Elaborate card stands, easels, and mechanical drums that could display moving credit rolls were used. The lighting and proper alignment of artwork and camera was a cumbersome process. With the advent of computers, electronic graphics systems have been developed that allow graphic designers and artists to produce television images directly from a keyboard or an electronic drawing surface, often called a **graphics pad** or a **tablet**, without touching physical materials.

When electronic character generators first became available in the late 1960s, they were usually located in or near the television studio or postproduction room. They were generally considered to be another piece of production equipment, to be operated by production personnel. The task of creating the graphics often was left to people who had no graphic training or background. This arrangement often produced less than optimal results. As systems have become more sophisticated, this is less likely to happen.

In many television production situations today, electronic graphics is a separate division of the production or art department. The area is often staffed by people with graphic arts training, experience with computer graphics, and perhaps some television production experience as well.

Graphics systems have changed dramatically in the last 10 years. Advances in digital technology have fostered this change. In fact, the graphic capabilities of today's personal microcomputers far exceeds that of the most advanced character generators of 15 years ago. It is difficult to keep pace with such rapid development. The focus of the discussion here is on the function served by graphics in the production process, on the basic operating principles and components common to most graphics systems, and on the ways you can use graphics to enhance and advance the communication of ideas, events, stories, and personalities through the television system.

What Graphics Do

Graphics are an integral part of most television productions; you have probably seen few television presentations that had none. In many ways, they have become conventions. You expect to see graphic titles at the beginning and ending of most television programs; you expect to see **lower third titles** that identify the person talking; you expect to see the numbers and team names that give you the score of a ball game.

Many times there are good reasons for using the same conventional approaches. At other times, conventions are used because they are safe and easier than trying to find a better way.

In your productions, use graphics whenever they can enhance the process of communication. The ways graphics can be used separate into three general areas:

1. Direct communication
2. Reinforcement or enhancement of other production elements
3. Establishment of the look or style of a production

Direct Communication The words, symbols, or drawings must have meaning for the intended audience. This is obvious, and when this is accomplished, the simple appearance of the graphic is all that is required to communicate the intended message.

Individual words, numbers, or symbols can be displayed on the television screen in isolation and be quite effective in communicating their meaning to the audience, especially when they are used in the broader context of other pictures and sounds that are part of the production.

Sometimes the words or symbols themselves are less important than the simple fact that a graphic, any graphic, appeared. For many years, motion pictures always concluded with a graphic title, "The End." Obvious, and

THAT'S HOW MTV DOES IT!

Music Television (MTV) became an influential force on television production in the 1980s. The techniques and strong visual style used in the production of the **music videos** shown on this popular cable service were imitated by many producers working in other areas of television.

This influence was clearly illustrated by an experiment I conducted with a class of advanced television production students. Each was assigned to produce a music video, including graphic titles as appropriate.

Every student in the class used a graphic title spelling out the name of the song and performer at the beginning and end of the production. And they all placed this information in the lower left-hand corner of the screen.

As was readily apparent, this placement had quickly become the accepted convention because that was the way MTV did it.

everyone knew it was time to get up and leave the theater. That convention is no longer in use. Motion pictures now usually conclude with a lengthy **credit roll** identifying the people and organizations involved in making the film. Many moviegoers now leave their seats as soon as the credits start to roll. It is the new graphic cue for the end of the film.

Abstract concepts can be communicated effectively through charts, drawings, and illustrations that are products of the creator's imagination and are able to stand alone as the principle communication device.

Reinforcement or Enhancement

Graphics are often used as an example for a concept presented in another way. They can be a specific illustration of a broader idea. For example, budget breakdowns are shown with pie charts. The chart can illustrate percentages more effectively than simple spoken words.

Graphics can be used to emphasize selected portions of other visual images by underlining, pointing out, or circling elements. Many sports productions currently use a system called a **telestrator**, which allows a commentator to draw lines directly onto the images of the instant replay screen to call the viewers' attention to specific player movements or actions.

Sportscasters use a telestrator to diagram movements or plays.

News shows routinely identify newsmakers verbally and reinforce that identification with a graphic title added at the bottom of the screen.

Style and Look

Television productions, by their nature, tend to contain a wide variety of images. That's what makes them visually interesting. But sometimes that variety may confuse the viewer with a program lacking unity. Graphics that are done in a consistent style can help alleviate the problem. Consistent type styles, consistent colors, consistent composition, all help to unify and "package" the production.

Advertisers take full advantage of this "look" concept by making sure there is a clear connection between graphic style seen in television and print ads and the appearance of the product in the marketplace where the consumer sees it at the point of sale.

Graphics Generators

Most television graphics are created by electronic graphics systems and most production facilities have this equipment. While operating methods and capabilities are quite diverse, certain common characteristics can be discussed.

Functions of the Graphics System

The graphics system serves two primary functions:

1. *Create and store images.* You will use the graphics system to produce the images that you have decided will facilitate the communication process. The nature of those images and their appearance varies greatly depending upon the design of the equipment in use. Since this process often will be time consuming and involve trial and error, the images will be prepared in advance of their inclusion in the final television production. Once prepared, the images must be stored until needed.
2. *Retrieve and deliver images.* During the actual assembly of the final television presentation, the graphics system will be capable of retrieving the images produced earlier and delivering a video signal into the larger television production system upon demand. The speed and flexibility of doing this again depends on the design of the particular piece of equipment.

Basic System Components

The system will generally have these basic components:

1. Input device
2. Processor or generator
3. Monitor
4. Storage system

The basic **input device** for a character generator is the standard typewriter or word processor keyboard. Generally, in addition to the standard letters, numbers, and symbols, the keyboard will also feature specialized function keys that give operating commands to the graphics system. More advanced systems will have graphics tablets that allow the operator to draw images on the screen. Some systems are able to capture images from a camera for manipulation.

The **processor** or **generator** is the heart of the system: The input is processed into electronic signals that will result in the desired images.

The images being created will ultimately be seen on a television screen. In order to operate the system, then, a **monitor** must be available so that the results of inputs from the keyboard or graphics tablet can be seen while they are being created.

Like computers, graphics generators require operating systems that must be accessed periodically to run the system. This information will be stored internally in the **resident memory** or, if its volume warrants, additional **disk storage** may be provided.

The system must also provide some means of storing the images created. Again, this may be done through internal memory or through **disk drives**. Naturally, images that are stored must be accessible for use when needed. As you can imagine, complex graphics systems with sophisticated capabilities require large storage systems.

Once the desired graphic image has been created and stored, the system will have a separate procedure that allows retrieval of the signal. The graphic images then can be integrated and combined with the other elements included in the total production package.

Operating Procedures

Most systems are structured in a way that allows the creation of **pages** of graphic information: individual screens or frames of two-dimensional images that can be composed or edited and stored and retrieved, by page number, file name, or other system.

Within that frame, capabilities vary drastically, although almost any system will have the capability to produce all the standard symbols available on a typical typewriter or word-processor keyboard such as letters of the alphabet, numerals, symbols of punctuation, and mathematic and scientific symbols. There will generally be a variety of **font styles,** or different kinds of type face, as well as a means to adjust the size and spacing of the symbols.

Many systems offer a variety of colors for the symbols and the backgrounds upon which they are displayed.

A page of type and graphics can roll, crawl, or be shown completely.

Various composition options usually are included, for example, horizontal and vertical centering and right and left margin justification. Most offer several display modes as well. Pages can be displayed completely or line by line. Most are able to **roll** through a sequence of pages so that the information scrolls up continuously from the bottom of the screen, as shown in Figure 5.2. Some also are able to **crawl** a sequence of continuous text on a single line near the bottom of the screen as shown in Figure 5.3.

Many systems are menu driven in the same manner as are computer systems, periodically presenting the user with a list of operating options from which to choose before moving on to a different function or activity. There is a multitude of possible operating methods. As with all other tools in the production machine, it is important that you learn and understand the capabilities of your equipment if you expect to use it effectively.

Figure 5.2. A credit roll is commonly used at the conclusion of a television program to smoothly display the names of those who contributed to the production.

Considerations in Creating Graphics

The most important considerations in the development of television **graphics** are whether the images will enhance the communication process and whether graphics are the most appropriate visual means. In the case of abstract concepts, graphics are the *only* visual means.

More specifically, will the image work within the limitations of the television system? Does it lend itself to the aspect ratio of television? Can it be displayed in only two dimensions effectively? Is motion critical and, if so, is there a way to use the system to animate the graphics?

Graphics is another area of production in which you are encouraged to experiment. Some generally accepted guidelines for using graphics are presented below, but they should not be considered as restrictions.

Readability   The technical limitations of the video image have already been discussed. Graphics must be easily readable in spite of those limitations. Lettering must be large enough to read comfortably from a normal viewing distance of six to eight feet. Fine detail in charts and graphs must be kept within the resolv-

Figure 5.3. A graphic crawl is often used to relay information that may not be a part of the production. Broadcast stations frequently crawl weather bulletins over programs in progress.

ing power of the television monitor. Subtle distinctions between colors must be discernable.

Timing   If something is important enough to deserve graphic presentation, then give the viewer time to see and understand it. Nothing is more frustrating to a viewer than to have an interesting graphic flashed on the screen so briefly that its content cannot be determined. More will be said about this in chapter 9 on program assembly.

Redundancy   Graphics can reinforce important concepts, as mentioned before. But some-
Graphics must be pertinent, accurate, and readable without being distracting or redundant.   times they become annoying to the viewer when they unnecessarily dupli-
cate information already presented in another way. For example, if your program began with an opening graphic title announcing *The John Doe Show,* followed by a camera shot of John Doe walking onto the set and say-ing, "Welcome to the show, I'm John Doe," do you really need a lower third title that spells out John Doe, host of *The John Doe Show?*

Pertinence   If you show a graphic, viewers will read it. Make sure that the graphic does not distract from some other, more important program element. For example, don't add a lower third title just at the most critical point in the interview when the police chief is confessing his drug addiction. Don't show the quarterback's passing statistics right after the linebacker makes a great tackle on the fullback—because if you do, most viewers will read the graphic and miss the answer to the question or the instant replay.

Sports is an area where statistics often reveal much about success or failure. Producers of television sports use graphics to tell the statistical story. Admittedly, many sports fans are obsessed with statistics. As graphics systems have become more sophisticated in the 1980s, sports producers have found novel ways to display more and more statistics. At the same time, the storage capacity of the systems has increased, allowing preparation and retrieval of ever more material. The end result has been that often it is difficult to "see the game through the graphics."

Accuracy   Perhaps above all other guidelines, make sure that material presented graphically is correct. Nothing distracts more from your credibility as a producer than numbers that don't add up, words that are misspelled, or titles that are incorrect. Mistakes are visible for all to see when presented graphically.

ADVANCED VIDEO GENERATOR SYSTEMS

Especially in the area of graphics, advanced technology has made significant contributions to the three-dimensional appearance of visual images and has expanded the use of animation. Elaborate **paint box** graphics systems are now capable of deriving an image from flat or three-dimensional artwork captured by camera or stored on videotape. That initial image can then be manipulated by painting with the graphics pad or tablet, enlarged, reduced, repositioned, or reshaded with different colors using the systems **color palette**, which generates a full spectrum of coloring options. This capability allows television artists to create unique images from almost any piece of original material as well as to use the system to render their creative impulses directly into the television system.

Chapter 7 covers the video switching equipment that is used to mix and combine visual images. In that chapter, more is said about **digital video effects** (DVE), another of the advanced systems that make manipulation of size and screen position possible. Many of the effects that appear three-dimensional are the product of DVE.

In your beginning projects, you are unlikely to have access to this kind of equipment. You will need to find other ways to express and create the images you need. But remember, no matter what equipment limitations you face, your imagination and creativity should face no limitations. Good ideas can generally be expressed within the framework of whatever facilities are available.

AUDIO GENERATORS/SYNTHESIZERS

Audio synthesizers create music and special sound effects.

No explosion in the use of **audio synthesizers** for television production has paralleled electronic graphics use. While most television production facilities have some form of graphics generator, only a few of the most sophisticated are likely to have audio synthesizers that can create sounds directly. In part that may be due to the fact that so much sound is available on tape, record, and compact disc. It may also be because of the lack of emphasis on sound, alluded to earlier.

As sound grows in importance in television production, you can expect increasing use of synthetic sounds in the form of music and special **sound effects**, just as the past 10 years has seen a dramatic change in graphics in response to the technological advances with graphics generators.

MONITORING SYSTEMS

Types of Monitoring Systems

Monitoring systems are of two types—electronic displays of the electrical signal itself and conventional physical reproduction of an optical image on the television screen or an audible sound produced by a speaker:

1. Signal
2. Picture and sound

Signal Monitoring

The test equipment used by technicians in the maintenance and calibration of the visual and audio signals consists of many sophisticated electronic devices. Two common video **waveform monitors**, both of which produce primarily quantitative displays, are the **oscilloscope**, which is used to display a number of different parameters of the video signal, and the **vectorscope**, which deals specifically with the color components. You have already learned about one of the most important audio signal monitors, the VU meter, used by both technical and production personnel. These devices all display a visual representation of the video and audio signals that can be helpful in calibrating the various pieces of processing equipment. They do not reproduce the actual pictures and sounds.

Picture and Sound Monitoring

The equipment used to make the final judgments about the video and audio signals are television monitors and sound speakers. These units convert the electrical signals into visible images and audible sounds that can be perceived by the human eye and ear.

In order for any valid judgments to be made using a monitoring system, its user must confirm that the system is accurately reproducing the signals involved. For that reason, test signals are used to calibrate and adjust the processing and monitoring equipment in television systems.

TEST SIGNALS

Calibration of the System

The final adjustment of the television screen is left in the hands of the audience. By adjusting the tint, color, and brightness controls on the TV set, the viewer can significantly alter the reproduction of the video signal.

However, this creates a potential for error during the production process. For example, how do you know that your camera has been properly white balanced and is rendering the colors on the scene correctly? You look at the results on a color television **monitor**, right? But how do you know that the monitor is properly adjusted? Perhaps someone has misadjusted the tint and brightness controls, altering the reproduction of the camera's output.

Monitors are checked for accuracy using color bars and reference tones.

The answer to all of these questions is, if you have doubt about the pictures and sounds being displayed, you must check the monitoring system against a standardized reference for accuracy. Otherwise, you must operate on blind faith in your ability to follow the camera adjustment procedures.

Standardized **test signals** are used to calibrate the processing and monitoring systems. **Color bars** are the most common video test signal; **reference tones** are used for audio.

Color Bars

The pattern of color blocks pictured on the front cover of this book is a standard video reference signal. It is electronically created by a device called a **test signal generator**. The colors come from the precise generation of selected frequencies within the electronic signal that produce the pattern when displayed on a properly adjusted color television monitor.

Video Display Adjustment

Four dimensions of the video display can be adjusted with this signal:

1. Brightness
2. Contrast
3. Tint
4. Color saturation

Adjustments to the monitor do not affect the strength of the electric signal.

Don't confuse the adjustment of the video display with the adjustment of the video signal itself, which can also be adjusted in these dimensions. Technical personnel normally assure that the output from a test signal generator is accurate by using waveform monitors that will show the results of adjustments being made to the generator. These waveform displays are primarily quantitative in nature. Figure 5.4 shows the monitor display and the

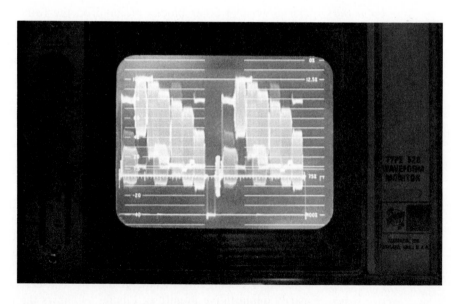

Figure 5.4. Video and waveform displays, of 100-percent color bars.

waveform image for the standard color bar signal with the video gain set at 100 percent. If the video gain of the test signal generator is then reduced by half, the monitor display and waveform imaging would appear as in Figure 5.5.

Notice that lowering the gain of the input signal has the same effect on the monitor display as turning down the contrast would have. But when the gain is lowered, all monitors displaying that signal would look like Figure 5.5, even though the monitor itself was properly adjusted.

Color bars provide a reliable reference for technicians to use when adjusting all the signal processing equipment within the video system. As a production person, you will use this same signal to adjust the video monitoring system. To do so requires only that you know what the signal should look like on the screen when the television monitor is properly adjusted. Figure 5.6 illustrates some of the key areas to use as a reference when adjusting the four dimensions on the monitor. You will want to refer back to the color version of the color bar display on the front cover as well.

Adjusting: Brightness

To adjust your monitor using this reference signal, start with the **brightness** control and turn it up until the black block just starts to turn gray; then turn it back to black.

Contrast

Next, turn up the **contrast** until the white block stops getting any brighter and set it at that point.

Tint

Now, adjust the **tint** or hue control until the individual color blocks are rendered according to the labels in Figure 5.6. Some find it easier to adjust tint using only the two blue blocks in the lower left corner of the display. When tint is set properly, those two blocks are the same shade of blue.

Color saturation

The last adjustment is **color saturation** or intensity. That is generally set to individual taste, though you will notice that if the color is turned up too high, the vivid colors begin to "bleed over" into adjacent blocks.

Remember, the adjustments you have made affect the monitor only. The test signal itself is unaffected. Once this process is completed and the resulting color bar display is correct, you can use the monitor as a means of making qualitative judgments about the color rendition of any signal displayed. If your camera output looks blue on the properly adjusted monitor, it probably means that the camera is not white balanced correctly.

Reference Tones

Using an oscillator, you should set the reference tone at 100 percent modulation on the VU meter.

The most common audio test signal is a reference tone produced by a tone generator. This piece of equipment uses an **oscillator** to create specific frequencies in the audio signal that will produce standard audible tones. The primary purpose in using the tone is to make a quantitative judgment as to the loudness of the signal. The tone is normally generated at 100 percent modulation and can be used to adjust the various audio processing equipment for proper calibration. When the tone is processed through the audio system and the VU meter indicates a steady 100 percent signal, the tone is using the full capacity of the system and any further increase in the volume of the signal through amplification will result in distortion. This is normally done using the VU meter described in chapter 4 and shown in Figure 5.7.

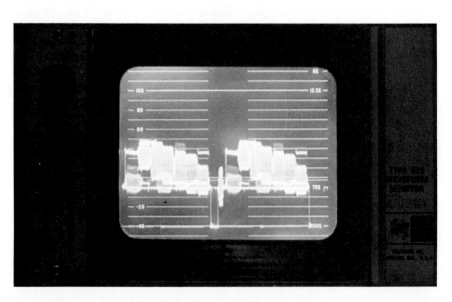

Figure 5.5. Video and waveform displays, of 50 percent color bars.

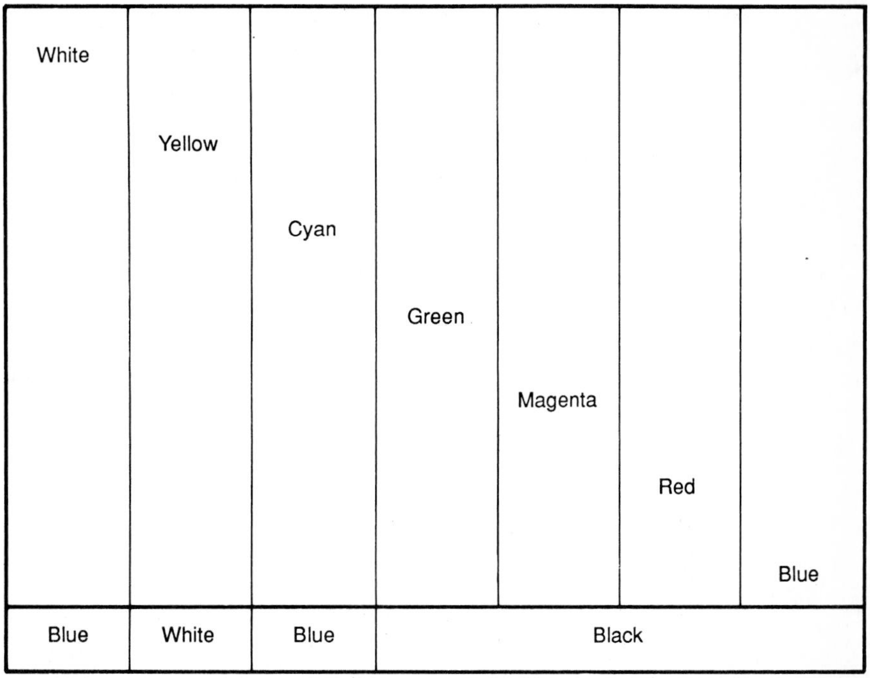

White
Yellow
Cyan
Green
Magenta
Red
Blue
Blue
White
Blue
Black

Figure 5.6. Standard color bars (see front cover for color photo).

VU
-20
-10
-7
-5
-3
-2
-1
0
+1
+2
+3
VU
PROGRAM AUDIO

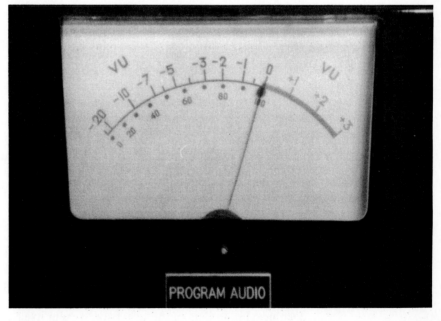

Figure 5.7. The 100 percent/0 decibel reference tone is using the full capacity of the audio system.

Once the VU meter has been calibrated with this standard reference, the loudness of all other audio sources can be adjusted using the meter to keep them within the desired range. This prevents **overmodulation** of the audio signal, which can lead to distortion during reproduction.

Similarly, any monitoring system can be adjusted by setting speaker volume according to personal taste, using the reference tone. Once set, the relative loudness of various sounds can be judged without regard to the volume control on the speaker itself. If a sound seems too weak, adjustment should be made to the microphone position or the amplification of the input signal, not to the speaker volume control.

These test signals are normally used by production personnel during the rehearsal and set-up phases of production. They are references provided for the adjustment of the monitoring systems that will be used during the production. Once production begins, judgments can be made with confidence that the video monitor or speaker being used is properly calibrated and producing an accurate rendition of the actual signal being made.

When programs are being put on magnetic tape, test signals are routinely recorded on the beginning of the tape before the actual start of program materials. Typically, 20 to 30 seconds of color bars and reference tone will suffice. That way, they can be used as a reference for properly adjusting the equipment used later to play back the material.

The test signals just described are unique to the television system. They do not exist in the real world until synthesized by the appropriate equipment and converted to images and sounds that can be detected by your eyes and ears. They are intended for use by technicians and production personnel as a means of calibrating the production machine. They are not normally intended for the use of the final audience of a production.

SUMMARY

This chapter has introduced several new tools of the production machine. All have the capability to produce television images and sounds directly through a generator or synthesizer in response to inputs from an operator. Monitoring systems are critical to the operation of these tools and this chapter has discussed ways of calibrating those monitoring systems to assure you that "what you see and hear is *really* what you get."

These generators provide another means of creating images and sounds for use in the communication process. Things that would be difficult or impossible to capture in the natural world are often easily created with these tools. They offer a wonderful opportunity for creative and imaginative users to find new and better ways to communicate with their audience. While there are guidelines to keep in mind, there are few restrictions beyond the technical limitations of the television system itself.

In chapter 1, the danger of being seduced by the operation of the television production equipment was mentioned. A reminder is in order at this point. Users of generators are prone to experiment and stretch the capacity of the equipment. That process is entertaining and challenging. In the pursuit of ever more elaborate new images and sounds, however, some lose sight of the original communications goal. The example used earlier with regard to statistics and sports is pertinent here. As a production person, no matter what the capabilities of the graphics system, remember that the first priority is to show the audience the game that results in those statistics.

Preplanning is crucial in all aspects of television production. Preparation of materials in advance of final program assembly is always a good idea. With images and sounds that are being created wholly within the television system, there is ample opportunity to experiment, create, rework, and store them in advance of the final production deadline. Remember, just as with most other elements of an effective television presentation, synthetic graphics and sounds don't just happen; they are the product of careful planning and efficient preparation.

REVIEW QUESTIONS

1. Give examples of how graphics can be used for direct communication in a television production.
2. Why are monitoring systems so important to the use of synthesizers and generators?
3. Give examples of how graphics can be used to reinforce or enhance a concept or idea.
4. What is the "look" of a production?
5. Briefly explain the two primary functions of a television graphics system.
6. List the components of a basic graphics system. Describe the function of each.
7. What is the most important consideration in the development of television graphics?
8. Why has there been no dramatic increase in the use of synthesized sound to parallel the explosion in electronic graphics?
9. What is the function of signal monitoring equipment?
10. Why should production personnel know about the proper use of test signals?

CHAPTER 6

Storage and Retrieval Systems

This chapter introduces the third major category of television production tools: storage and retrieval systems. Tools in this general category — using video and audio tapes, records, compact discs, film, and slides — do not create original images or capture naturally occurring sights and sounds. They capture the outputs from the tools that do those things. These systems can reproduce materials previously captured or created by other machines. Images and sounds that have been stored on videotapes, for example, become available to every producer who has access to the equipment necessary to retrieve them.

HISTORICAL PERSPECTIVE

Until recently, the process of recording pictures and sounds has been lengthy and cumbersome. The development of photography in the nineteenth century made possible for the first time the capturing of still images. Early sound recordings were made by mechanically carving grooves in a rotating cylinder. In the early twentieth century, motion pictures made the images move and, shortly thereafter, added sound. The optical/chemical process of photography and film made possible the storing of images and sounds, but the process was extremely time consuming. The development of electronic audio and video systems made possible instant hearing and seeing via live radio and television broadcasts.

Initially, there was no convenient way to store the electronic audio and video signals. Early sound recordings were made on cumbersome recording discs covered with acetate or wire recorders with very poor quality reproduction. Early television programs were captured with the kinescope process mentioned earlier.

Magnetic Recording and Playback

Simultaneous recording of a production, immediate playback, and easy storage and editing are possible with magnetic recording.

In the late 1930s, the process of **magnetic recording and playback** was developed. Unlike the crude etching of cylinders and discs and the time-consuming chemical process of motion picture development, **magnetic recording** stored the electronic signals in a magnetic pattern that was created on the surface of a tape coated with iron oxide particles. These particles could store a positive or negative charge in a manner that captured the frequencies and amplitudes of the electronic signals. The time reference for the fluctuation of the electronic signals could be stored by moving the tape at a predetermined speed. When the tape was played back at the same speed, the patterns on the tape could be read and converted back to the electronic signals.

Because the magnetic recording process predates the development of video cameras, sound signals were the first materials recorded. Tape quickly became a production tool as well as a storage and distribution method for the radio industry. Programs could easily be saved for later playback, and program segments could be recorded in advance for inclusion in a later production. By physically separating various sections of the tape and then reassembling them by **splicing** them together in a new order, the tape was **edited**.

Development of Videotape

Videotape recording, storing pictures and sound together, was introduced in the mid-1950s. There has been steady refinement of the process and the equipment, and the quality of the signal recorded and played back has improved dramatically. The size and cost of the equipment has gone down while its reliability has gone up.

Chapter 1 talked about the revolution that magnetic recording created in television. Suddenly, users of the television system could control time and space. Programs could be done at one time and shown at another, just as had been done with audio tapes in radio. Videotapes containing programs could be transported from one television station to another for later showing. Duplicate copies of videotape programs could be made and distributed. Television stations used videotape recording and playback to record programs from the networks for later playback at more convenient times, and they also acquired prerecorded programs on videotape from suppliers.

In the 1960s, videotape became a production tool in television, just as audiotape had in radio. Previously recorded material could be replayed as part of a subsequent production. Technology was developed to electronically edit videotape, that is, to arrange images and sounds from one tape into a new combination on another tape and to assemble production elements from a number of different sources into a unique, final production.

Field Recording

As technology improved, audio and then video recording equipment became smaller and more portable. Location recording became easier, and more production moved out of the studio. Images and sounds could be captured in the field with cameras and microphones, recorded on magnetic tape, and taken to a production facility for editing and reassembly on videotape.

Slow Motion   Videotape technology also created another revolution when it became possible to record action in real time and then replay it at a slower speed, producing slow motion. This introduced a totally new dimension to production. Television producers have used slow motion for entertainment and to give audiences new insights into many activities.

Technical Limitations   As various manufacturers have developed recording techniques and processes, they have often used different methods, for instance, in the way the magnetic information is placed on the tape (the specific use of tape width or channels), the speed of the tape, and the arrangement of the various technical components of the recording and playback system. The result has been

*Differences in **videotape** formats creates incompatibility.*   a variety of **videotape formats**, listed on pages 158–159, which has often resulted in compatibility problems: tapes recorded on one type of machine in one format will not necessarily play back on another. Although this is a problem as new systems are introduced, the marketplace gradually tends to sort these out; one format becomes dominant and ultimately becomes the standard.

Magnetic recording makes possible the duplication and copying of signals from one tape to another. That is one of the most important functions of the process and the means by which videotape editing is accomplished. But duplication of video and audio carries a price. Each copy suffers a slight loss of signal quality due to the inherit limitations of the electronic process. Depending upon the sophistication of the equipment used, this may be hardly noticeable or very objectionable, but duplication diminishes some technical quality of the pictures and sounds compared with the original.

Most television producers make extensive use of video and audio recording and playback. As you will see, most producers also use other retrieval systems to take advantage of materials already available in some other form. Records, compact discs, 16-millimeter motion picture film, 35-millimeter slides, all provide images and sounds that have been stored and can be retrieved and converted to television signals for use in television productions. These represent a significant resource that can be used to enhance the television production.

USING STORAGE AND RETRIEVAL SYSTEMS

While all the systems presented here are important to the production process, you will find that the functional role of videotape is pivotal. You will use it to temporarily store images and sounds, you will use it as a source of archival materials, you will use it as a tool to manipulate and rearrange images and sounds, and you will probably use it to store the final version of your production. You will record on videotape in the field and in the studio. You will edit from one videotape machine to another. You will replay materials from videotape into studio productions that are being done live or being stored on tape. You will use it to make additional copies of finished productions. It's hard to imagine the television production process without the use of videotape.

Functions of Storage and Retrieval Systems

Storage and retrieval tools make production easier and expand its potential. They serve four important functions that you will probably utilize in every project you do:

1. Control
2. Access
3. Portability
4. Duplication

Control   The most obvious function of storage/retrieval systems is control. In the storage mode, magnetic recording allows you to capture images and sounds, put them on the shelf, and recall them whenever they are needed. It gives you the control of both time and space that is one of the greatest powers of the television system.

In the retrieval mode, all these tools allow you to reuse an image or sound as often as necessary.

In addition, magnetic recording allows you to redo something as many times as necessary to achieve the results desired. Those production elements that are successful can be reused; those that are not can be eliminated.

These storage/retrieval tools also allow you to give the audience new insight into subjects by repeating the display of information or by slowing down or stopping the action so that images can be dissected and analyzed.

Access   A huge library of images and sounds is available that have been stored in one technological form or another. At your disposal will be images and sounds already recorded for inclusion in your production.

Portability   Storage and retrieval systems provide a convenient way of transporting images and sounds not only from one location to another but also, within the context of a production, from one point in time to another.

As a storage system, the equipment is quite portable so the options as to where you will collect images and sounds is largely unrestricted. Video and audio can now be recorded almost anywhere.

Duplication   Copies of most images and sounds can be made using storage and retrieval tools, making broad distribution of programs possible. Copying is also the primary method of editing.

It is not feasible to describe all the ways that these tools can be used in a television production. The problem that you will face in deciding what meets your needs will be one of overabundance, not of scarcity. Once again, the danger of seduction looms. Learning to operate this equipment is exciting. Having access to all the images and sounds can be intoxicating. There is a natural tendency to want to use it all.

But again, your job is to decide which images and sounds will most effectively communicate your message. Once you know, these tools are available to help obtain that image or sound.

THE MAGNETIC RECORDING AND PLAYBACK PROCESS

*Magnetic energy alters tapes by creating a **pattern** of electrically charged particles.*

You have already been introduced to ways some production tools produce an electrical signal. Such signals can be stored on audio- and videotapes through a process called magnetic recording and can be retrieved through playback. Between the recording and the playback, the signals are in limbo, stored in a **pattern** of charged particles on the surface of a tape. When the tape is played back, the patterns re-create the original electrical signals, and you see and hear the resulting pictures and sounds on video monitors and sound speakers. The pattern is still on the tape. If you play it another time, the same pictures and sounds result. However, if the tape is placed too close to a source of electromagnetic energy, the pattern will be disturbed and will no longer produce the desired playback. If you choose to rerecord the tape, the old pattern will be erased and replaced by a new one representing the new signals.

Magnetic Recording and Playback Equipment

The equipment used to accomplish this process includes five basic components:

1. Input section
2. Tape transport
3. Record and playback heads
4. Output section
5. Operating controls

Storage Process

Input gain is the relative strength of the video or audio signal to be recorded.

Recording starts with the video or audio signal to be stored. The signal will be routed to the **input** of the recorder. Most recorders have monitoring systems that display both the input signal and the actual pictures and sounds. By monitoring the signal, you will be able to adjust the strength of the signal to match the requirements of the recorder, usually through a control that can be used to adjust **input gain**. Once the signal strength is adjusted, the signal is processed into a form useable by a **record head**, which is the component of the recorder that creates the magnetic pattern that stores the input signal. When the record head is turned on and comes in contact with the surface of a recording tape loaded onto the **tape transport** (which moves the tape through the recording machine), then the record head magnetizes and arranges the particles of iron oxide on the tape into a pattern that represents the electronic signal.

Heads Most audio recorders actually have three fixed heads that contact the tape as it moves through the machine:

1. Erase head
2. Record head
3. Playback head

Figure 6.1 labels the heads on an open-reel audio recorder; this system does not use cassettes or cartridges but rather two reels or spools to supply and take up the tape.

*The **erase head** prepares tape for the recording of new patterns by the record head.*

The **erase head** contacts the tape first. If the machine is in the record mode, the erase head is turned on and neutralizes the charge of any particles on the tape. It prepares the tape to receive a new pattern.

The **record head** then creates a new pattern in response to the input signal.

Figure 6.1. This Otari open-reel machine can record and play back two-track stereo. The four-track head can be selected for playback only of tapes recorded on another machine. The selection of playback heads is made with a two-position switch not visible in the photo.

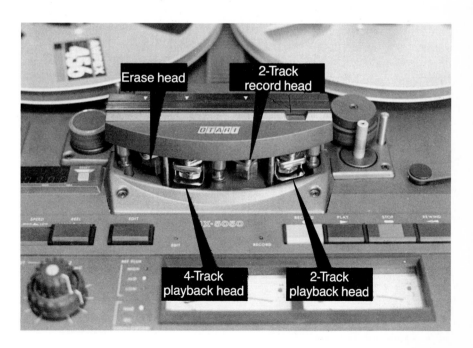

The **playback head** reads the pattern just recorded and produces an immediate output to a monitor.

Tracks   As you know from previous chapters, input signals change and fluctuate. The magnetic recording stores those changes by moving the tape at a constant rate. As the tape moves past the record head, the pattern generated is stored on the oxide, creating a **track** of magnetic patterns.

An **open-reel** audio recorder may use the full width of the tape to create this linear track, or trail of information. This method would produce the best quality recording for any given tape width, since it would distribute the information over the most particles. This is important because the greater the oxide density, the less potential for loss due to shedding of individual particles as the tape ages and is constantly subjected to the wear of being passed over the various surfaces within the recording machine.

If the recording is to be made in **stereo**, at least two distinct channels of information must be created on the tape, as illustrated in Figure 6.2.

Tape Speed   In order for this system to be reliable and accurate, the speed of the tape must be carefully regulated. Tape speed stability is of major concern in all recording. It is so critical with video recording that a special reference signal called **control track** is recorded on the moving tape as a means of regulating the tape speed and synchronizing the various tape functions when the tape is played back later. This is discussed more fully under "Retrieval Process," page 152.

*The **control track** provides critical regulation of videotape speed.*

Moving Video Heads   Video recording is especially complex, since both the tape and the record head are moving. Much more information must be recorded to store the video signal than was required for the audio signal, and moving the head as well as the tape results in a series of diagonal tracks across the tape: the head moves diagonally on the tape and this allows more recording room. Move the tape rapidly and you provide greater space upon which to store the magnetic patterns. The alternative would be to make the tape very wide. In fact, early videotape was 2 inches wide and moved through the machine at 15 inches per second. The video signal was recorded by four separate heads mounted on a spinning wheel that created 32 individual tracks on the

Figure 6.2. In the two-track stereo mode, the machine pictured in Figure 6.1 would utilize the full width of the 1/4-inch tape to create two distinct tracks of information.

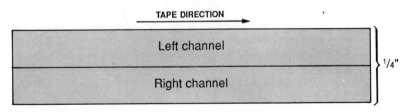

TAPE DIRECTION

Left channel

Right channel

$1/4"$

tape just to store the information necessary to reproduce a single frame of video information. Such a recording system is diagrammed in Figure 6.3. These **quadruplex** or four-headed machines were the first practical video tape recorders developed. Some were still in use by broadcast stations in the 1980s.

More modern technology has resulted in narrower tape moving at slower speeds and fewer video heads recording *longer* diagonal tracks on the tape. Most video machines have two heads mounted on a rotating assembly that results in each, exactly synchronized, making diagonal tracks upon the surface of the tape as it moves by. They're known as **helical scan** machines. The two heads are mounted 180 degrees apart on the **headwheel** or **scanner** so that one head is always in contact with the tape. (Both the record and playback functions are commonly performed by each head.) The fairly common 3/4-inch U-matic tape format stores all the information for one field of video in one long diagonal track, as shown in Figure 6.4. Two of these tracks combine to create one complete frame.

Video tape recorders must also record audio signals. This is commonly accomplished in the same way that audio-only machines record, by utilizing a fixed audio record head that creates a single lateral or linear track of magnetic patterns on some portion of the tape. More advanced systems may have two or even three individual audio tracks in addition to the section of the tape used for the video tracks, and at least one other track designated for the control track (see Figure 6.4).

In television production, the action of starting a tape in motion is called **rolling the tape.** Since tape speed is so critical, it's important to remember that most tape machines will require a **preroll** time of from two to five seconds when the tape is first set in motion, before the speed stabilizes. This is important, since material recorded prior to the tape speed being stabilized

Preroll before actual recording to stabilize tape speed.

Figure 6.3. Quadruplex videotape recording track configuration.

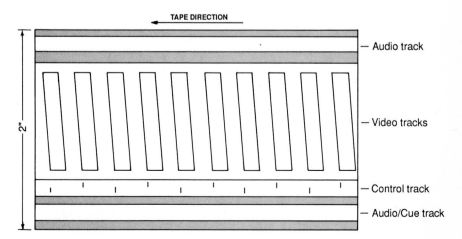

TAPE DIRECTION

2"

— Audio track

— Video tracks

— Control track

— Audio/Cue track

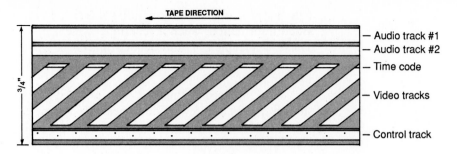

Figure 6.4. Track configuration of the 3/4-inch U-matic videotape recording.

is not retrievable. The practical application of this is that you should make sure that the recording machine is rolling before you turn on the input signal. If you're recording your voice from a microphone, pause briefly to let the tape stabilize before you begin speaking. If you are shooting video in the field, roll the tape for at least five seconds before you start the action in front of the camera, or move the camera.

Retrieval Process

The other half of the process is called playback. The playback machine must move the tape at the same speed at which it was recorded, align the various **playback heads** with the correct tracks on the tape, and read the magnetic patterns so as to convert them back to the video and audio signals that were originally part of the input. When that process is completed, the playback machine's **output** can be used, just as the signal from any other source, as part of a production. The images and sounds are perceptible on monitoring systems and can be integrated with other images and sounds.

Some adjustments, as you have learned, can be made to the input signal; most machines will process and amplify the *output* signal as well, to bring it up to the intensity of other signals within the production system.

Playback Heads In most audio recorders, the playback head reads the recording immediately after it is made and produces an output signal from the pattern just created. This allows the operator to immediately confirm that the recording is being made. This same playback head is used in the normal playback mode as well. On most professional-quality recorders, you will be able to switch the monitoring system back and forth between input and output while recording to compare the sounds going in with the sounds coming back from the tape. There will be a slight time delay, since the signal for any given sound had to travel the short distance between the record and playback heads before being reproduced.

Because of the complexity of moving heads on video machines and the fact that the same heads record and play back, the instant playback feature was not available on video tape recorders until approximately 1980. Some manufacturers now mount a third playback-only head, immediately behind one of the dual-purpose heads, to monitor the recording. It's sometimes called a **confidence head** because it allows the operator to ensure that the recording is being made as expected.

Prior to the development of this system, video tape recordings could be checked only after a production was completed. If something was wrong with the machine or with the tape itself, you didn't know until the recording was over. You can imagine the frustration of early users of videotape who would produce entire programs, only to find that some of the oxide had rubbed off the tape backing and become attached to the video head, effectively clogging it and rendering the recording unusable. The only alternative was to clean the machine, insert another tape, and try again.

Control Track   The **control track** placed on the videotape during recording is critical to accurate playback. The synchronization of the tape speed and the alignment of the proper head on the proper track can be accomplished only when the playback machine can correctly read and follow the timing provided by the control track. Most machines will have a **tracking control** that allows the user to make small adjustments to correctly line up the playback with the material on the tape.

Nonstandard Playback   Some machines are capable of **slow-motion playback** and **still frame.** Put simply, these machines use special processing and tape transports to move the tape more slowly than normal so that the playback heads pass over the same signal more than once. As you can imagine, if one pass of the 3/4-inch playback head produces one frame of video, and the tape is stopped so that it passes over that same head repeatedly, the resulting output would be one continuous reproduction of that single frame. If the tape moves forward more slowly than normal, you will see the same frame displayed several times before moving to the next, which in turn will be shown several times. Building on the persistence-of-vision concept, the preception will be of continuous motion at a slower speed.

When the tape moves at irregular speeds, special **time-based correctors** are required to stabilize the picture and to compensate for the unusual tape speed. Most time-base correctors also have additional processing circuits to adjust the nature and strength of the output signal (color level, for example).

Operating Modes and Procedures

Most tape machines have record, playback, fast forward, rewind, stop, and eject controls.   While magnetic recording and playback systems may have a variety of operating modes and procedures, most will also share some common ones. You should learn the specific capabilities of the equipment you will be using.

Tape Loading   The tape will be either wound onto reels or enclosed within a **cassette** or **cartridge.** In the first case you will need to know how to load the reel of tape onto the transport and thread the tape through the **tape path** to a **take-up**

reel, which gathers the tape after it has been used. The tape is used beginning to end and, normally, after use, it is **rewound** back onto the original supply reel so as to be ready for the next use. Figure 6.5 shows a typical tape path for an open-reel audio tape machine.

In the second case, the tape comes from a specialized package that provides supply and take-up reels internally. Loading cassettes and cartridges is easy; simply insert the unit and the machine will thread itself. When finished, press the **eject** or **tape release** button.

The process the videotape machine uses to extract the tape from a cassette and thread it into the tape transport is complex and time consuming. That causes delay between the time the cassette is pushed into position and the time it is ready for use. This delay, coupled with the time required to preroll the tape, means that several seconds will elapse between the loading of a cassette and its readiness for use.

Tape Position   Most machines will have some form of **tape counter,** used to identify and/or mark specific points along the length of the tape. This will usually be a visual display that shows the length of tape footage or the time calibrated to the length and speed of the tape. This counter can be reset to zero at the discretion of the operator. It provides a convenient though imprecise indication of location on the tape.

Figure 6.5. Unlike self-threading cassettes and cartridges, open-reel tapes must be properly threaded into the tape transport by hand.

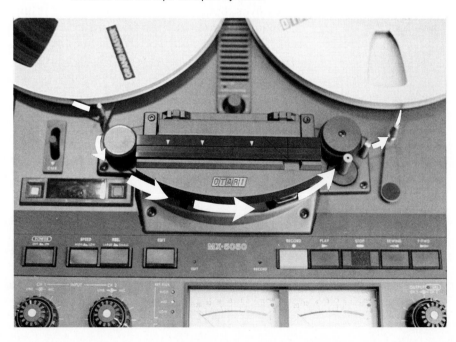

Controls will be provided to **fast forward** or **rewind** the tape at high speed to expedite the process of locating the desired tape position. Typically, you will not see or hear the material on the tape during high-speed positioning of the tape. To terminate the high-speed positioning you will normally need to press the **stop** control.

For example, you load a videocassette into the machine and want to find certain material for playback that is two minutes from the beginning of the tape. You press the reset button on the tape counter to zero, press fast forward and watch the counter until it reaches approximately two minutes, press the stop button, then press play and find the exact beginning of the material you want. Once the tape is in the desired position you will choose one of the normal operating modes.

Record

There are safeguards against inadvertent recording or erasing.

Most recorders have a safety system that requires you to depress two controls simultaneously to activate the record mode. Since recording will erase any material previously stored on the tape, this safety feature prevents you from inadvertently hitting one wrong button and accidentally erasing material that you want to preserve. As an added reminder, many will feature a red button for the record control and may also have a red indicator light to warn the operator that the machine is recording.

Additional protection is provided with some types of videocassettes. The cassette itself may include a **record tab,** a plastic button or flange on the container that can be removed to prevent inadvertent recording. Videotape users have been embarrassed to learn that what they thought was a machine malfunction turned out to be the result of a missing record tab.

When the record mode is selected, the input section processes the incoming signal, the tape is put into motion at its normal speed, the record head is turned on, and the signal is recorded as outlined earlier. The monitoring system displays the signal coming into the input system; some machines can be switched to display playback of the material immediately after it is recorded. This monitoring selection may be marked as EE/recorder, input/output, or source/tape.

Play

Pressing the play button will cause the machine to turn on the playback head, start the tape at normal playback speed, and turn on the output section to process the signal from the tape into a useable video or audio signal. You will see and/or hear the results through the monitoring system.

Cue

Many open-reel audio tape machines have a control that turns on the playback head and pulls the tape up against the head without activating the tape transport. This feature allows you to move the tape back and forth by hand at a slow speed to precisely locate information on the tape by listening to the audio monitor.

Shuttle or Search

Most videotape machines have a control that turns on the playback head and allows you to move the tape at variable speeds from very slow frame-by-frame display to two or more times normal speed while seeing the pictures and hearing the sound reproduced through the monitoring system. Usually the tape can be moved forward or backward. This feature allows quick and precise cueing of the tape.

Still or Pause

Pausing too long will wear out videotape.

When the tape transport is not moving the tape but the tape is loaded and in contact with the heads, a continuous display of the single field of video recorded at that point on the tape will be visible.

It's important to understand that this feature requires that the playback head be in contact with the tape. If the tape is not moving, the video heads (which move) will be constantly rubbing against the same spot on the tape, causing excessive wear on the tape and the heads. For that reason, many machines have an automatic cut-off that will release the tension on the tape if the tape is not moved within two or three minutes.

Slow Motion

On some videotape machines, the shuttle control used for cueing can also be used to play back the material on the tape in slow motion. The operator controls the speed at which the tape is moved past the heads, effectively slowing the display of the images.

STORAGE AND RETRIEVAL EQUIPMENT: OPERATING CHARACTERISTICS

Most television production facilities have a diverse assortment of storage and retrieval equipment. In addition to the magnetic audio and video record and playback machines just discussed, most will have turntables for records, audio cassette machines, cartridge machines, compact disc players, and slide and film projectors integrated into a system called a film multiplexer. Since many different manufacturers make this equipment, you should familiarize yourself with the unique operating characteristics of various products.

Audio

You will probably have the opportunity to use a lot of different audio production equipment. Some of these tools will be capable of both storage and retrieval; others will be retrieval only and will access prestored signals from other sources. Your job as an audio operator will consist of knowing how to **load** the various sound sources (tapes, cassettes, cartridges, CDs, records) and how to operate the machine to **cue up** the desired portion of the material on the source, adjust the input and output levels as necessary, and activate the machine to either record or playback, as required.

Open-Reel Audiotape Machine

The open-reel audiotape machine is the basic machine, sometimes called **reel-to-reel** machines or **audiotape recorders (ATRs),** discussed earlier in the chapter. It is the general-purpose workhorse of many production operations because of its excellent quality and versatility. It can be used to edit audiotape as well (see chapter 7).

Cartridge Machine

Usually called a **cart machine,** this is a specialized machine developed for use by broadcasters to both record and play back. It uses a continuous loop of 1/4-inch audiotape prepackaged to various lengths in a plastic cartridge. The tape can be quickly loaded by simply pushing the cartridge into the machine, and it is immediately ready for use. Since the tape itself is a continuous loop, with no beginning and end, cart machines use special **cue tones** that are recorded onto the tape at the start of each recording as a means of finding the beginning of specific material. After a cart is recorded, the playback machine advances the tape until it detects a cue tone and then stops the tape, ready for its next play.

Cart machines have no erase head. Therefore, before recording on the cart, you must **bulk erase**: a powerful electromagnet removes the old cue tones and sound signals.

Carts are generally used for recording short audio segments. The running time of the cart is tailored to the length of the segment so that the cart will **recue** shortly after the end of the segment—it will be positioned ready for immediate reuse. As you can imagine, putting more than one segment on a cart can become confusing since the only way to determine what segment is cued up is to play it. If it is the one you want, you must play through the entire loop to find it again. For that reason, many users put only one segment on each cart.

Cart machines recue automatically, making them ideal for fast-paced studio production.

Operationally, the cart is extremely convenient. If the cart is already cued, meaning that it has been played through once to make sure the loop is positioned at the proper cue tone, then when you need it in the production, you just load it into the machine and push the play button at the appropriate time. The sound playback starts instantly. When the segment is over, remove the cart, put in the next one, and you're ready. Carts are excellent for fast-paced studio productions.

Cassette Machines

Production facilities often use audio cassette machines to both record and play back materials. The same 1/8-inch tape cassettes available to consumers are used. The tape is self-contained in a plastic cassette, though it is not formed into a loop like the **cartridge.** Most cassette machines are reversible, meaning the cassette can be turned over and more information recorded or played back when the tape moves in the opposite direction. Only half the width of the tape is used for each direction of travel.

Cassettes are very convenient and, if high-quality tape and machines are used, produce good sound. They are, however, susceptible to tape speed fluctuations and somewhat difficult to cue up.

Turntables

Many of the musical selections and sound effects you may need for a production will be readily available on record. Most production facilities have a conventional **turntable** that allows you to retrieve the signal from the record and integrate it into your production directly, or transfer it to one of the other tape formats for later or more convenient use.

The output from the turntable will need to be amplified to make it compatible with other audio signals. This normally is accomplished with a sound mixer in the same manner that the signal from the microphone is boosted. More is said about this process in chapter 7.

Compact Disc Player   Many facilities now use **compact discs** (CDs) where they formerly used records. Because of the CD's method of storage and retrieval, sound quality is greatly improved and cueing easier.

The machine will have the conventional start and stop, fast forward, and rewind controls. Most will also be able to search directly to a particular selection in response to a control input from the operator.

Additional sounds can be retrieved from the audio signals that accompany videotape and motion picture film, which have the capacity to include synchronized sound. The audio signals are retrieved through playback heads mounted in the videotape player or the film projector and then routed to monitoring and mixing equipment for inclusion in your production.

Video

Videotape Machines   The numerous videotape formats are commonly differentiated by the size of the tape they use.

As with audio machines, the operator needs to know how to load the tape into the tape transport, how to use the controls to cue up the tape, and how to use the monitoring system to adjust the input and output levels to record and play back the desired material. Depending upon the nature of the production, the operator will need to start and stop the machine as required, and in the case of slow-motion replays, may be required to judge the playback speed as well as the specific portion of the tape to be replayed. When you work as a videotape editor, you also will be operating the machines and making edit decisions. The editing process is covered in chapter 7.

Common videotape   You may be working with any of several videotape formats in your pro-
formats.   duction facility. Some common ones include:

> **8-millimeter** — a consumer-grade format that uses small videocassettes and very lightweight, easy-to-operate **camcorders** (the camera and recorder are contained in a single unit). Eight-millimeter editing systems are available.
>
> **1/2-inch VHS** — a common consumer-grade machine that became the dominant format in the late 1980s in the United States. The tape is 1/2-inch wide and enclosed in a plastic cassette. These machines record and play back. They may have one or two audio channels. Some have an editing function.
>
> **1/2-inch Betamax** — a competing consumer-grade format developed by

the Sony Corporation. Not as widely used as VHS, and Beta tapes are not compatible with VHS.

1/2-inch S-VHS — a derivative of the original VHS format that provides improved video and audio quality.

1/2-inch Betacam — a professional-quality derivative of the original Sony Betamax format. Betacam is currently considered one of the best formats for television news because it is recorded by a one-piece camcorder that combines the video camera and the video tape recorder into a single unit. Camcorders are convenient and the signal quality is very good.

1/2-inch MII — another broadcast-quality format that utilizes camcorders and produces very high quality. A competitor of Betacam.

Because of the size of the tape transport mechanism and associated electronics required with the following formats, camcorders are not available. Instead, the video tape recorder is a separate unit connected by cable to the camera.

3/4-inch U-matic — one of the most common formats. Uses a 3/4-inch-wide videotape contained in a plastic cassette. The machines are produced by several manufacturers and are widely used at all levels of television production. This 3/4-inch format has been in use since the late 1960s and is standardized so that compatibility is not a problem.

The 3/4-inch videotape format produces good-quality signals because of the wide tape and high tape speeds. When the output from a 3/4-inch machine is routed through a time-base corrector, it can deliver professional-quality pictures. It is widely used by broadcast news organizations because the machines are small and portable and because the tapes are easily edited. The 3/4-inch machines normally have two separate audio channels.

Portable 3/4-inch recorders require a slightly smaller size videocassette with a total tape time limited to 20 minutes. These are called *minicassettes* and can be used in any U-matic machine. The larger 30- and 60-minute videocassettes cannot be loaded into the portable machines.

One-inch — a high-quality tape format that became popular as a post-production format in the 1980s. It uses 1-inch-wide open-reel tape, produces superior slow-motion and still frame images, and processes the signals very efficiently. There is minimal signal degradation when making copies. Depending on the exact equipment in use, one-inch may have as many as three separate audio tracks in addition to the usual video and control track signals.

Quad — Quadruplex is the original videotape format that uses two-inch-wide open-reel tape. Quad has been the standard in broadcast television for many years, although its technical quality has been surpassed by some newer formats. The large size of both the tape and the machines make it primarily a studio system. Quad tape is difficult to edit and provides only a single audio channel.

Operating Principles

You will need to learn and understand the operating characteristics of the videotape format in use at your facility. Regardless of the format you are using, some basic operating principles apply:

Compatibility You must have the correct format machine to play back tapes acquired outside your facility. Naturally, if the tape to be played was recorded on a machine that exists in your facility, there should be no problem.

Control Track Just as a train runs on railroad tracks, videotape runs on a control track. Tapes must have a properly recorded control track in order to be useable. In the section on editing in chapter 7, you will learn about some of the problems that can develop when control track recording is mishandled.

Preroll Most videotapes require speed stability to produce normal recording and playback. Since the tape must accelerate to the proper speed when it is started, some interval is required between the starting of the videotape and the time at which it is stabilized and useable.

Figure 6.6. A typical slate created with a character generator. The slate summarizes the contents of the tape.

Figure 6.7. This film multiplexer system projects the optical image from the 16-millimeter film projectors (the upright units at the outer edges of the photo) or the 35-millimeter slide projector (the double drum unit in the foreground) into the special video camera located in the housing below the video monitor. The multiplexer itself is housed in the rectangular unit in the center of the system.

Tape Checks From the earlier disussion of video recording, you know that one of your concerns in using videotape is to make sure that material is properly recorded. Videotape has become much more reliable since its introduction, but unless your equipment includes a confidence head, you will want to stop the machine after a recording session and playback some portion to confirm that a useable signal was recorded.

Bars and Tone Since the tape being recorded may be played back several different times or by different machines, common practice is to record reference signals at the beginning of the tape to serve as a guide in properly adjusting the playback equipment later.

Slates Most television producers also record **slates** on the beginning of tapes to provide a convenient summary of what the tape contains. A typical slate is shown in Figure 6.6.

Slates are typically created with a character generator or some kind of camera card. When feasible, you may also have someone read the information on the slate into a microphone to create an audio slate. By doing this, the videotape operator or editor can quickly determine that the correct tape has been loaded onto the machine.

Film and Slides

The optical media of **film** and **slides** provide another source of images and sounds that have been previously stored. Before the development of lightweight portable video cameras and recorders, 16-millimeter film was the primary portable storage system used by television, especially news. That function is largely gone, but much visual material is still stored on film and many facilities will have a special projector system called a **film multiplexer**, as shown in Figure 6.7. This system allows the projection of the optical image into a television camera, which in turn produces a video signal compatible with all the other video sources. Many films have an accompanying synchronous audio track that can be retrieved and handled, along with the other audio signals already discussed.

*Film and slides can be transferred onto videotape using a **film multiplexer**.*

A source of static images is 35-millimeter slides, which can be projected through the film multiplexer in the same manner as 16-millimeter motion picture film.

Films and slides can be introduced directly into a television studio production or they can be transferred to videotape for later retrieval or editing.

ON ASSIGNMENT

Consider this practical example of how the concepts and procedures just presented about videotape recording can be applied to a typical assignment.

You are part of a production team assigned to gather man-on-the-street interviews of citizen reaction to various candidates for a public office. Excerpts will be taken from the interviews and edited together to build a news story about how the candidates stand one week prior to the election.

You are assigned to be the videotape operator/sound person. A field producer/reporter will arrange the interviews and ask the questions, and a camera operator will shoot the pictures and be responsible for the lighting. The location is near the entrance to a busy shopping mall.

You are working with a portable 3/4-inch recorder and a hand-held microphone. The producer gives you a stack of videocassettes on which to record the interviews.

The first task is to set up and connect the system. Once the camera operator has positioned the camera, you place the recorder nearby, insert the batteries to power the machine, and connect the video and audio inputs. The video will come through a cable connected directly to the camera. The audio will come from the hand microphone via the cable to the recorder.

Once the connections are made, you connect the headphones to the recorder and turn on the machine. You ask the camera operator to turn on the camera and switch on the internal color bar generator to provide a reference signal. You note that you are getting the proper video signal on the video input level meter.

Now you ask the camera operator to speak into the microphone so you can confirm that it works and set an approximate level. While looking at the VU meter for audio channel one, you adjust the input gain control until the signal is peaking at 100 percent modulation. You then adjust the monitor level of your headphones to a comfortable volume.

With inputs connected and set, you load the first tape into the recorder, set the counter to zero, and press play/record to make a test recording. Again, the camera operator speaks into the microphone and, for convenience, states the information necessary to identify the material to be recorded, creating a sound slate.

That process takes about 20 seconds. You stop the recorder and rewind the tape to zero. Now the camera operator switches the camera viewfinder to return video. When you press the play button, the color bars just recorded are observed in the viewfinder and you hear the sound of the audio slate in the headphones. The recording seems useable so you stop the tape at the end of the color bars, reset the counter to zero, and are ready to record the first interview when the reporter returns.

As the session proceeds, you adjust input gain as necessary and monitor the quality of the recording through the headphones. You check each tape at the end in the same fashion if possible, then record a short segment of color bars and slate at the beginning of each succeeding tape. Either you or the reporter make notes of the person recorded on each tape and you attach a label to the cassette itself to identify it by number, name, or whatever system you choose.

At the conclusion of the session, you return to the postproduction room with confidence that you have recorded the material and that it will be relatively easy to locate on the various tapes.

SUMMARY

This chapter has introduced a lot of new equipment. Though the methods and techniques used to accomplish the task may vary, all of these tools retrieve images and sounds that have been stored in one form or another. The equipment recovers the information and reproduces a corresponding video or audio signal that can be integrated into a television production along with the signals from pickup devices and from synthesizers and generators.

Some of the tools have the added capability of recording video and audio signals magnetically so they can be stored for later editing, playback, duplication, and/or distribution.

The result of this process is great flexibility and capacity in the television production machine. These tools make possible the manipulation of images and sounds from many sources.

Unfortunately, this equipment may contribute to the distortion discussed in chapter 1. These tools shift time, they make possible the rearrangement of images and sounds, and they introduce pictures and sounds from diverse sources. Questions of authorship, elimination of context, and misleading juxtaposition are all possible with storage and retrieval systems. Users assume considerable ethical responsibility to use them in an honest and fair way and to avoid the distortion and misrepresentation that so easily happens. These responsibilities are discussed more thoroughly in later chapters.

REVIEW QUESTIONS

1. Give a general description of how the magnetic recording process stores and retrieves pictures and sounds.
2. What is a videotape format? Give some examples.
3. What is the function of control track in the videotape recording and playback process?
4. Why is it necessary to move the magnetic tape during recording and playback?
5. Why is a preroll necessary with some videotape formats?
6. Explain the distinction between the input and output signals of a magnetic recorder.
7. What is a confidence head?
8. Describe in general terms how some videotape playback equipment can display pictures and sounds in slow motion.
9. Audio cartridges must be bulk erased before each use. Why?
10. Explain the function of a film multiplexer.
11. Why does videotape play a pivotal role in the television production process?
12. List four important functions of storage and retrieval tools. Briefly discuss each.

CHAPTER 7

Mixing, Switching, and Editing

You have been introduced to most of the television production tools in the previous six chapters. Although each can function in limited ways separately, effective productions are achieved through the blending and combining of images and sounds from different sources.

Mixing, switching, and editing tools bring all the others together.

Through **mixing** (of audio), **switching** (of video), and **editing** (of both), you select, manipulate, and mold pictures and sounds into finished productions that allow viewers to experience events, stories, ideas, and personalities. It is through these tools that you will usually exercise the final control over the way various elements fit together.

Much of the activity to be discussed in this chapter happens at the production facility, in studio control rooms and postproduction rooms. It is in these facilities that options can be explored, combinations considered, and plans executed or rejected.

A production can be assembled in "real time" — as it is being distributed, such as in a live broadcast. It can also be done word by word, shot by shot, utilizing the control of time possible with videotape.

Planning is essential, but be open to discoveries and inspiration during the editing process.

Later, part 2 will deal with program assembly. Emphasis will be placed upon the need to plan the form of the production before getting to the mixing, switching, and editing phase. When you bring all of the production elements to the final assembly stage, you need to have a plan. But as you will learn with your initial projects, sometimes better ideas come out of the ongoing process. Other production personnel contribute ideas. Experimentation with the equipment often reveals better ways of blending sources. Call it inspiration; call it luck. The process is not a rigid, sterile one. It involves *synthesis*. In the hands of creative and imaginative people, the sum can be greater than its parts. The relationships established between pictures and sounds create a new experience for the viewer that none of the individual elements could do by itself.

Again, the danger of seduction is high. The potential of becoming enthralled with "pushing the buttons" is great. As you learn to use these tools, you must keep that in mind.

THE FUNCTION OF MIXING, SWITCHING, AND EDITING

Mixing, switching, and editing tools perform three basic functions in the television production process:

1. Selection
2. Transition
3. Combination

Selection   Mixing, switching, and editing equipment provide a means of gathering signals from a variety of sources into a common processing unit where selection decisions are executed. Producers, directors, and editors use these tools to determine which pictures and sounds will be seen and heard at any given time within the production.

Transition   These tools offer several options for making the transition from one sound or image to another. The ways in which transitions are made can influence the audience's perception of the relationship between them and contribute a variety of connotations to a given audio or video sequence.

Combination   These tools also make possible the blending of several separate images or sounds into a new, composite image or sound. These combinations, called **special effects**, can have a profound impact on the message communicated.

Each of these functions is discussed in the context of various mixing, switching, and editing tools and procedures.

MIXING

This section deals with the mechanics of audio equipment and procedures — the process of blending, combining, and selecting audio sources. Mixing adjusts various audio signals into a compatible range and combines them into new, composite signals. Mixing is a mechanical process that requires a certain amount of manual dexterity and the ability to concentrate on a complex task. But mixing itself is a creative activity, since many of the required judgments and decisions must be made by the **audio operator** and are beyond the direct control of the producer or director. That's why clear communication of goals and objectives is essential before a production session begins.

Sound mixing has become more complex as more and more production has moved into the field. When images are captured in the natural environment, audiences expect to hear the accompanying natural sounds. As producers strive to communicate primarily through pictures, mixing and blending the companion sounds to enhance the experience of the viewer becomes a real challenge. Smoothing out the discontinuity of sounds gathered at different places, at varying levels, and with inconsistent quality, while at the same time blending in music, recorded sound effects, and the human voice of a narrator or on camera talent, makes the task formidable. On the other hand, this complexity is what creates the overall sound environment that is so important to effective production.

You will be learning in greater detail how sound is used creatively to further the communication process. First, however, it's important that you understand the role played by the audio operator. During the sound-gathering process, each sound must be preserved separately, if possible, so that no options are eliminated by premature mixing. Once two sounds are mixed and stored together, it is generally not possible to separate them unless you can go back to an original source that isolates the individual sounds. Most mixing is done in the studio or postproduction room. Every facility is different and procedures and techniques are tailored to the unique characteristics there. You will probably have several opportunities to operate the audio system available to you and to become comfortable with the process.

Components of the Audio Console/Mixer

The primary piece of equipment used to accomplish the mixing process is called an **audio console**, **audio mixer**, or just **mixer**. The simplest mixers have several basic components:

1. Input channels
2. Signal processing
3. Potentiometers
4. Monitoring
5. Output channels

These components are usually assembled within an enclosure or housing that makes provision for cable connections, power supplies, and a structure within which to mount the components. Most mixers have a control panel that makes the system easy to operate. Figure 7.1 shows two types of audio mixers. The portable mixer can be used in many different settings. The studio unit is a more permanent installation typically found in control rooms and editing rooms. Sometimes, the audio mixer is isolated in a separate control room to provide a better environment in which to hear the sound quality.

Input Channels

*A **mixer** can handle the inputs from 4 to 30 or more sources . . .*

Audio **mixers**, by definition, must have the capacity to receive signals from at least 2 different audio sources. In fact, most will have input channels for at least 4 sources and may have as many as 30 or more. Typically, some of the channels will be used for microphone **inputs**, some for generators and

Figure 7.1. A battery-powered four-input portable audio mixer used in field production; and a 12-input studio audio console with individual channel equalization.

synthesizers, and some will be used for the signals from tape machines and turntables.

Signal Processing   The signal produced by the various audio sources may vary in strength. Therefore, the mixer must boost or reduce each signal to make it compatible with the others. You will recall from chapter 4 that microphones have a relatively weak signal that must be amplified to a useable level. Most mixers have preamplifiers that boost the input signal from microphones. Conversely, some tape machines have built-in amplifiers that produce a signal that is too strong, and in some cases the mixer will have **audio pads** that will reduce the signal strength back into the compatible range. Amplifiers and pads provide the initial "course" adjustment of the inputs necessary to bring them within the operating range of the mixer.

Potentiometers
vary each signal's
*strength with **pots** . . .*   Each input channel will also have a **potentiometer**, or **pot**, which is used to make fine adjustments to the relative strength of each signal. These are usually controlled through use of a rotating knob that increases the signal strength as it is turned clockwise, or a sliding **fader** that does the same thing in a linear fashion. Figure 7.2 shows a pot of each type.

Monitoring
***audition** sound quality*
*through **monitors** . . .*   In order to mix the audio signals the operator must have a **signal monitor**, usually a VU meter, to display the effects of changes made with the pots, and a program monitor through which the reproduced sounds can be heard. This monitoring system will be capable of displaying the signal and reproducing the sounds from any of the input channels. When more than one pot is open, the monitors will show and reproduce the combined sound signals.

More elaborate mixers have separate monitoring systems than can display several sources independently or that can be used to **audition** a signal or mix prior to introducing that signal into the final mix.

Output Channels
*and finally route **output***
sound to storage or
distribution.   Once the sources have been mixed, the resulting combined signal, or output, is amplified as required by the specific installation and is then routed to its ultimate destination, which may be a storage system, or directly to an audience as is the case with a live broadcast or cable presentation.

Figure 7.3 is a simple schematic diagram of an audio mixing system and the flow of the various audio signals through that system.

On Assignment

Consider a simple example. You want to mix music with your voice. The music will come from a record on the turntable connected to channel one on the mixer. Your voice has been recorded on a tape cartridge that comes through on channel two. The mix you are trying to accomplish will have the music and voice start simultaneously, with the voice at normal level and the music playing as background **under** the voice.

Figure 7.2. The portable mixer has rotary potentiometers (pots); the studio console has linear faders on each channel.

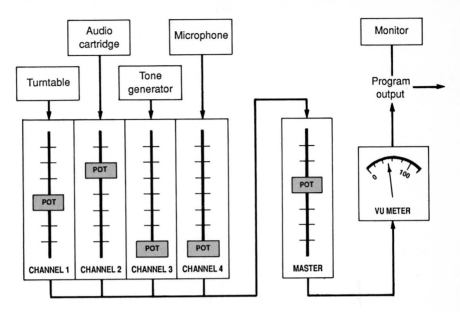

Figure 7.3. Basic audio mixing system.

To set up this mix, the first step is to play each source to determine and set an approximate level using the VU meter. Then each source is recued to the desired starting point and again played together with each pot open to the preselected setting. You listen to the resulting mix and decide if it is appropriate. Perhaps the music is still a bit too loud. You turn down the pot for channel one, reducing the strength of the music signal until it no longer competes with the voice but rather falls comfortably into the background. The VU meter indicates that the resulting mix is within the acceptable range since the peak indications during the loudest spoken parts are just below 100 percent modulation.

Now that both sources have been adjusted, they are recued once again and are ready for use when needed. Since the goal here is to store that mix on open-reel tape, you load a blank tape on the open-reel machine and check that the mixer output is being routed into the input of the recorder.

Before recording the mix, the input level of the recorder must be set. Since the mixer has a reference tone generator that is available on channel three, you open that pot and set the tone level at 100 percent modulation on the mixer's VU meter. Now you check the recorder input with the VU meter on the recorder and adjust input gain until it matches the levels indicated on the mixer's program line meter. Now the system is ready.

You turn off the tone and start the recorder. As a reference, you open the channel three pot again and record the 100 percent tone on the tape for 10 seconds. Next, you close the pot and set the pots on channels one and two to the preselected settings. Then you start the turntable and the audio cartridge machine simultaneously. As they play, you may need to make minor adjustments to either pot to maintain acceptable peak levels and to produce the desired ratio between the loudness of the voice and the music. This is known as **riding gain**.

When the mix is completed, you close the pots on channels one and two, let a bit of silence record on the tape beyond the end of the mix, then stop the recorder. You rewind the tape just recorded, switch the open-reel machine's monitor to playback, and listen to the mix as it is played from the tape just made.

Specific Functions

Selection

The audio mixer is used to select from a variety of audio sources. It gives the producer control over the audio elements of the production. The basic way it is used to accomplish that task is by simply turning the signals on and off. Each channel on the mixer has a pot that can be turned all the way down. Many have a separate **toggle switch** that allows the operator to turn each channel on and off with the pot preset to the desired level. In this way, several different sources can be selected, one at a time, or in various combinations.

Transitions

In most productions, audio mixing will be used to smooth the transitions between sources and to blend them together. As you can imagine, with spoken language it is fairly simple to switch between voices during pauses between words. But with continuous sounds like music or many natural sounds, to simply turn them on or off would make for very abrupt transitions. For that reason, these transitions are usually accomplished with **audio fades**, in which the pot is used to gradually increase or decrease the sounds. A typical example would be when music is used at the beginning of a production and then gradually faded out under the voices of the on-camera talent as they begin to speak.

Cross fades and music beds are common audio mixing techniques.

When two or more continuous sources need to be interchanged, the technique is called a **cross fade**. As the first sound gradually decreases, the second gradually increases. This results in a less abrupt transition.

Combination

Continuous sounds such as music are often used as background for voices. This is sometimes referred to as a **music bed** — the music sets the mood and adds interest to the overall sound. This technique requires that the music input channels be adjusted to a relatively low level of modulation, while at the same time the voice input channels are operated at normal levels. There are no hard and fast rules for the ratio between them; it depends entirely upon the nature of each sound and the overall effect desired. The audio operator must make a subjective judgment by listening to the resulting mix on the monitoring system while at the same time watching the VU meter to assure that the peak levels are kept within limits.

Foldback Monitoring   In some situations, it is desirable for on-camera talent to be able to hear other audio sources in addition to their own voices. This is often the case with sports events, for example, where an announcer needs to hear the sounds of the event being picked up by other microphones. A system called an **interruptible program line (IPL)** or an **interruptible foldback (IFB)** is often used. The program output from the audio console is routed back to a set of headphones worn by the announcer. This system usually includes a feature that allows the program's producer or director to interrupt the program sounds and speak to the announcer through the headphones directly for cueing purposes. Great care must be taken not to interrupt with cues while the announcer is talking. You can imagine how confusing it would be to try to call the action of a sports event while listening to someone talk to you about something else.

Most studio installations have monitors that amplify the program audio output on a speaker in the studio. These installations typically include a **muting** system that cuts off this speaker whenever one of the studio microphone channels is activated. This prevents audio **feedback**, in which the microphone's output is reintroduced into its receiving element, resulting in a high-pitched squeal.

Operating the Audio Mixer

As audio operator, you will have several responsibilities in both field and studio productions. Field work is primarily a gathering process. Studio and postproduction usually involve more complex mixing.

Because of the subjective nature of sound quality and the judgment required to mix sounds effectively, you will play an important part in the overall effectiveness of a production. It is important that you have a clear understanding from the producer and/or director of the sound goals before the production begins. Your responsibilities will be to:

1. Connect the audio system
2. Test audio sources and set levels
3. Respond to cues and directions during production
4. Monitor audio levels/listen to program output
5. Check any recordings at the conclusion of production

Connect the   At the beginning of a production you will assemble and connect the required
Audio System   equipment. Microphones must be chosen and **mike lines** run to connect with the audio mixer. You will need to position the mikes on the set or help on-camera performers put on lavalier mikes if they are used.

You will make sure that all generators and playback systems are connected to the appropriate channels of the mixer. In many installations an **audio patch bay** is used to increase flexibility and allow a variety of configurations to be used. Various sound equipment can then be added to or deleted from the system so that some input channels can be used for either microphones or playback sources. You will be responsible for tailoring the set-up to meet the needs of this particular production.

You are also responsible for assembling the records, CDs, and tapes that will be used in the production. Make sure you understand the order in which they will be used and the appropriate point in the material to be cued up.

Test the System   Once the system is ready, you are responsible for testing all the inputs. Microphones should be checked and approximate levels obtained by asking performers to speak, while you watch the VU meter and set the pot. Be aware that many persons, especially nonprofessional guests, will speak much more loudly during an actual production after they overcome their initial nervousness.

All playback materials should be played to obtain levels and then recued to the desired point. If there is a lot of this material, those items to be used later should be assembled in a logical order near the equipment so they can be efficiently loaded and cued up during the production.

Cues and Directions   Once the edit session or the studio rehearsal begins, your job is to respond to the cues and directions from the editor, producer, or director. Every production facility or organization has its own peculiar terminology and procedures, but some fairly common ones are:

> **Standby** — this means get ready. Normally the standby will be preceded by the directions for what you are supposed to get ready to do.
>
> **Open/close mikes** — mike pots are opened and closed to the predetermined settings, or toggle switches are turned on or off.
>
> **Fade up** — the pot for the desired source is gradually opened to the predetermined level, as outlined earlier.
>
> **Fade under** — the pot for the desired source is gradually closed until a setting is reached at which the sound is audible in the background or under some more dominant sound.
>
> **Fade out** — the pot for the desired source is gradually closed all the way. Often this will occur simultaneously with a similar fading of the picture. If so, the sound should fade at the same pace as the picture.
>
> **Cross fade** — one pot is closed and another opened gradually so that a smooth transition is achieved.
>
> **Roll or spin** — this cue requires that you open the pot for the playback source desired and simultaneously start the playback source. Sometimes these playbacks will be started and then faded up.
>
> **Take VTR or sound tape** — in most situations, videotape playback is controlled by another production crew member. You will have worked with that person earlier during set-up to obtain audio levels from tape playback. When you are told to take the audio from VTR, sound tape, or just "sound it," the cue will normally follow a separate

cue that started the VTR playback. Sometimes VTR audio is faded just like other audio-only sources.

Monitor Levels and Sound Quality

During the production session, you are solely responsible for the audio portion of the program. It's up to you to make sure that signal levels are kept within the acceptable range on the output VU meter. You must continually listen to the resulting sound mix and make the judgments necessary to achieve the desired goals.

With all the other activities already outlined, that's not easy. In most productions, you'll be busy. Not only must you operate all the equipment and listen to the cues and commands over the intercom, but also you must pay attention to the end results. Live studio production can be very demanding if numerous audio sources are involved and the production runs continuously. Edit sessions are less arduous, though the control provided by the editing process often means that even more complex sound combinations and precise mixes are required.

Check Audio Recordings

At the conclusion of any production session where a program is recorded, you should check the quality of the final recording immediately after it is concluded. If problems are found, corrections must be made and the production redone if possible. Depending on whether you have playback monitoring available as the recording is being made, you may be able to check the recording during production.

After the Production

One of the most important aspects of production you must learn is that the job is not done until everything is put away, all the tapes are rewound, and the production facility restored to its normal condition for the next user. Take care to remove batteries from microphones, recoil cables, and remove tapes and records from the audio console area. Discard or return scripts and cue sheets to the producer. Leave the audio system in the condition in which you would like to find it.

SWITCHING

The video counterpart of the audio console/mixer is the **video switcher**. This piece of equipment allows the selection, mixing, and blending of video signals into a new combination of images. Video switchers, when operated in real time, create the visual sequences that tell stories and capture events by joining images from a variety of video sources in new ways. As with audio mixing, most video switching is done in studio and postproduction facilities, although some productions, like live sports events, require the assembly of a complex video production facility in the field that can be combined through a video switcher.

All types of switchers perform the same basic function—to make transitions between images.

The video **switcher** allows production personnel to execute the visual design of a production by tying all the sources together and making them technically compatible. It also provides a variety of switching modes so that the transitions between images or the way they are combined can be accomplished in a number of different ways. By joining together a sequence of images, you can create a complete and unique visual environment for the viewer. Even if the individual scenes are not directly related, the viewer is mentally able to join the images into a unified impression. Naturally, the better the images and the more skillfully they are assembled, the more effective the communication of the experience will be.

Like all other production equipment, the video switcher is a tool with which to execute preconceived designs. (Creating those designs and planning their execution are discussed later in this book.) The switcher is only as effective as the images that it handles. Many production students become infatuated with the many ways the switcher can handle the images and attempt to create interest with special effects and rapid switching; to "dazzle the audience with their footwork," so to speak. Generally, this overuse of switching techniques calls attention to itself and distracts from the overall effectiveness of the presentation. In contrast, well-done transitions and effects can be so appropriate to the situation that viewers will be unaware that anything out of the ordinary has been done; instead, their attention will be upon the content of the visual images and the message being communicated.

Components of the Video Switcher

Notice the considerable similarity between the components of the audio console and the video switcher. Basic video switcher components are:

1. Input channels
2. Buses
3. Monitoring
4. Effects generators
5. Output channels

All these components will be assembled in a housing or console that includes a control panel from which the switching system can be operated. Typically, video switchers are mounted into countertops in production control rooms or editing rooms. Figure 7.4 shows two types of video switchers.

Input Channels

The video switcher has input channels that receive the signals from all the video sources described in previous chapters. Each input channel can be selected by pressing a single button on the operating panel. There will be at least one button for each input, such as cameras, character generators, and videotape machines.

The switcher will normally generate specialized internal signals. Two of the most common are **black** and **color background**. Black is simply the video

Figure 7.4. A basic video switcher with single mix/effects bus, program, and preview buses; and a more complex multiple bus switcher with digital video effects.

signal that results in a totally blank screen. Most programs begin by fading up from black to the first image and conclude by a fade back to black. The counterpart of black in audio is silence. Either black or silence can be used as a transitional device. Viewers accept as a symbol of time passing a brief fade to black and/or silence before the scene fades back up to a new setting and time.

Color background is a full screen of solid color. The color can be selected with the controls on the switcher from the full range of the spectrum. It is often used as a background for titles and graphics created on the character generator or for creating a variety of special effects.

In order for the various video signals to be switched and combined, they must be technically compatible. This is accomplished in most video switchers through a process called **gen-lock**, in which all the sources are referenced to the same synchronizing generator so that the scanning and frame rates are all the same. If the sources are not gen-locked, glitches can occur as different sources are selected that may be at different positions in the scanning process.

Buses   The input channels and the buttons that control them are arranged into groupings called **buses**. This is typically a row of buttons that all connect to a common video output so that any input can be selected and instantaneous switches made between them. These instantaneous transitions are called **takes** or **cuts** and will be discussed later in this section. Figure 7.5 shows a diagram of a single-bus video switcher.

Monitoring   Since the video switcher, unlike the audio console, does not control the levels of the video signals, no signal monitoring is normally provided. However, most installations have individual **source monitors** for each input and at least one **preview monitor** and one **program monitor** that can be selected to show the outputs from different buses. Often the source monitors will be black and white and the others will be color.

The source monitors allow control room personnel to see each source prior to making a selection. The preview monitor is normally used to preset special effects, preview special image combinations, or see sources to check their color before they are selected. It is controlled by a separate **preview**

Figure 7.5. Single-bus video switcher.

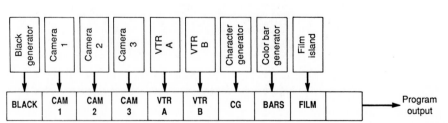

bus. The program monitor displays the final output of the switcher and shows the result of the switching process as the audience will see it.

Effects Generators   To expand beyond the simple-one-at-a-time capability of the basic switcher bus, **mix/effects (M/E) buses** are added to most production switchers. A basic M/E bus will consist of two identical input buses that share one output. The bus feeding the output is selected by a **fader bar** that can be positioned to either bus. The effect created by the movement and positioning of the fader bar is determined by the mode selected. An explanation of some basic effects follows later in this chapter. In Figure 7.6, a preview bus and an M/E bus have been added to the basic switcher shown in Figure 7.5. Since all inputs appear on each bus, any one can be selected on either bus. The fader bar is used to move from one set of inputs to another, so that one image is gradually replaced by the second image.

The manner in which this transition occurs depends upon the various effects modes that are possible with the video switcher in use.

Dissolves   Most switchers will be able to **dissolve**: the first picture gradually becomes transparent and the second image gradually appears. The second image also is transparent until the fader bars have been completely moved to the new bus, at which time the first image is gone and the second is solid. Figure 7.7 shows the effect created when the switcher is halfway through a dissolve. At the midpoint of a dissolve, both images are transparent. If the fader bars were stopped halfway, as shown, so that the images remained superimposed, the effect would be called a **super**.

Figure 7.6. Video switcher with mix/effects bus.

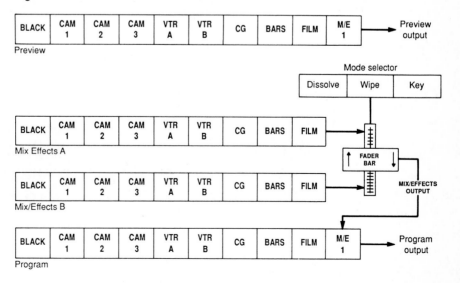

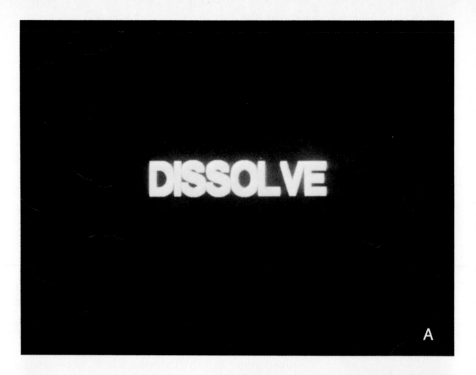

Figure 7.7. The dissolve starts with picture A on one bus. As the fader bar is moved toward the other bus, both pictures are superimposed and combine to form picture B with each image being transparent. As the fader reaches the opposite bus, picture A is totally replaced by picture C.

Figure 7.7 *(continued)*

Wipes   Another basic transition available on most switchers is called a **wipe**. Wipes generally create a geometric pattern that forms the transition line between two video sources. As the fader bar is moved from one bus to the other, the selected pattern wipes away one image and replaces it with another. Figure 7.8 shows a simple horizontal wipe. Similar to the super, if the fader bar is stopped in the middle position, the effect is to divide the screen into halves. This is called a **split screen**.

Keys   A third common effect available with most special effects generators is called a **key**. Figure 7.9 (p. 184) shows a graphic title created with a character generator keyed over a generator output. In this configuration, the output from both buses is visible. With the key effect, the white portion of the graphic title is visible but the dark portion has been replaced by the video signal from the generator. Unlike the super, the keyed title is not transparent but rather a solid image.

Downstream Effects   Another fairly common special effects component is called a **downstream keyer**, or **DSK**. This component is situated at the output of the switcher and generally has few input sources. Its function is usually either to fade the program output in and out of black or to key a selected source over the

Figure 7.8. The wipe starts with picture A on one bus. As the fader bar is moved toward the other bus, the screen is split horizontally with a portion of each picture being visible as in picture B. As the fader reaches the opposite bus, picture A is completely wiped away by picture C.

Figure 7.8 *(continued)*

program output. Figure 7.10 shows a DSK added to the switcher diagrammed earlier.

Outputs The signal that ultimately is produced by the video switcher is called the
program output. This is the signal in its final form, which will be stored on
videotape or routed directly to the audience. By using source and preview
monitors, you are able to prepare in advance the individual images and special effects before they are seen on the program output.

Methods and Procedures

A Simple To begin to appreciate what even a basic switcher can do, consider this ex-
Program Opening ample. Refer back to Figure 7.10 as necessary.

Your program will begin with a camera shot and a title keyed over. You
want to fade from black up to this combined image. You put the DSK in
black by positioning the fader bar on the DSK input bus with black selected.
The DSK mode selector should be on fade. Now select key on the M/E bus
mode selector, CG on M/E bus A, and the appropriate camera on M/E bus
B. Position the M/E fader bar to bus A to activate the key. Check the effect
by selecting M/E one on the preview bus and looking at the preview monitor.

Figure 7.9. The key effect displays picture A over picture B. The color bars fill in all but the white lettered area of picture A. The white letters in picture C are solid rather than transparent, as in the dissolve in Figure 7.7.

Figure 7.9 *(continued)*

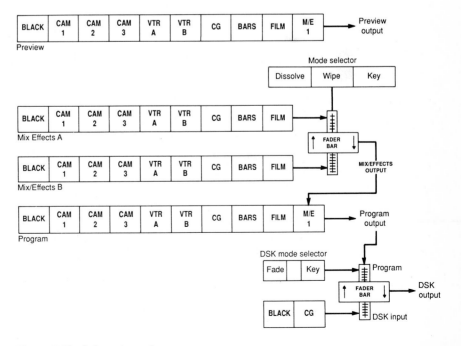

Figure 7.10. A downstream keyer.

Switching allows manipulation of images and control of program impact.

If it looks correct then select M/E one on the program bus as well. You are now ready. Figure 7.11 shows the switcher as it should be preset for this opening.

For the opening, move the DSK fader from input to program and look at the program monitor. You will see the effect fade up from black.

The dissolve, wipe, and key are basic special effects. This is an area in which technological development has made dramatic advances possible in recent years. Sophisticated switchers are capable of complex manipulation of the images from various sources and can combine many at one time into a single frame. The decisions you make as to which images to show and when to show them is the essence of video production.

Specific Functions

The video switcher can be used to select and combine sources in real time as would be the case in a live television production. It can also be used when the program is being edited onto videotape for storage. Videotape editing will be covered in the next section of this chapter.

The switcher provides the television producer with control of the visual elements of a production. Preview and source monitors allow the control room personnel to see all the available options. By the *manner* in which the switcher is used, the images the audience ultimately sees are determined.

Figure 7.11. Video switcher preset for program opening.

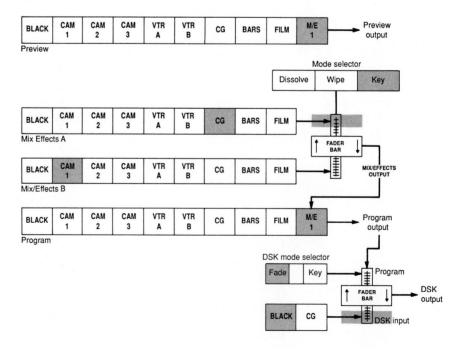

Take Transitions   The simplest manner in which a transition can be done is called a **take** or **cut**. If you select any single source available on the switcher, the program line can instantaneously display its image. If a program started with a blank screen, then a take to a camera shot would make its image appear immediately. If you switched to a second camera and a take transition was used, it would abruptly replace the previous image. Fast-paced programs like game shows, news programs, sports, and up-tempo music usually contain numerous shots joined together by take transitions that yield an up-beat, rhythmic presentation. When the images selected create a logical sequence, most viewers are unaware that they have actually seen several different views.

Consider, for example, a simple interview or dialogue between two people. If you were observing this activity in person, you would probably make note of the relative position of the participants and the setting in which the discussion was taking place. Then as the two began to talk, you would focus and shift your attention between them. If the discussion became more animated, you would become more interested and more sharply focus your attention on them.

Television coverage of the same situation would attempt to create a you-are-there experience for the viewer. An establishing shot or shots would be used to show the relative position of the two participants and the setting in which the discussion was taking place. The production would follow the discussion with take transitions between individual shots of the person talking, occasional reaction shots of the person listening, and then an occasional wider shot to re-establish the relationship between the two. As the discussion became more intense, the shots would close in to allow the viewer to see the emotions on the faces. Close-up reaction shots would be included. As the pace of the conversation increased, the takes between shots would become more rapid. In this way, the same experience that you might have in person is conveyed by television.

Fades   The most common use of the **fade** is at the open and close of a program, when the video starts with black and then gradually fades to the first image. This gives the viewer an opportunity to get ready. At the end of the program, a slow fade to black again gives the viewer time to reflect upon the final scenes as the program ends. Fades out of and into black have become accepted conventions for the start and finish of programs.

Dissolve Transitions

Take transitions usually occur within a scene; dissolves often denote a change of time or place between scenes.

To soften and smooth the change between two images, a dissolve transition can be used. It does what a fade does, except that a dissolve is used to fade between images. It can be used to replace the take when there is discontinuity between two images. It can also give the viewer a different impression of the relationship between two images. A dissolve normally is used when two images thus joined represent different times or different places. The dissolve tells the viewer that a time shift or change of location has occurred even though each image may contain some of the same visual elements.

For example, a dramatic program includes a scene that takes place in a living room involving actors A and B. That scene is immediately followed by another scene, with actors A and C in a different room, which is supposed to occur a few hours later. The first scene ends with a close-up of actor A and the next begins with a similar shot in the new setting. To make a take transition between the two would be confusing since actor A would have suddenly jumped from one room to the other. A slow dissolve from one shot to the other would communicate to the viewer the passage of time and smoothly move actor A from one scene to the other.

The dissolve allows artistic overlap between images and can be used effectively to create a cohesive and powerful visual message. But it is prone to abuse. Many producers join incompatible images using a dissolve. An old adage of television, which should be retired, says, "If you can't solve it, dissolve it." The theory is that if images do not fit well together, the dissolve will hide that fact. It doesn't work. If the images do not fit well together, find different images.

To communicate a more definite change in time and place, you might choose to fade to black and back up between shots. But the fade to black can also mean the end of one story and the beginning of another. The longer the time spent in black, the more the audience expects entirely new material to follow.

Combinations

The switcher not only makes transitions between images; it also permits the display of more than one image simultaneously. The **key** effect permits the addition of a second image overlaying the first. Dissolves and wipes that are stopped in midtransition result in multiple-image display. Sophisticated switching equipment using DVE is capable of compressing or expanding individual frames or repositioning them within the frame and displaying four or even more individual images simultaneously. Experiment with your particular equipment to discover the full range of special effects capabilities. Part 3 will deal with the reasoning behind the decision to use various transitions and effects. It is important that you learn the capabilities of the switchers you will be using prior to planning your initial production projects.

Operating the Video Switcher

A TD operates, suggests, and implements, but does not independently direct.

The production person who operates the video switcher is usually called the **switcher** or the **technical director (TD)**. That person's job is to operate the equipment in response to cues from a director. Sometimes, in fairly simple productions, directors will do their own switching. In the editing room, the switcher will sometimes be automated and operated by the edit controller, discussed in the next section. At other times, it will be operated by the editor or the producer.

Note that the technical director does not make directing decisions but rather executes someone else's decisions. A good TD knows how to operate the equipment and has the manual dexterity to make the appropriate control settings quickly and efficiently. That does not mean that the person in this position has no role in the production process. Quite the contrary. Because the TD sees all the images and knows the capabilities of the video switcher, he or she is in an ideal position to make suggestions and to assist the director or producer in exploring options.

In some production operations, the TD may have the added responsibility of starting and stopping video retrieval sources like videotape machines and film projectors. Again, this will be done in response to cues from a director, and in most cases the loading and cueing of the sources will be handled by another individual.

As you can imagine, switching is an exciting and demanding task in a fast-paced, complex, real-time production. Responding efficiently to the director's cues can be very challenging. Every director is different but most will follow the standard procedure of giving "ready" cues before each execute command. Complex special effects that must be preset will usually be preceded by a standby cue, which gives the TD time to set the switcher controls. If retrieval sources require prerolling, a separate roll or start cue will be given before the switching transition to that source. Good TDs have the ability to think ahead and, like directors, are constantly anticipating and preparing for the next switching task.

EDITING

Postproduction editing constructs the program.

The editing process affords the greatest degree of control over the selection and construction of video and audio. Once images and sounds have been stored on magnetic tape, they can be retrieved and rearranged, mixed and blended, into new combinations through the editing process and ultimately stored in the new combination on magnetic tape. Unlike the editing done during real-time productions when decisions must be made instantaneously, editing on magnetic tape allows precise frame-by-frame control and the luxury of previewing and redoing transitions and effects.

As with the audio console and the video switcher, the person who operates the editing equipment executes the selection decisions that have been made; the editor makes the images and sounds appear in the order and fashion deemed appropriate. In many situations, producers do their own editing; in others, the job is done by a specialist. The decision-making process behind editing — and how it relates to the stages from retrieval of stored images to the final version of the program — is the focus of Chapter 11. Here we explore operation of editing equipment.

Components of the Videotape Editing System

Combining selections from several videotapes produces an edit master tape.

Videotape editing is done through selective duplication of materials from one videotape to another. Images and sounds are located on a playback source and then duplicated or combined into the new sequence on a second tape called the **master tape**.

The most basic editing system will have these components:

1. Playback sources
2. Recorder
3. Controller
4. Monitor

Using this production method means that programs are assembled with duplicate images. Remember, there is a technical penalty associated with duplicating video and audio signals on succeeding generations of magnetic tape. Care must always be taken, no matter what the quality of the system, to minimize the generation loss in the editing process. Avoid making copies of copies. Go back to the original recording of the material whenever possible.

The alternative to the duplication process is to physically cut and splice the magnetic tape to rearrange the order of the material. This process is still used in some audio applications, particularly in audio tape editing where great precision is required and preservation of signal quality is essential.

The flow of various signals in the basic editing system is shown in Figure 7.12. Refer to it as each of the system components is explained.

Figure 7.12. The edit process using the system configuration shown here starts at the edit controller. Here the edit mode is chosen and tape position selected and designated. The controller then sends the appropriate edit mode commands to the record VTR. It also sends tape position commands to both VTRs, which respond by positioning the tapes for the desired edit. The controller knows when the tapes are in position from the control track information it receives back from the VTRs.

Once the tapes are in position, the controller sends commands to the machines to execute the edit. It confirms that the machines are synchronized and then turns on the record function at the beginning of the edit interval. During the edit, the record VTR will duplicate any source VTR output signals received at any of the recorder inputs programmed to record.

At the conclusion of the edit interval, the controller will turn off the record function and reset the system to either review the edit just completed or proceed with a new edit.

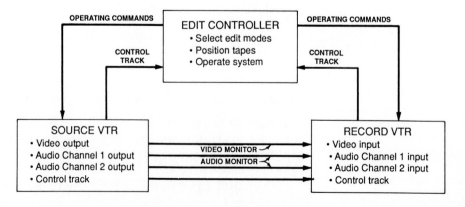

OPERATING COMMANDS

EDIT CONTROLLER
• Select edit modes
• Position tapes
• Operate system

CONTROL TRACK

OPERATING COMMANDS

CONTROL TRACK

SOURCE VTR
• Video output
• Audio Channel 1 output
• Audio Channel 2 output
• Control track

VIDEO MONITOR
AUDIO MONITOR

RECORD VTR
• Video input
• Audio Channel 1 input
• Audio Channel 2 input
• Control track

THE MICROSCOPE AND LAB COAT

In the early days of videotape recording, technicians would occasionally cut and splice videotape. This was generally done only out of desperation when a videotape had been damaged.

The process was extremely cumbersome. The quadruplex machines in use at the time had four video heads and each head made four passes over the surface of the videotape just to store the information necessary to re-create one field of video. Splicing this tape required that the corresponding head tracks be precisely aligned when joined again.

To aid in seeing these tracks, a liquid was spread on the videotape to make them more visible. The editor looked at the respective tape ends through a microscope in an attempt to find the correct tracks.

Once that was done, the videotape had to be precisely trimmed so that the tape ends butted together. The editor would then clamp the tape ends in place on a special splicing block and apply a very thin adhesive tape to hold them together. Because even small dust particles under this tape could cause problems with a splice, most editors wore special gloves and lab coats when doing this task.

The tape, as spliced, could then be run through the videotape player. In my experience, these edits were always noticeable, usually resulting in some "break up" of the tape playback. They certainly were impractical as a production technique though occasionally necessary to avert an irretrievable loss.

Obviously, this technique was a far cry from the simple electronic videotape editing available today.

Playback Sources   The basic editing system has two video tape recorders: the first plays back video and audio signals for selection and duplication through the editing process. In many cases this machine will be a playback-only machine with no recording capability.

More elaborate systems often have several playback VTRs, sometimes of different formats, to afford greater flexibility in playing a variety of materials acquired from diversified sources.

The retrieval sources must be compatible with the circuitry and operating system of the controller. In some cases, machines from one manufacturer cannot be used in an editing system designed by another.

Recorder   The other VTR in the basic system records the images and sounds in the new order. As with the playback machine, the recorder must be compatible with the operating system of the controller. The machine must also be capable of making **electronic edits** consistent with the various editing modes of the controller.

The flow of signals within the editing system is normally one-way only.

The playback machine cannot be used to record and the record machine cannot be used for playback.

Controller
The selection of functions and the operation of the editing system are governed by a **controller**. A typical controller is shown in Figure 7.13.

The controller is usually housed in a console that contains all the operating controls for the system as well as the circuitry necessary to control the system. This unit performs three basic editing functions:

1. Select edit mode
2. Position tapes
3. Synchronize and operate other system components

Select edit mode.
Most editing systems have two edit modes: **assemble edit** and **insert edit**. The controller can set the system to operate in either of these modes. Assemble edit places each new image at the end of the last, in a sequence; insert edit places a new image between two others, affecting the previous recordings. Methods of accomplishing this are given later in this chapter.

Position tapes.
The controller is also used to position the tapes in preparation for an

Figure 7.13. This controller for a 1/2-inch VHS videotape editing system includes tape counters plus video and audio monitoring for source and record VTRs. Edit modes, tape position, and edit programming can all be done with this unit.

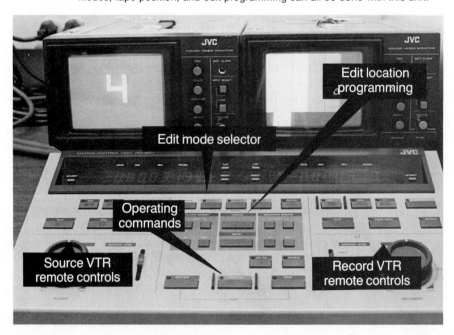

edit. The operating system will allow the controller to **shuttle** or **search** the tapes on each VTR forward and backward at various speeds. Speeds as slow as one frame at a time to several times normal play speed are generally possible.

Using the monitoring system, the editor can thus find the material to be edited and the position into which it will be edited by shuttling, playing, and rewinding each tape as necessary.

Since the controller cannot "see" or "hear" the monitoring system, some means of marking the desired tape positions must be provided once they are identified. This is generally accomplished by using a tape counter system that reads out in minutes, seconds, and frames and which can be reset at the discretion of the operator.

The counter actually uses the control track on the tape as a reference by which to count. Once the counter has been set, any position on the tape can be identified by a specific counter reading. These locations can be stored in the controller's internal memory as a place either to start or to end an edit. In a simple edit system, once **edit-in** and **edit-out** locations have been defined and stored, the controller is able to position the tapes to those locations for the programmed edit.

*During **off-line editing**, a time code can be keyed over the video image for easy reference.*

More advanced editing systems use **time code** as a reference in lieu of control track. Time code is an electronic signal that is recorded upon the tape in one of the audio channels or a separate address track. When played back it reads out in hours, minutes, seconds, and frames. Every location on the tape can be identified by the time code number recorded on it at that point. These **addresses** are not changeable as with the control track counter. Once recorded on the tape, they will not change.

If control track counter readings are used, the control track counter must be reset at the beginning of each tape so that it is the zero reference point. Lack of time code will make the editing go more slowly since each time a new tape is loaded it will have to start from zero on the counter, that is, from the very beginning of the tape. With time code, a cassette can simply be loaded, the time code reading determined, and the tape forwarded or rewound as necessary.

Time code is more precise than control track reference. Since it is fixed and contained within a signal recorded on the tape, it is transferred in the duplication process just as are other tape signals. As a result, *copies* of original tapes with time code can be used to plan editing sequences. These copies or comparatively low-quality **work tapes** can be used for preview and planning, making editing decisions, and listing time code numbers that will provide the basis for the final editing.

On-line editing produces the master tape audiences will see; off-line editing creates a blueprint for on-line editing.

The editing done with work tapes is called **off-line editing**. Edit planning takes place in simple viewing and editing rooms. Once the edit list (a list of images and sounds still needed) is ready, the final editing of the master tapes can be done using the full editing facility to produce the final, high-quality "edit master" that will be shown on the air. This is **on-line** editing. Both stages are detailed in Chapter 11.

Synchronize and operate system.   Once the edit mode (assemble edit or insert edit) is selected and the tape positions at which the edit is to begin and end have been programmed into the controller, most systems give the operator the option to preview or to perform the programmed edit.

When the preview or the perform function is initiated, the electronic controller will rewind both the recorder and the source VTR to the address given for the start of the edit.

Videotape editing is complicated by the fact that the transfer of signals from the source tape to the edit master tape must be done while the tapes are both in motion. They must be carefully synchronized to arrive at the start point for an edit at the same time and must run at the same speed during the edit. The controller makes this precision possible.

Once both tapes are at the start point for an edit, most systems will back them up a few seconds to provide preroll time. Both machines will have the same length of preroll. The machines will be started simultaneously, and the controller will read and compute the counter or time code readouts to assure that the tapes are running at the proper speed and will reach the starting point for the edit at the same time. When that point is reached, the record function will be activated on the recorder, in whatever edit mode was selected. The recorder will record the material being played back from the source until the controller reaches the address given for the end of the edit. At that point, it will turn off the record function and then stop both machines a few seconds beyond the end of the edit.

Most controllers will then give the operator the option to **review** the edit. When this function is selected, the controller rewinds the record tape to a position a few seconds preceding the previous edit point and replays the edit master so that the operator can see the edit as it was actually recorded upon the tape. Once the review is completed, the controller is ready to begin the process once again.

Monitoring   As with the other television systems discussed earlier, the editing system must have a video and audio monitoring system. In addition, it must have counter or time code readouts and **annunciator lights** to indicate which system modes and functions have been selected. These displays are typically included on the operating panel of the controller. Some time code systems display the numbers in a small window within the video monitor display, allowing the operator to see the time code display along with the video on the television screen. This facilitates editing, and the time code display can be removed when the editing process is completed and the material is distributed.

Advanced Systems

The **single source** system described in this section is a basic one. More elaborate systems have **multiple source** VTRs, complex switching and audio mixing capabilities, graphics generators, and other elements, all operated by

THE HUMAN CONTROLLER

One of the first editing systems I worked with was equiped with the electronics required to make simple edits. Both quadruplex tape machines were located side by side in the videotape room of the small television station where I worked as producer/director. There was no electronic controller, but we had Harold.

The system was simple. I would work with Harold to find the edit-in and edit-out points on the source and record tapes. Then he would mark them using the crude tape timers driven by rollers that turned by contact with the tape. These were quite prone to slippage. Harold would write the counter numbers on a scrap of paper and then cue up the respective machines.

Harold was a very methodical man. He would set the source VTR for a 10-second preroll to the edit-in point. He would set the record VTR for an 8-second preroll. Then he would position himself precisely in front of the start button for the source machine, push the play button and immediately turn to his right, take two carefully measured strides to the record machine, and push its start button. That took two seconds. So the machines were synchronized!

Harold would then watch the tape counter on the record VTR and approximately 1/2 second before the edit-in time, he would push the edit button. (There was about a 1/2-second delay between the pushing of the button and the activation of the record function.) Once the edit commenced, Harold would patiently watch the counter for the edit-out point and then push the stop button.

Crude as this may sound, we were able to do some fairly tight editing. But each edit took 5 to 10 minutes, so it was a slow process. Fortunately, Harold was a very nice man, because we spent a lot of time together. Modern electronic controllers may be more precise, but they aren't as friendly.

sophisticated controllers. Multiple source–editing systems greatly expand your editing possibilities with increased storage of edit decisions, automatic synchronization of each source VTR, and interfacing between different VTR formats. For instance, two source VTRs, labelled A and B, can be synchronized so that special effects like dissolves and wipes can be accomplished in the editing room, a technique known as **A/B rolling**. Because the basic system is probably the only one you will have access to, the following discussion outlines its editing capabilities.

Methods and Procedures

Most single-source editors have two edit modes: **assemble** and **insert**. These systems are sometimes called **cuts-only** editors since they are capable only of making instantaneous cut or take transitions.

Assemble Editing   Assemble editing constructs a program piece by piece in a sequence. The individual images and sound components are retrieved and transferred onto the final tape in the order of presentation.

A typical 3/4-inch video tape recorder records a video channel, two audio channels, and a control track channel. When assemble editing, the machine will record all of these channels simultaneously. The recording function will be turned on and off by the controller at specific times. When a scene is transferred from a playback source to the recorder, the assemble edit recording will last until the end of the scene. Then the machine can be stopped and another playback scene prepared. When it is played back for transfer, the assemble editor will turn on the record function precisely at the end of the previous scene as it was recorded on the master tape, then turn it off again at the end of the second scene, and so on.

When the master tape is played back, the two scenes are connected by a simple take or cut transition with no technical discontinuity between them. The images and sounds are connected in the same manner as with a video switcher or a sound mixer.

The technical continuity of this process is made possible by the control track. It is the reference signal that synchronizes the various tape functions and serves as a guide for the editing system. During an assemble edit, the controller uses the **control track** to synchronize both the source VTR and the record VTR. It also uses the control track from the source VTR in creating the new control track on the record VTR once the machine goes into the assemble edit mode. In this way, the assemble editing process builds a control track at the same time that the video and audio is being formed into a continuous flow of program elements. When the process is complete, the tape will include a continuous control track. When the edit master tape is played back later, there will be no indication that the control track was assembled step by step. Similarly, the video and audio channels will run continuously, giving the appearance that the program was created in real time.

Assemble editing creates a control track piece by piece that will appear continuous.

An Example: Spot Reels. A common practice in commercial television is to put together commercial reels, special tapes that contain all of the commercial spot announcements that will be inserted into a program to be produced later in real time. A football game broadcast might include as many as 20 different commercials. They are commonly assembled on one master tape to facilitate their playback during the live broadcast.

The process usually starts with a master tape and a stack of individual commercial tapes. The editor assemble edits all of them, in the correct order, onto the master reel. Typically, each spot runs 20 to 30 seconds.

If you are assigned this task, this is how you should proceed. After assembling all the required tapes and confirming the correct sequence, you load the first commercial into the source VTR and load your master tape into the record VTR. Then you record the color bars and reference tone onto the beginning of the master tape for reference. Next, play the first commercial, check the slate to make sure you have the right tape, and then cue it up to the beginning of the spot. That is the point at which you begin the transfer. You cue the master tape to the end of the color bars and tone, again designating that point as the place where the transfer should begin. The position of each tape denotes the start point for the assemble edit, so you program those locations into the controller. Now select the assemble edit mode; then push the **perform** or edit button on the controller.

At this time, the controller takes over and backs both VTRs up to a point five seconds before the selected start point for the transfer. Once each tape is precisely in position, the controller starts both and synchronizes them so they will reach the edit point simultaneously. When that point is reached, the controller turns on the record function on the record VTR and begins recording the video, both audio channels, and a control track as they are being played back from the source or playback VTR. At the end of the commercial spot, you press the **end** button to tell the controller that the edit can be stopped.

Now you rewind and unload the first commercial and replace it with the second. You find the beginning of the commercial and cue the player to that point. You reposition the recorder to the end of the copy of the first commercial that is now on your edit master tape and designate that point as the start of the next edit. Again, press perform. The controller backs up the tapes, rolls them forward, and begins the transfer, just as before. After the second spot is transferred, you again press end.

To check the edits, you rewind the master tape to the very beginning. When the tape is played back you will see color bars and tone, and then the first commercial, followed immediately by the second, with no interruption between them. If the edits are acceptable, you continue the process until all the commercials have been assembled on the single tape.

Some editors check every edit after it is completed; others do so periodically during the editing session. Ultimately, every edit should be checked during a complete playback of the edited tape. Of course, if a problem has developed somewhere in the middle of the session and you have waited till the end to check, you may face the prospect of redoing a lot of edits.

Working with one edited tape instead of 20 or more makes the ultimate playback of the commercials simpler and more efficient during the live broadcast.

Assemble editing is often used in this way to quickly combine a series of previously recorded or edited program segments into a finished production. It is also sometimes used during multicamera studio production to allow the various program segments to be created in a start/stop fashion. This technique is especially useful, for example, when major set or costume changes are required in the middle of a production.

It can also be a lifesaver when major production errors must be corrected. In that situation, the videotape can be cued for an assemble edit at the desired point before the error, and, as the edit is executed, the studio production sequence resumes. The end result will appear as though it were done in real time.

Insert Editing   Insert editing is similar to the assemble editing process but with some very important differences. In both, a video channel and two audio channels can be recorded. But in the insert mode, each channel can be recorded independently, which means that sounds can be recorded separately in each channel and video can be inserted at the same point in a program where audio has already been recorded.

In the insert mode, the control track is not recorded. The control track must be on the tape before insert editing begins, because the control track provides the reference for all the other tape functions, including the precise location of the independently selected edit points in the video and audio channels. The record machine reads the control track from the tape upon which it is recording. Therefore, tapes to be used for **insert editing** must have a **control track** recorded on them in advance of the editing session. At most facilities, the process of prerecording this reference signal is referred to as *laying black, blacking a tape*, or simply recording control track. The task is commonly accomplished by recording the black signal from a switcher onto the edit master tape before starting the actual editing session.

Insert editing uses a previously recorded control track as a reference for inserting material.

An Example: Adding File Footage. An example illustrates the insert mode. Assume that you are working in a TV news department. The reporter has assemble edited a short story about the winning record of a local high school football coach. The tape includes an on-camera introduction by the reporter followed by some **actualities** or sound bites excerpted from an interview done earlier with the coach. Your task is to go back to the videotape files and find some game footage of the specific games mentioned by the coach in the story. That material will be inserted at the appropriate points in the story.

After locating the **file tapes**, you go to the edit room and load the reporter's edit master in the recorder and the file tape with the highlights in the source VTR. You play the edit master tape and listen as the coach describes a big game against the rival team. You note that he talks about that game for 20 seconds. You now play the highlight tape and find a sequence of a touchdown play from that game and then footage of the coach celebrating with his players after the score. There's more than 20 seconds of that, so you find the best portion and cue up to the beginning of the 20 seconds you will use. Now back to the recorder to designate the start point, which will be at the point where you hear the coach start to describe the rivalry with the opponent. You advance the tape to the end of that section and designate the end or edit-out point where the insert will stop.

Now to the controller where you select insert edit, video and audio channel two. By doing this you will preserve the coach's voice, which is already in channel one. No new control track is recorded during this insert editing, but one already exists from the previous assemble editing done by the reporter.

In order to check the timing and to set the audio level of the football action sounds under the coach's voice, you **preview** the edit. As the controller previews the edit, you note that the timing of the video insert fits nicely. You also adjust the record level of channel two while listening to the combined sounds from playback of the coach's voice in channel one and the natural football sound from the insert in channel two. Once the record level is set and the timing appears correct, you instruct the controller to perform the edit.

When the edit is complete, you press the review button. The edited master now shows the coach talking first; then the game action and sounds appear as he begins to describe the specific game. His voice continues as the pictures and sounds of the game action unfold. At the end of the 20-second insert of game action, the footage of the coach reappears and the game action and sound are gone.

Insert editing greatly expands the flexibility of the process. It is used when independent manipulation of video or audio is required. It also permits reediting of materials in an earlier portion of a tape. Changes can be made in an earlier section while preserving the edited sequences before and after the reworked section.

Using the Editing System

From the preceding discussion you can appreciate the control that videotape editing gives you over the final content of a program. But that control is of little value unless you know the nature of the raw material available, are familiar with ways to shape it, and, first and foremost, have a clear understanding of what you are trying to say in the edited version. Editing *begins* with a clear definition of the message to be communicated. Once a goal has been established, an analysis of the raw material is possible. This reviewing of the videotape and progress toward the final version of your production is covered in chapter 11 of part 3, "Putting the Machine to Work."

Thanks to the storage and retrieval capacity of magnetic recording, no editing decision is necessarily final. Combinations and sequences can be created, evaluated, saved, or rejected. It is because so many options are available that having a clearly defined goal at the outset is critical. Without one, the editing process could wander and explore options with no purpose other than exploration. But the editing process is not a sterile, assembly-line procedure. On the contrary, it can be an extremely creative effort in which new ideas develop and preliminary plans are *enhanced* by options that become obvious as the editing moves along.

SUMMARY

This chapter has introduced the equipment and techniques used in mixing, switching, and editing images and sounds into sequences that create television productions. When used effectively, these capabilities lead to the creation of presentations that give sounds and images new meaning.

Through the use of this equipment, producers select images and sounds to be seen or heard at specific times within a production, how the transitions from one source to another will be made, and how and when special effects will be included.

You have now been introduced to the basic television production facilities, operating procedures, and terminology.

The last section of this book explores the role of the television producer and director who will use the production machine. The potential of the machine can be realized only when its users establish clearly defined communication goals, plan productions thoroughly, and conduct the production process in an imaginative and decisive manner.

Learning how the production machine runs is not the end; it is the beginning. These tools and the skill to use them are valuable only when they are used to communicate to audiences ideas and events, stories and personalities. As Edward R. Murrow, pioneer broadcast newsman for CBS, so eloquently put it:

> This instrument can teach, it can illuminate; yes, it can even inspire. But it can do so only to the extent that humans are determined to use it to those ends. Otherwise it is merely wires and lights in a box.[1]

NOTES

1.   Edward R. Murrow, addressing the Radio Television News Directors Association, October 15, 1958. As quoted in *Introduction to Mass Communications*, Jay Black and Frederick C. Whitney (Dubuque, Iowa: Wm. C. Brown Company Publishers, 1983), p. 233.

REVIEW QUESTIONS

1.   What is the general function of mixing, switching, and editing systems in the television production process?
2.   What is "real time"?
3.   Give examples of how a mixer, a switcher, and an editor can be used to execute selection decisions?
4.   What is the importance of the manner chosen to make transitions from one image or sound to another?
5.   What are special effects?
6.   What is the technical function of mixing? the aesthetic function?
7.   List and describe the components of a basic audio mixing system.
8.   Why is careful attention to the sound monitor essential during mixing?
9.   Outline the audio operator's responsibilities in a television production.
10.   What impact has the increased use of natural sound had on the audio mixing process?
11.   List and describe the components of a basic video switching system.

12. What is black and how is it used?
13. Describe two types of common transitions possible with most basic video switchers.
14. What is the role of the technical director in a television studio production?
15. The video switcher is an especially seductive production tool. Why?
16. Why is videotape editing the most precise way of assembling video and audio into a finished production?
17. List and describe the components of a basic videotape editing system.
18. What is time code?
19. Explain the distinction between an assemble edit and an insert edit.

PART TWO

Program Assembly Procedures

Now that you have been introduced to all the basic television production tools and their normal operating procedures and characteristics, you can begin to put them to work — to combine them into systems that allow you to gather, create, and assemble images and sounds into television presentations and programs.

This section discusses the two most common methods of assembling production elements into a finished product: field/postproduction and studio production. The third method, usually called *remote production,* involves complex portable television systems that can be combined into a complete production facility at a location away from the studio. Remote production is beyond the scope of this introductory text.

Knowing when and why to use a particular production method is covered in part 3 of this book. The purpose of the discussion in part 2 is to give you a sense of how the various production tools, and the people who operate them, can be coordinated into a productive machine.

Chapter 1 explored the importance of teamwork. The program assembly process, especially in the case of studio production, is heavily dependent upon *cooperation and coordination* of the efforts of many people using a lot of different yet interrelated equipment. This section introduces the role played by various members of the production team and the function that each performs so that the production process can run smoothly. In each chapter we go "on assignment" and trace the various procedures and responsibilities you might encounter during a typical production.

CHAPTER 8

Field and Postproduction

As television equipment has become more portable and more reliable, television production has moved steadily away from the studio and into the field, where images and sounds can be gathered in real settings. Being able to go where the action is makes television truly a window on the world. Though doing production on location means that producers must sacrifice some of the control afforded by the studio, the immediacy and flexibility gained is of far greater value in many situations.

News events are the most obvious example. Television news has always involved a lot of field production, first with motion picture film and later with portable videotape, often referred to as **electronic news gathering** or **ENG.** Today's television news crews, with satellite uplinks, portable microwave transmitters, and light and rugged camcorders, can go almost anywhere to cover a story. ENG often involves coverage of a breaking event, such as an earthquake or crime scene that affords little or no opportunity for preparation. ENG crews are routinely faced with less than ideal lighting or sound conditions. They must adapt to the situation at hand, sometimes compromising production quality in the interest of getting the story.

*More than ever, **field production** is used to gather news and sports and shoot commercials and TV shows.*

Television can go to where the action and the people are, rather than bringing them to a studio. Not just news, almost any type of television production can be done on location — dramatic programs, sports, commercials. The discussion here is about single-camera **electronic field production** or **EFP**, which uses much of the same equipment as ENG but usually affords more control. EFP crews usually have time to execute the location work according to predetermined plans, using the best available techniques.

*In **remote production** studio-type facilities are brought to a location.*

Another kind of field production is called **remote production**. It involves assembling a more complete facility *on location* to handle a production that cannot be brought to the studio or that cannot be covered by just one or two individual cameras. Large multicamera television vans with complete editing facilities and switching and mixing systems can be set up on location. In effect, remote production takes the entire television facility to the site of the production.

THE PROCESS

The typical field production is done by a small team, sometimes by one person, who shoots on location and then brings the **raw tape** that results to a postproduction facility, where it can be edited and molded into a finished program.

As with all television production, the EFP process begins with the formulation of a plan. Part 3 will deal in more depth with the planning process. Suffice it to say here that at the outset, the communication goal must be established, the audience defined, and the production schedule outlined.

Systems to Be Used

The approach you use in meeting any assignment will be limited by the equipment available. But even the simplest production facility will have a portable camera and recorder with a selection of support equipment, videotape, and other essential supplies and a compatible videotape editing system with at least one source and one record VTR.

Personnel

Even the most basic equipment, in the hands of creative, ambitious, and responsible people, can produce very effective television production. Personnel, to a much greater extent than equipment, determine the success of any project.

People, not sophisticated equipment, are what make good TV productions.

Field and postproduction can be done by one person working alone, though such an approach makes the process much more difficult. It also robs the project of the synthesis that can so often occur when two or more people are applying their energy and imagination to a common goal.

The mechanics of working alone in the field can be cumbersome. Single-unit camcorders make the process simpler by reducing the clutter of equipment. But, dividing attention between the demands of reporting a story, and the mechanics of the equipment can still be burdensome. For that reason, most EFP/ENG work involves at least two people who divide the various tasks between them.

On most of your early assignments you will probably be working with a partner. Communication between you is critical to the successful completion of the assignment. You both must know what the goal is and who is responsible for each of the components that will go into the final product. The most effective partnerships develop when ideas and concerns can be openly shared in the interest of doing the best job possible.

As with any group activity, one person will need to have the ultimate responsibility and make decisions where there is disagreement.

The following narrative takes you through a fairly typical field/post-production activity. The tools and techniques outlined earlier will now be integrated.

ON ASSIGNMENT

You are working for a commercial production company in a small city. Your assignment today is to shoot and edit a 30-second television commercial for a local car dealer. The spot was written by a local advertising agency that has contracted with your company to do the production work and deliver a master tape to them for showing to the client.

The manager assigns you to complete the project with the help of one production assistant, an intern from the local university.

The equipment   You have use of the company's new video camera, a unit equiped with a CCD image sensor, and the newest 3/4-inch recorder, which features a confidence head. A portable color monitor will also be available, but you must return all the equipment by noon, since it is scheduled for another crew in the afternoon.

The postproduction room is booked for your use in the afternoon. It has a basic 3/4-inch cuts-only edit system with a single-source VTR and a character generator (CG) that can key titles over the source VTR or over color backgrounds.

The manager tells you that the ad agency people are scheduled to watch the commercial with the client at 4:30 this afternoon in the company's viewing room. He would like to see it before that. You set 3:30 P.M. as a goal by which to have something finished for his review.

Preproduction

You head for your office with copies of the script and ideas already starting to form in your mind. Your assistant is waiting and you hand him a copy to read. Figure 8.1 shows the script as you received it. It is formatted in fairly typical fashion with the left half of the page reserved for the video portion of the production and the right half for the audio. The actual narration is typed in all capital letters. Various descriptions and instructions for both the video and audio are included.

Background on the client   The agency has been working with this client for some time and the graphic style and the music called for on the script are the same ones used in other spots that you have produced. You already have the music on videotape and some of the graphics are already on the floppy disk for the character generator.

Since the agency knows your work, they have given you some latitude in the shots to be used and the way they will be edited. There's nothing especially difficult about the assignment. Good camera angles, good lighting, crisp sound, and tight editing should produce the desired results. Care must

Client: Linda's Auto Sports World
Spot: Spring Convertibles
Runs: :30
Air Dates: April 26–30

Close-ups, Convertible	(Standard Music up under)
	VO SPRINGTIME IS A GREAT TIME TO BE OUTDOORS. SO PUT THE TOP DOWN . . . CELEBRATE THE SEASON. CONVERTIBLES ARE BACK . . . AND WE'VE GOT 'EM.
Linda OC with Car	OC FIVE DIFFERENT MODELS ARE IN STOCK RIGHT NOW. COME ON IN AND TRY ONE. YOU CAN DRIVE AWAY IN THE OPEN AIR TOO!
Drives away in the car	(Music up full)
WS of Dealership	
Key Graphics (Linda's Auto Sports World)	
Black	(Music fades out)

Figure 8.1. Sample script for commercial.

be taken to help the car dealer do her best with the on-camera portion. From past experience you know that she sometimes is rushed to get back to business and needs to focus her attention on the production for a few minutes in order to do her best.

You spend a few minutes discussing ideas of how to shoot the spot and work out a time schedule with your assistant. It's 9:00 A.M. You need to be at the shooting location by 9:30 and back before noon. With drive time, you'll have about two hours to shoot. That should be plenty of time.

A short break for lunch and then you'll have until 3:30 P.M. to edit the spot in the postproduction room.

It may be a little tight, but the schedule seems workable.

Collecting the Tools

You and the assistant spend a short time assigning responsibility for collecting all the necessary equipment and supplies.

Divide responsibilities beforehand.

He will gather the camera gear, VTR, microphones, lighting reflectors, batteries, and cables. You agree to take both a lavalier and a shotgun microphone and to decide which to use at the location. This spot is supposed to be shot outdoors, so no lights are needed; the weather forecast is for clear, sunny skies all morning. You plan to shoot with battery power but will take AC power supplies and extention cables as a backup.

While your assistant is loading the equipment into the company van, you head to the supply room for new videotapes on which to record the material. Next stop is the copy machine for additional copies of the script that will be needed by the owner/talent. Then you go to your office to call and confirm with the car dealer that she is expecting you at 9:30 A.M. and that the vehicle to be included in the commercial will be washed and available. Everything is confirmed.

It's 9:15 and you meet at the van. This intern is good. He has everything packed in its carrying case and secured inside of the van so that it is well protected.

As you drive to the dealership, you review responsibilities for the actual production. He will set up audio and VTR. You will set up the camera and take care of the setting, the talent, and the lighting. Since you have worked together before, you know that you communicate very well and have been successful in the past. Obviously, you will make the final decisions where necessary.

Location Set-up

Upon arrival at the location, you check in with the owner and discuss the overall plan. She would like to shoot in the northwest corner of the car dealership lot, which is adjacent to a park with a lake and some trees. The featured vehicle is a sporty convertible and the park background would fit nicely with the recreational, open-air theme of the commercial.

Check the location for possible problems before shooting.

You walk to that area to have a look. It's away from the noise of the street, though there is some noise from the auto service department nearby. If the car is parked right at the edge of the paving, it should allow several good angles that will have the park as background. There are some fairly long shadows now but in another 45 minutes the sun should be high enough that the lighting will look fine. The talent will need to be facing south to have the best lighting.

The location will work. You ask your assistant to move the van to the location and have someone move the convertible as well. In looking at the car itself, you decide that it looks good coming toward you and going away, but is least attractive when viewed from the side.

You proceed to the owner's office to discuss the script. She's busy on the phone and signing sales orders at the same time. After a short time, she finishes and is ready to talk over the shooting. Most of the commercial is voice-over. Her voice will be heard while the audience sees the car. Only the last line is to be done with her on-camera. All the narration will be recorded in the same location so that the sound quality is consistent, but the on-camera part can be done in a separate take. The rest can be done from the script if necessary. She asks her secretary to prepare a **cue card** for the line to be given on-camera as a prompting aid. You ask her to rehearse the lines and to come out to the location in 15 to 20 minutes.

As you walk back out to the corner of the lot, you're thinking of ways you can create some action in this spot. Move the car? Have the talent move? Something to keep it from being so static. With more time, you might try to find a place to shoot the car on the road, but today it will have to be done right here.

Also on your way back you stop to talk with the service manager to see about noise from his department during the shoot. The shop crew takes a coffee break at 10:30 A.M., so it will be relatively quiet then. If necessary, he can close the main service door briefly to help isolate the shooting location.

The car is now in position. As you walk around it, it is obvious that this location was a good choice. The background looks very good and much of the park is actually on higher ground than the lot, so you should be able to get some good low-angle camera shots, which will emphasize the sleekness of the car.

Set up and double check all the equipment.

Your assistant has much of the equipment unpacked already. You set up the camera tripod, mount the camera and battery pack, and connect the cable between the camera and VTR. You switch the camera to standby, see that the indicator shows a fully charged battery, and use a piece of **lens tissue** to clean the lens before production begins. This particular tripod has a **fluid head**, so you loosen the pan and tilt locks and move the head briskly to warm up the fluid in the head so the camera will move smoothly and freely.

The VTR is ready and the microphone is connected. You have decided to try the shotgun mike first, since you're thinking of having the dealer walk into the shot and drive away. Tape number one is labeled and loaded in the machine.

You switch on the camera and select the color bar mode sending the test signal to the VTR. The video meter indicates that the signal is fine. Your assistant asks you to count to 10 while he points the shotgun microphone at you and sets a level. Nothing! Check the connections? All fine. Battery? That's it. This shotgun is a condenser microphone and must have a small battery installed to power the preamplifier. You replace the battery with a spare. Now the microphone level looks fine.

*Remember to **slate** your production details over the **color bars**.*

After rolling the tape in the record mode, over the **color bars**, you make an audio slate with the client's name and the nature of the production, the date, and the tape number. Your assistant rewinds the tape and monitors the sound playback while you select return video in the camera monitor. The test recording indicates that the system is working properly. But what about the color? Your assistant connects the color monitor while you turn on the camera, select the daylight filter, uncap the lens, and set the white balance and exposure. You place the standard white card against the windshield of the car, zoom in until the white fills the frame, check to make sure that the lens iris is set on automatic and that the light meter in the camera viewfinder indicates that the exposure is correct, and then go through the recommended white balance procedure. This particular camera sets automatically with the push of one switch.

Production

It's now 10:15 A.M. While you wait for the dealer to come out, you look back over the script and make some plans. With the setting as it is and the car positioned on the edge of the lot, it will work well to shoot all the close-ups later as the sun moves a little higher. Therefore, you'll shoot out of sequence and have the dealer do the voice-over and on-camera shots first. The action will involve her walking into a medium shot, opening the door and delivering the on-camera line, and then getting in, starting the car, and driving out of the shot past the camera.

For those shots, you position the camera near the left front fender of the car, with the tripod adjusted down so that the camera is at about the level of the fender, looking up slightly.

You ask your assistant to stand where the dealer will be with the door open and check the shot with the camera. The shadows on the **camera left** side of his face (the left side of his face as seen through the viewfinder) are very dark, so you use a reflector, sometimes called a *shiny board,* to reflect some diffuse sunlight into that area. You'll need someone to hold that reflector when you do the actual taping. For now, you prop it up on the hood of the car and return to look at the results through the camera. Looks good. And it also looks good on the color monitor, but you ask the assistant to hold up the white card in front of his face and reset the white balance again. You're ready to shoot.

The dealer is late. You put the camera on standby again to conserve the battery. Back to the office to get her and to recruit the secretary to hold the shiny board. It's nearly 10:30 A.M. and you want to take advantage of the shop's coffee break.

She's just getting off the phone. The secretary can help. It's back to the car.

While you discuss the staging of the shot with the dealer, your assistant tapes the cue card to the tripod just beneath the camera lens. A brief instruction to the secretary about holding the shiny board and then you go to the camera. Better safe than sorry, so you ask her to hold the card while you white balance one more time. Your assistant asks the dealer to rehearse the on-camera line so that he can set the audio level. He has positioned the VTR about half-way between the camera and the talent so that he can see the meters on the machine and also hold the shotgun close enough to her with the fishpole. He will be able to see the color monitor and thus will avoid getting the microphone into the shot. The levels are correct and he thinks the sound quality is acceptable.

You decide to record a take and then review it for both video and audio quality. But first, a rehearsal. This takes some coordination since you want to start on a slightly looser shot and then zoom in a bit as the talent walks into the shot. At the conclusion of her line, you will zoom back smoothly as she gets in, starts the car, and drives away.

A walk-through will identify problems before actual shooting.

A **walk-through** points out some problems. The microphone cable must be moved to the right, out of the shot. The secretary must back away as the dealer sits down in the car, to be out of the path of the car. And the dealer must speed up the start and drive action. Two more walk-throughs smooth out the action, and the dealer's delivery is getting better. She is focusing on the matter at hand now.

Things are still quiet in the shop. You decide to tape the next one. It goes pretty well, although you were a little jerky on the zoom-in. Another try. That was pretty good. Maybe you had better review the two you've shot and listen to the sound quality. Tape looks and sounds good. The talent would like to do one more so you set everything up again and do it. A quick check confirms that this one is good too, and she is especially happy with her performance on the last one.

Locking down is securing the pan and tilt brakes on the camera.

Next, you have the dealer stand in the same spot by the car door and deliver the lines from the script that will be used as voice-over narration. The video will not be used, so you leave the camera **locked down** on a wide shot while you do several takes of this material. You ask her to slate each take. Right in the middle of the second take, your assistant says "cut" because he's picking up noise from the shop, which is back at work. You walk over and ask the service manager to close the big door for five minutes while you complete the voice-overs. He's agreeable.

Back to the set—three more takes, and the dealer's job is done. She will tell the service manager to reopen the door on her way back to the office. You thank both her and the secretary. It's almost 11:00 A.M.

Mark the tape number of every recording for easy reference later.

Your assistant has packed up the microphone and cables, since there is no more production sound to be recorded. Now he is free to help with moving the camera and holding the shiny board. You take a moment to mark on the script the tape number and takes for each of the sound bites you have just completed.

Now it's time to get the close-ups called for in the script. You move around the car and reposition the camera as needed. Every shot is done on the tripod so the camera will be steady. Some shots include camera movement, but you always hold the shot still for several seconds before and after the camera move so that the static shot could also be used. This will give you some options in the editing room. Just to be safe, you recheck white balance frequently, slate each shot with a simple voice slate picked up by the microphone mounted on top of the camera, and check the tape playback occasionally on the color monitor. In the middle of this work, the tape-end light comes on in the viewfinder, indicating you're almost out of tape.

A few extra shots will allow for more options while editing.

You label and load a second tape, record color bars and a slate, and continue shooting until finished. Now you recheck the script. Do you have everything that is required? You have the wide shot of the dealership from previous shoots on tape in your office, but the seasons don't quite match. There's time, so you decide to move the gear and get that shot on the way back to the office.

You repack all the equipment, ask someone to return the car, and check to make sure that the location is left just as you found it. A quick stop at the office to say goodbye and thank everyone for their cooperation. Then across the street and up the hill to get the wide shot—and you're done with the field production. It's 11:35 A.M. You'll have the equipment back on time for the next crew.

Postproduction

After lunch you gather the things you'll need in the editing room: the tapes that were recorded this morning, a new tape upon which to assemble the master of the spot, the floppy disk for the CG, the tape that contains the standard music used in these spots, and the scripts and notes from this morning's shoot.

Upon arrival in the editing room, you check the system by selecting color bars and reference tone on the input for the recorder. The levels appear correct on the waveform monitors and the VU meter. You make a minor adjustment to the tint of the color picture monitor and adjust the speaker volume.

After loading the blank master tape in the recorder, you select black and silence on the input and start the recording to "lay black" on the videotape, since you will be insert editing.

While that is being done, you review the script and formulate a plan. The first thing to do is edit the music, voice-overs, and on-camera segments in sequence on the tape. These are the elements that will need to be carefully timed and mixed to blend smoothly and fit within the overall running time of the commercial, which is to be 30 seconds. When the sound from the on-camera segments is edited, the video will be edited simultaneously to preserve the lip sync.

Once the sound track is complete, the remainder of the video can be inserted and synchronized with the appropriate sound.

*Prepare a **leader** before actual editing.*
The master tape is now ready. It has black, silence, and control track recorded upon it. The following preliminary steps will create a **leader** at the beginning of the tape. This will provide future users with test signals for adjusting playback equipment and monitors, information about the content of the tape, and a convenient countdown for cueing up the tape for precise playback.

Rewind the tape to the beginning and select insert edit on the controller. Insert editing will allow you to build the video and audio channels individually or in various combinations as necessary or convenient. For this first edit you will insert video and audio in both channels. You again put color bars and reference tone on the input selector.

Now you press the search control for the recorder and reset the tape counter to zero. With the shuttle control, you advance the master tape approximately 10 seconds from the start. You stop it there and mark that as your edit-in point. Now you shuttle forward another 20 seconds and mark that as your edit-out point. You now program the controller to insert color bars and tone for 20 seconds between those two addresses. You push the perform button and the controller executes the edit.

Since this is the first edit of the session, you next press the review button to check the quality of the edits and the recording just made. It appears fine.

Now you press stop on the recorder to release the tape tension while you type up a slate on the character generator. The slate is shown in Figure 8.2. Once the slate is ready, you select CG on the recorder input, program the edit-in and edit-out points, and insert edit the slate immediately after the color bars.

Next, you load the **countdown tape**, which is a graphic sequence of the numbers 9 to 2, on the source VTR and cue it up to the beginning. You mark the edit-in point on the source VTR and then shuttle forward to the end of the countdown and mark the edit-out point.

For sound, you select the source VTR on the recorder input and play back the countdown to adjust the audio level of the intermittent **beep tones** that accompany the numbers. Once that is set, you stop the source VTR, shuttle the recorder to the end of the slate you just recorded, and mark an edit-in point. Since the controller now has three addresses, it will automatically compute the fourth address, the edit-out point for the recorder, based on the running time of the material between the in and out points already selected on the source VTR.

You press the perform button and the controller cues both tapes up for

Figure 8.2. This graphic slate describes the content of the videotape. It is created with the character generator and inserted on the master tape before the commercial is edited.

a five-second preroll to the selected edit-in points. When both tapes are in position, it starts them simultaneously and synchronizes their speeds. At the edit-in point, it turns on the record function and inserts the video and audio from the countdown tape onto the master immediately after the slate. This completes preparation of the leader.

Sequence of editing procedures

Now you're ready to edit the spot. You load the tape from this morning's shoot into the source VTR to review and to time the various takes. You plan to use the last take of the on-camera material, which runs 13 seconds. The best take on the rest of the narration runs another 10 seconds. Therefore, the prerecorded music will be up at full level for 7 seconds at the end of the spot.

Your usual approach is to put voices in audio channel one and music and natural sound in audio channel two when you edit this type of material. That way the voices can be recorded at normal levels and the music and natural sound can be added later at background or full level, as required. Sound is edited before video in this situation, since the length of the individual shots is dictated by the narration rather than the action in the video.

For this spot, the dealer's voice will be edited first. You select insert audio channel one on the controller and adjust the input level for that channel while the source VTR plays back the voice-over take to be used. Then you mark the edit-in and edit-out points on the source VTR.

*Using the two **audio** channels, separate voice from other sound.*

This narration starts right at the beginning of the commercial so, using the tape counter, you establish a zero point that is 2 seconds beyond the 2 of the countdown. That way, the commercial will start precisely where the countdown, if continued visually, would reach zero. Now you mark the edit-in point on the master tape. You push the perform button, and the controller inserts the 10 seconds of voice-over. You check the edit to make sure that it is in the correct location on the master tape.

Next, you reprogram the edit mode on the controller to insert video as well as channel one audio. You cue up the third take of the on-camera material, the one the dealer agreed was the best, and mark the edit points. Then you cue up the recorder to the end of the voice-over material just edited and mark the edit-in point on the recorder. You are careful to leave a slight pause so that the transition from one line to the next will seem natural. Then you press perform and complete the edit.

All the narration is now on the tape. You turn off the insert mode for channel one audio and turn it on for channel two audio. You also turn off video insert. You eject the source tape and load the one that contains the music. You find the piece that runs exactly 30 seconds and mark the edit points; you then cue it up and play it back while adjusting the input level for channel two on the recorder. You set the level to peak at 100 percent modulation. It will be at that level for the last 7 seconds of the edit, but will start out at background level under the narration.

Now you mark the edit-in point on the record VTR at the zero point on the counter, the address that you designated earlier as the starting point for the commercial.

Preview edits before commiting them to tape.

Since you will need to manually adjust the audio level from background to full in the middle of the edit, you preview the entire sequence first to determine levels and practice making the level change at the appropriate time. The controller cues both machines and rolls them forward to the edit-in point. At that point you hear the music as it is being processed by the input section of the recorder. You also hear the playback of the narration previously recorded in channel one as it is being processed by the output section of the recorder. This allows you to adjust the record level of channel two to produce the desired mix with the narration. You note where that level is on the VU meter for channel two. At the end of the narration you adjust the channel two record level up to the 100 percent modulation setting so that the spot will end with the music up full for 7 seconds.

When the preview of the edit is complete, you move the channel two level back to the proper setting for the beginning of the commercial and press the perform button. The controller recues the tapes and rolls the edit. The music is playing under the narration. You watch the tape counter and listen to the narration. When it ends at 23 seconds into the edit, you smoothly raise the record level of channel two to the predetermined 100 percent modulation setting. At 30 seconds, the music ends precisely at the edit-out point.

You press the review button and listen to the completed sound track. The music runs the full 30 seconds but is at background level until the voice ends. Then it comes up to full level to the end of the spot.

Now to complete the video portion. It is 2:30 P.M. You select insert video on the controller and turn off insert on both audio channels. From now on you will be editing video only and listening to the playback of the mixed audio track as a reference for selecting edit points and pacing the video of the spot.

You load the floppy disk in the CG and call up the first page of graphics required. Then you load the tape with the new wide shot of the dealership that was shot this morning in the source VTR. You select the edit points and then select CG output on the recorder input. This will allow you to key graphics over the images being played back by the source VTR. When you edit, you will insert the graphics and wide shot into the video channel at the point where the music starts.

As you work your way through the rest of the video, you use the rhythm of the music to pace the edits of the various close-ups. Special care is required on the last edit prior to the on-camera portion of the spot. Remember, that video is already recorded on the master so the edit-out point for the last shot that precedes it must be marked correctly so as not to overlap with any of the on-camera material already on the master tape.

Always review the final edited sequence for mistakes and glitches.

You complete this final edit at 3:15 P.M. Now to have a look at the edited sequence. You rewind the master tape to the beginning, press play, and lean back to judge the overall effect that has been created. It looks pretty good although there is one close-up that is a little shaky. You must have used the wrong take on that one, so you go back and check the source tape. Yes, there is a better take, so you recue the master and program an edit to insert the better take in place of the one used earlier.

You rewind the tape and call the manager to view the tape with you. You ask your production assistant from this morning to watch too. The consensus is that the spot looks good and will be presented to the agency and the client in the viewing room at 4:30 P.M. Since no further editing will be required, you take care to remove the **record tab** from the bottom of the master tape to prevent inadvertent recording on the tape. You rewind all the tapes, clean up the papers and general debris in the editing room, and head for your office.

At the viewing, you will show the tape and discuss the results with the agency and the client. If changes are necessary, you will make them tomorrow morning. If none are required, you will make duplicate copies for the agency and the various media outlets that will be running the commercial. Then you'll file the master tape in the company's library.

SUMMARY

This chapter has detailed a fairly typical field/postproduction assignment. Many who work in television production spend their days doing this kind of work.

This assignment was a mixture of creativity, careful planning, technical skill, and coordination of the activities of several people. Time was a factor. And if you had the feeling that it passed rather quickly, that is the way it usually happens. Especially in the postproduction phase, time seems to fly when you're editing and faced with an immediate deadline.

In developing this scenario, many more problems could have been introduced. Experienced production people would probably say that this project went more smoothly than most. That may be true. No one has yet found a cure for Murphy's law. But the more time spent planning and anticipating problems, the more smoothly productions will go.

The evaluation portion of the project is pivotal. No matter how hard you worked, no matter how good or bad the idea may have been, the bottom line is how the finished videotape looks and sounds. Each person who views it will have a slightly different reaction, but if the general reaction is the one desired, then the original goal has probably been achieved.

As this assignment illustrates, field/postproduction does allow considerable independence to the producer. Especially in the editing room, you have considerable freedom to experiment and to work at your own pace. But you also shoulder most of the responsibility for the successful outcome of the project and must face the ultimate evaluation of your boss, the client, and the audience.

The next chapter describes studio production. Teamwork and coordination are much more critical in that setting, although they are essential in any television production. Consider the time and effort as well as the quality of the results if the automobile commercial done here with field/postproduction were attempted using the studio production approach.

REVIEW QUESTIONS

1. Why is television production increasingly done on location rather than in studios?
2. What impact has that change had on the overall production process?
3. Briefly describe the field production process.
4. How do you plan a field and postproduction assignment?
5. List the steps normally taken in executing a simple field and postproduction assignment.
6. Describe some of the activities involved in each step.

CHAPTER 9

Studio Production

Studio production was the dominant method of production in the early days of television. Before the development of videotape recording, most studio productions were delivered to an audience in real time through live broadcasting. But in the 1990s, live studio production is the exception rather than the rule.

Studios are still often used and offer many advantages for certain kinds of productions, particularly where distractions would cause problems. Lighting, sound, weather, and extraneous activity can be controlled in a studio. Generally, technical support personnel and facilities are more readily available, too.

Studios offer a controlled environment.

Studios also offer a protected environment in which to experiment. They can provide a workshop atmosphere in which production people can mingle and practice their craft without interruption from the outside world.

Many times, studios are used to produce individual segments or individual shots that will be used later in postproduction and editing of a program. Sometimes they serve as a centralized "anchor position" to which many different elements can be brought for assembly and integration. The resulting production can then be stored on videotape and/or it can be delivered directly to a distribution system. The most common use of a studio at many broadcast television stations is for local **newscasts**. All the various reports and production elements that make up the day's news are gathered and funneled through the studio production facility for delivery to the audience. Newscasts are also the most common live production in broadcasting.

THE PROCESS

As with all television productions, studio productions begin with a plan. The person responsible for developing the plan and implementing it is called the **producer** (the producer's role is expanded upon in chapter 10). With studio production, the producer faces the task of communicating the production goals to many more people than with field production, since studio production involves a lot of personnel. Each person has a distinct role to play, but experienced producers know that all will do their job better if they have an understanding of the "big picture" and how their job fits into the total production plan.

Communication is the key for effective studio production.

Studio production is similar to team sports or other group activities with all the attendant **group dynamics**. In addition to having a well-thought-out communications plan and the technical skills to execute that plan, producers who use the studio approach must also be skilled in coordinating the activities of others and dealing with the interpersonal relations necessary to make the studio machine run smoothly.

The System

A basic television production studio system will have a special studio room that is isolated from outside sound, has adequate air conditioning, and has power for a lighting system. The studio will usually have at least two cameras with mounts and an assortment of basic microphones. Most will have at least one video **floor monitor** and a speaker system for channeling production sound back into the studio when appropriate. Some also have a **squawk box system** for communication between the studio and the control room.

There will be one or more adjacent control rooms that house the video switching and audio mixing equipment, graphics generators, storage and retrieval equipment, and work areas for production personnel.

If the studio is to be used for live production, it will be connected to a distribution system. For example, at most broadcast stations, the production studio and control room are connected with a **master control** room where the distribution function is handled. Independent studios often contract with **mobile satellite uplinks** that can be brought to the studio site and connected with the control room for direct delivery of the studio signals to a satellite distribution system.

Studios that are not connected with a distribution system always have videotape recording capability.

Personnel

As you've learned in earlier chapters, the various production tools often require individual operators. If the studio system is to be used in a real-time production, then several people will be needed.

*The **producer** assembles the tools and people; the **director** guides and coordinates them.*

Overall coordination of studio production is normally handled by a **director**, who implements the plans developed by the producer. (Frequently, producers do their own directing, although the two roles require quite different skills.) When the jobs are handled by separate people, the two normally work closely together during the planning of a production. The **producer** is responsible for gathering and delivering all the necessary production elements to the studio. They are then turned over to a director, who operates the studio production machine and assembles those elements according to the production plan. The director delegates responsibility as necessary to the various television equipment operators, who in turn do their jobs in response to cues and directions. Chapter 11 expands upon the role and function of the television director.

Directors usually assign at least one assistant who functions as a **floor director**. This person essentially functions as the director's physical presence on the studio floor. The director normally works from the control room, the one place from which all production tools and personnel can be seen, heard, and controlled.

Although it is impossible to detail the exact responsibilities that will be assigned to each production team member, some common roles and functions can be outlined in the description of a live studio production that follows.

ON ASSIGNMENT

It's 7:05 A.M. and studio A at KXYZ-TV is already filled with activity. The production crew is busy preparing for the broadcast of "Sunrise Edition," the station's five-day-a-week morning show, which airs live at 8:30 A.M. Despite the fact that the same crew works on nearly every show, Fred, the **production manager** at KXYZ-TV, puts out a crew call list the day before every production. (The list for today's show is shown in Figure 9.1.)

KXYZ-TV is a small-market station, so the set-up crew is made up of the same people who will fill many of the production positions during the broadcast. Christine, who will be floor directing today, is also responsible for studio staging and lighting.

One end of studio A is reserved for the "Sunrise Edition" set and it is normally left in place from day to day. Only on special occasions like election coverage or a telethon will the crew **strike the set** to make way for another production. The other end of the studio is occupied by the "Newscenter 8" set, which is also semipermanent. The news portion of "Sunrise Edition" originates from that set. A floor plan of the studio and the position of the sets is shown in Figure 9.2.

Today's show will follow the standard format, with Bill and Kathy, the show's hosts, anchoring the program from the main sit-down area, two pretaped feature segments, one interview guest in the studio, the usual news headlines from the news set, and a pumpkin-carving demonstration from the kitchen area. A **rundown sheet** for the program is shown in Figure 9.3 (p. 224). Some procedures introduced in this description are explained more fully.

Timing Methods

"Sunrise Edition" is a live broadcast that begins and ends at specific times in KXYZ-TV's broadcast schedule. Sarah, the show's director, coordinates with the station's **master control** operator to make sure that the program fits

PRODUCTION CREW ASSIGNMENTS

Day/Date: _____ *Thursday* _____

Start Time: _____ *7:00 am* _____ Air Time: _____ *8:30:00 am* _____

Program: SUNRISE EDITION   Studio: A

Producer: _____ *Kathy / Bill* _____

Director: _____ *Sarah* _____

Floor Director: _____ *Christine* _____

Technical Director: _____ *Fred* _____

Character Generator: _____ *Joyce* _____

Cameras: _____ *Linda* _____

_____ *Tom* _____

_____ *John* _____

_____

Teleprompter: _____ *Marcia* _____

Videotape: _____ *Amy* _____

Audio: _____ *Dave* _____

Notes: *Check lighting in kitchen area. Two-person demonstration at counter.*

Figure 9.1. "Sunrise Edition" crew call list.

within the assigned time slot. Master control room (MCR) is the area where the television distribution system is located for the station.

In planning and executing this particular show, the production team will utilize three separate forms of timing, as illustrated on the program rundown sheet.

Segment Time

*During **live** broadcasts, three timing methods are used: **segment time**, **back time**, and **running time**.*

Each program segment, including the commercial positions and the show's opening and closing, is timed separately. The time for any of the pretaped segments was fixed when they were recorded or edited, so the only flexibility for adjusting the overall timing comes from the live studio segments.

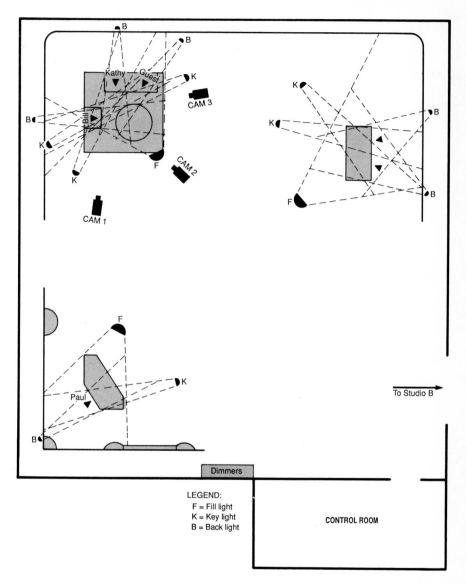

Figure 9.2. This floor plan of studio A at KXYZ-TV shows the location of sets and cameras along with a diagram of the lighting design for "Sunrise Edition." Clockwise from top left: "Sunrise Edition" set; the kitchen set; and the "Newscenter 8" set.

When all the segment times are added together, they must equal the total time alloted for the program.

Back Time   During the taped segments, Sarah will start a stopwatch preset to the segment time and will count down to zero. That technique allows her to prepare

SUNRISE EDITION   KXYZ-TV
Rundown Sheet

Content	Source	Segment Time	Back Time		Running Time	
			Start	End	Start	End
Opening	VTR	0:30	28:30		8:30:00	
				28:00		8:30:30
Kathy & Bill	Studio	1:30	28:00		8:30:30	
(30-second cue)			27:00		8:31:30	
				26:30		8:32:00
Position #1	MCR	2:00	26:30		8:32:00	
				24:30		8:34:00
Pumpkin	Studio	5:00	24:30		8:34:00	
(2-minute cue)			21:30		8:37:00	
(1-minute cue)			20:30		8:38:00	
(30-second cue)			20:00		8:38:30	
				19:30		8:39:00
Parade	VTR	3:00	19:30		8:39:00	
				16:30		8:42:00
Position #2	MCR	2:00	16:30		8:42:00	
				14:30		8:44:00
Interview	Studio	3:00	14:30		8:44:00	
(1-minute cue)			12:30		8:46:00	
(30-second cue)			12:00		8:46:30	
				11:30		8:47:00
School Feature	VTR	4:53	11:30		8:47:00	
				6:37		8:51:53

Figure 9.3. The rundown sheet for "Sunrise Edition" outlines each segment of the program with a description of the content and its source. VTR denotes material to be played back on videotape. All the live segments originate from the studio and thus include time cues to assure that they run the appropriate length of time. All the commercials are grouped into three segments that are handled by the KXYZ-TV master control room. There are separate columns for segment time, back time, and running time. This rundown helps the producers organize the program and summarizes that organization for the director.

and anticipate the end of each tape and be ready to move on to the next production element. By noting the **running time** as the tape starts, she can also calculate how far off from the schedule the production might be.

The intervals when pretaped segments are being run provide an opportunity to make adjustments, to discuss options with the producers, and to communicate required changes to the production team and on-camera talent.

Sarah also has back times for the total production. If one individual segment ends after the scheduled back time, then she knows that some adjustment has to be made to a later segment in order to finish at 8:28:30.

Program Running Time

In the same manner, a running time for the program is available to help determine if the segments are starting and ending as scheduled.

During production planning, Sarah worked out the running time at which each segment should end. That way she will know when to give back-time cues to Bill and Kathy. The pumpkin-carving segment is scheduled to run 5 minutes and end at 8:39:00, according to the rundown sheet, so Sarah knows that at 8:38:00 she should give a one-minute cue to Kathy.

As the timing becomes more complex and more critical, some directors assign a person to act as the **assistant director**. Among other things, that person usually handles all time calculations.

Time Cues

The floor director relays visual time cues to on-camera talent during a show.

As **floor director**, one of Christine's primary jobs is to communicate time **cues** to the on-camera talent. As mentioned earlier, many production facilities utilize an IPL or IFB system through which the director can talk to the talent. At KXYZ-TV, visual time cues are relayed to the performers by the floor director. While each production organization may have its own unique signals, those shown in Figure 9.4 are fairly standard. These cues are given at the times noted in the program rundown sheet so that on-camera talent can pace comments and questions to fit segments within the designated times.

It is critical that the floor director make sure that these cues are relayed to Bill and Kathy. The cues should be given as near to the lens of the camera as possible if the talent is talking into the camera. When the talent is looking elsewhere, perhaps at an interviewee, the floor director must move into a position from which the cue can be seen easily without becoming visible in one of the camera shots. Unless the floor director is told to do so, these cues are normally not shown to program guests.

Back on the set, Christine has checked all the standard lighting and discovered that one spotlight and one scoop from the kitchen area have been removed. (That part of the set hasn't been used since Monday.) Everything else looks all right, though she will double check the lighting on the interview guest once that person arrives.

The camera people have been assigned to help with the set-up, and Christine has put them to work. Linda and Tom have retrieved the borrowed lights from studio B and are working on the moveable scaffold to reattach them to the lighting grid. John is at the main studio dimmer board where he can turn on the lights as requested by Christine.

The lights are repositioned, aimed, and focused. Christine uses a light meter to obtain the appropriate light intensity. She steps back and looks at the results while Tom stands in to serve as a model. Linda has checked with Ken, the **engineer** assigned to maintain studio A, to confirm that the cameras are ready for use. Ken works for engineering, not for production, so he is

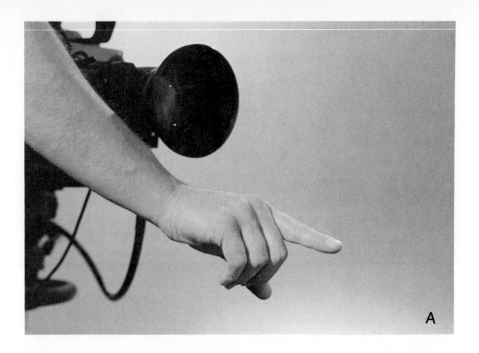

Figure 9.4. (A) A single finger pointed at the on-camera talent is the cue to begin. (B) Rotating the finger tells the on-camera talent to "wrap-up," to finish quickly. (C) A two-minute cue. The floor director and on-camera talent have already clarified whether this is a segment, back, or running time cue. (D) The half-circle formed by the open hand indicates half a minute. These cues are given close to the camera lens if the on-camera talent is talking to the camera. Care must be taken that they not be done in view of the camera.

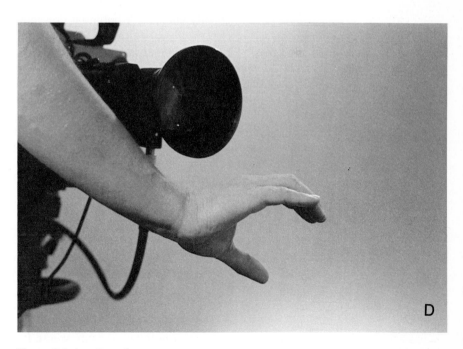

Figure 9.4 *(continued)*

not assigned to a specific production and is not listed on the production crew assignment sheet.

The cameras are ready and Linda moves camera two into position to shoot the kitchen area. John has gone into the control room to **punch up** camera two on the video switcher so that its picture will be visible on the studio monitor. The lighting looks fine.

It's 7:45 A.M. and Dave has begun to **string the mikes** to be used on the production. Lavalier microphones will be used for all of today's performers so three of them are placed on the interview set, one additional at the kitchen set, and the other on the news set. Linda helps with this task by speaking into each microphone after Dave returns to the control room so he can check that each works. He will need to take another level after the actual users have put on their mikes just before air time.

Tom and John move the other cameras out into position. After each production the cameras are moved back to their assigned parking place near the control room window and the camera cables are coiled neatly so that the cameras are out of the way during staging and lighting. This protects them from damage and makes it easier for engineering to work on them if necessary between productions.

Producers and directors work closely to prepare a show; production crews prepare the facility.

"Sunrise Edition" is produced by Bill and Kathy, who also serve as the show's co-anchors. Sarah assists with producing and is the show's director. These three work closely together to plan and organize the show, and they rely on the production crew to have the studio facility ready to go by air time. They usually arrive in the studio only a few minutes before 8:30 A.M. though Sarah usually checks for potential problems periodically during set-up.

Fred, the production manager, has assigned himself to work as the technical director today because the usual TD is on vacation. As head of the production department, he has broad responsibility for the scheduling of production crews and facilities. He fills in frequently so that he can stay involved with the various station productions and observe the performance of the production crew. After stopping by the "Sunrise Edition" office for a copy of today's rundown sheet, Fred gets to the control room at about 8:10 A.M. and begins the process of presetting the special effects that will be used on the video switcher. He also notifies Ken in engineering that the control room monitor for camera three is not working.

Joyce, in charge of the character generator, is already working in another section of the control room, loading the pages of graphics needed for today's show. There are lower third name titles for the guests, the weather and sports graphics for the news segment, and some addresses that will be given during the pumpkin-carving segment. The regularly used titles and names are already stored in the character generator's memory.

Amy, in charge of videotape, arrives next carrying an armfull of videotape cassettes. The two pretaped feature segments were supplied by Kathy, and four others came from the newsroom where Paul, the news **anchorman**, is finishing the script for his segment. Paul, like most newspeople, won't arrive on the set until just before he is scheduled so that he can have the latest information available on whatever stories he is following that day. It's not unusual for the show to begin, and even for the news segment to begin, without all of the videotape news packages being completed. Amy often gets a news package to load and run only minutes before it is used. She loads each of the cassettes into the playback machine, checks that it is correctly labeled and plays properly, and recues it to the starting point. As she does this, she works with Dave so that he can adjust the audio level of the playback VTR on the audio mixer.

*Teleprompters are generally used for longer copy; **cue cards** for shorter copy.*

Today's show doesn't have much scripted material. Bill and Kathy don't need scripts for most of the program. They will read assigned copy to introduce the pretaped segments. Those will be visible to them on the **teleprompters**, which are one-way mirrors mounted on the studio cameras. The main user of the teleprompter is Paul, whose entire script will be slowly displayed. The teleprompter allows him to read the script while appearing to look directly at the camera lens. Marcia methodically loads each tape of the script onto the machine and controls the speed of the display to match Paul's rate of reading. Figure 9.5 shows the set-up of the teleprompter system as it displays a script.

It is 8:20. Sarah is now in the control room and has asked the crew to move to their assigned positions and **get on the headsets**. Each production crew member will be able to communicate over the studio intercom system. During the production, much of the communication will consist of Sarah talking and everyone else listening and responding to her directions. Each can talk to her when necessary, but only essential communication between crew members will take place. The intercom is not the place to discuss last night's ball game, especially not in the middle of a live production.

Bill and Kathy have stopped by the restrooms to check their appearance and apply make-up as necessary. Bigger stations might have make-up people on the staff, but at KXYZ-TV, performers must do their own.

Christine has just returned from the lobby with the guests for today's show and she is helping them get comfortable. Dave has come into the studio to help each of them with their microphones. When they are set, he and Christine work together to have each guest speak into the microphones to get a level. From experience, Dave knows where to set the pots for the regulars on the show.

It is 8:25 A.M. when Bill and Kathy arrive. They talk briefly with their guests and then move into position for the opening of the show. The cameras are in position, lights are all on, and the studio video monitor is on and adjusted and positioned where it can be seen both from the interview area and the kitchen set. Christine makes sure Bill and Kathy have their mikes on and Dave gets a quick mike check to be sure they're still working.

The guests are seated just off the set, where they can move to their positions during the commercial breaks in the program.

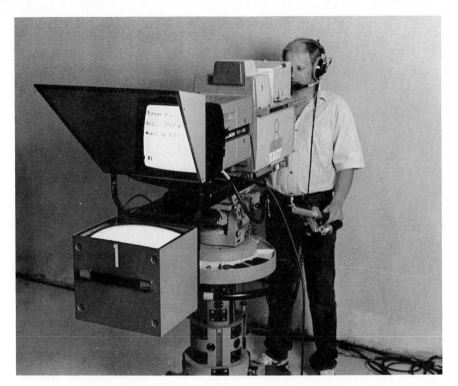

Figure 9.5. The teleprompter system utilizes a special black-and-white video camera (not shown) to shoot the pages of a script. That camera's output is then routed to the black-and-white monitor mounted below the lens of the studio camera. The resulting video display is reflected into a one-way mirror mounted directly in front of the studio camera's lens. The on-camera talent can then read the script while appearing to look directly at the lens.

It's quiet now in the studio. But in the control room, there is a steady flow of chatter, mostly coming from Sarah:

"Stand by all around. One minute to air. Ready tape opening on VTR A. Opening shots on cameras. I'll need Kathy's super first, then Bill. Ready to sound VTR A, then studio mikes. The opening seg is two minutes, then we're into the first position."

The commercials that are inserted into "Sunrise Edition" are grouped into positions. Each position usually contains three or four 30-second spot announcements that will be played from the special **videotape cartridge player** located in KXYZ-TV's MCR. During these commercial breaks the studio is not on the air, and the production crew uses these intervals to reposition and prepare for the next segment.

The master control operator selects the various sources from which programs originate, either from another studio, videotape, or an outside source.

Today the station is carrying a network morning talk show from 8:00 to 8:30 A.M. When that show ends, master control will select Studio A as the new program source and cue Sarah to start the production.

It is 8:29:45 A.M.

SARAH: "Fifteen seconds to air. Stand by to roll A. Stand by in the studio."

8:29:55 A.M.

SARAH:"Roll A. Ready to take it, with sound. Stand by in the studio."

Sarah looks up at the source monitor for VTR A and watches the leader count down from five.

8:30:00 A.M.

MASTER CONTROL: "You're on."

SARAH: "Take A with sound. Ready camera two. Ready to open the mikes and cue Bill."

Sarah surveys the camera monitors. "Camera one, tilt up slightly on Kathy. Two and three look good. Ready dissolve camera two. Ready A sound under."

The last graphic and the opening announcement on the show opening tape has disappeared.

"Open the mikes, cue Bill, dissolve two, A sound under."

Fred smoothly moves the fader bar on the video switcher and Dave lowers the VTR A sound to background level. Christine, who is standing beside camera two, points her finger and cues Bill just out of camera range beneath the lens.

BILL: "Good morning. Welcome to 'Sunrise Edition' for Thursday. . . ."

SARAH: "Ready Bill's CG over camera three."

Sarah glances at the CG monitor to confirm that the correct graphic is ready. Fred has already preset the key on mix/effects one with CG over camera three.

"Take CG over three. (*Pause*) Lose it."

As Bill and Kathy talk about today's show, Sarah switches between cameras one and three to follow the conversation.

8:01:30 A.M.

SARAH (*to master control*): "Ready position one. Christine, show Bill a 30-second cue. Ready camera two on a dolly out from the two shot at the break. Ready CG over camera two for the **bumper**. Ready bumper cart."

Bill sees the cue from Christine and knows that he has 30 seconds to lead into the first commercial break. A bumper is a video and/or audio transition often used before and after commercials. Frequently it contains excerpts from the main program to maintain viewer interest. "Sunrise Edition" uses only a music bumper.

Linda pushes the camera cable aside so that she can do the dolly back. Fred presets the key on M/E one. Dave has the bumper cart loaded; the pot is down and will be faded up after the cart is started.

SARAH: "Spin cart up under."

The bumper music from the audio cartridge fades in softly under Bill's voice.

BILL: "We'll be back with our first guest, and show you how to carve that Halloween pumpkin, right after these messages."

SARAH: "Music up full. Dissolve two. Start the dolly Linda. Take CG over two. Ready position one."

MASTER CONTROL: "Position one in five, four, three. . . ."

SARAH: "Fade to black. Fade audio out."

*During **commercial breaks**, adjustments and equipment checks can be made.*

During the commercial break, cameras two and three truck over to shoot the pumpkin-carving demonstration. Kathy moves over to that area while Christine escorts the guest onto the set. Dave makes a quick check of both microphones to make sure that no connections have come loose during the move. Tom turns the studio monitor slightly so that the guest can see it more easily during the actual carving. Amy has loaded the first taped feature in VTR A and it is ready for use following the live demonstration.

8:03:45

MASTER CONTROL: "Ready back to you in 15."

SARAH: "Stand by in the studio. We'll come back on camera one. Then Bill throws it to Kathy on camera three. Ready CG with the guest's name."

As she talks through this upcoming sequence, Sarah checks the various source monitors to confirm that the video elements are all in place. The rundown sheet shows that this next segment should run eight minutes; five for the demonstration and three on tape.

SARAH: "Ready open mike and cue Bill. Ready fade up camera one."

MASTER CONTROL: "You're on."

SARAH: "Open mikes. Cue Bill. Fade up camera one."

***Cues** should be given in the same order each time.*

Sarah gives the **cues** in the same order each time. Open the microphone first (so that Bill's first word will not be clipped), then cue Bill (there will be some delay while Christine reacts to the cue, points to Bill and he reacts), then take the camera (again some delay while Fred reacts). Using this priority sequence briskly usually results in the shot of Bill coming up just after he has received the cue and before he has actually started to speak.

Bill welcomes the audience back and introduces the pumpkin carving demonstration.

SARAH: "Ready mikes. Ready cue Kathy. Ready camera three."

BILL: ". . . is with Kathy right now."

SARAH: "Open mikes. Cue Kathy. Take camera three. Ready CG over camera two."

As the demonstration progresses, Sarah switches between cameras two and three with close-ups of Kathy and the guest, and with close-ups of the pumpkin they are working on. Christine relays back-time cues to Kathy so that she will know when to finish the segment and introduce the videotape feature scheduled next.

SARAH: "Ready to Roll A with the Thanksgiving Parade feature. Show Kathy 15 seconds."

KATHY: ". . . Thanksgiving parade."

SARAH: "Roll A. Ready to take it with sound."

KATHY: "'Sunrise Edition' reporter Mark Smith has that story."

SARAH: "Take A with sound. Good job crew! Christine, bring the next guest in. Camera three, move back to the interview set. Two, set up on the news desk. We're on tape here for three minutes. Then we'll come back to Bill and Kathy for the bumper into position two."

The production runs smoothly because all know their jobs and are very familiar with the routine of the program. Sarah is in charge, but she gets plenty of help from the crew members who know their roles and do many things with very little direction. Everyone is trying to anticipate problems and to prepare in advance of actions that will be required.

*The director makes sure the show is **running on time** and makes adjustments.*

In addition to directing the various production operations, Sarah is also responsible for **keeping track of time** to make sure that the program will devote the planned amount of time to the various segments and will end at the scheduled time. (In a larger station, Sarah would probably have an assistant director to help with this task.) Since some of the program elements are already on videotape, their time is fixed. She must therefore make minor changes in the live segments as necessary to make adjustments if the overall program is running short or long; for instance, the interview can be shortened a bit, a news story can be dropped, or the closing conversation about tomorrow's show between Bill and Kathy can be changed. Today's show is scheduled to end at 8:28:30.

8:26:38 A.M. The news segment is almost finished. Scores are being keyed over videotaped highlights from last night's National Basketball Association games as Paul reads them.

PAUL: "Seattle over Phoenix . . . 103 to 101."

SARAH: "Take two. Show Paul 15 seconds. Stand by on camera three with Kathy. Christine, tell them they'll have a little over a minute for the close. Ready mikes. Ready cue Kathy."

PAUL: ". . . and that does it for sports. Kathy."

SARAH: "Open mikes. Cue Kathy. Take camera three."

Bill and Kathy thank today's guests and talk about tomorrow's show.

SARAH: "Ready to roll VTR A. Ready dissolve A with sound. Ready dolly back on camera two."

KATHY: ". . . thanks for joining us."

SARAH: "Take camera two. Start your dolly. Roll A.

BILL: "We'll see you tomorrow."

SARAH: "Dissolve A with sound. You're clear in the studio. (*To Master Control.*) Back to you in 15 seconds. Ready fade to black. Ready fade audio."

Sarah watches the control room clock countdown. 8:28:27.

SARAH: "Fade to black. Fade the audio."

8:28:30. Master control goes into the **station break** preceding the next program.

SARAH: "We're clear. Nice job everyone. Thanks a lot! Let's strike the studio."

Bill and Kathy thank their guests; then Christine escorts them back to the lobby.

After a few minutes to relax and unwind from the production, Sarah, Kathy, and Bill will meet in the "Sunrise Edition" office to discuss today's show. They'll talk about the overall program content and analyze any production problems that may have developed. Then they will spend the rest of the day preparing for tomorrow's show.

The production crew cleans up the studio. The cameras are pulled back out of the way and parked. Linda and Tom clean up the mess from the pumpkin in the kitchen set while John helps Dave recoil the microphone cables and put away the mikes.

Amy rewinds all of the videotapes and returns them to Sarah. Fred asks the crew to gather in the studio when they are finished to discuss today's production. This show went very well, although he is going to ask Christine to make some adjustments to the lighting on the kitchen set before tomorrow.

Most of the production crew will take a short break and then move into studio B, where they are scheduled to work with a different producer on some local commercials. That will run until 11:30 A.M.; then they'll come back to studio A for production of the "Newscenter 8 Midday Report" at noon.

Discussion of Procedures

"Sunrise Edition" was done live. If there had been problems or mistakes, the viewers at home would have seen them. Some stations might elect to do such a program on videotape, which would offer the option of doing the entire program over or of pausing in the middle of the production to make corrections. But that would require a very early start time for the videotaping to allow for this more time-consuming approach. KXYZ-TV decided that it would be difficult to have guests come in so early; furthermore, the live production offers greater immediacy.

The example is fairly typical of the way television studio production is done at a small-market broadcast station. As with field production, anyone who has worked in such a situation knows things don't always run so smoothly. The equipment sometimes does not work. Guests fail to arrive. Tapes are mistimed. A thousand different things can happen to cause problems. Dealing with these problems and making the show look good in spite of them is a measure of the skill and professionalism of the production team. Below are a few other things to keep in mind.

Computing Time   One of the skills that production people must master is the adding and subtracting of times. Since time is calculated in minutes and seconds, it can sometimes be confusing.

Consider this example from "Sunrise Edition." The school feature was supposed to run 4:53 minutes. That is the segment time shown on the rundown sheet. In the middle of the production, suppose the editor came to the control room and told Sarah that he wrote down the time incorrectly. It actually runs 4:35 minutes. Since it's almost time to insert the feature, Sarah must recalculate program times during its playback to adjust for the mistake.

She gets into the school feature on time. Using running time, when will the tape end?

$$
\begin{array}{r}
8{:}47{:}00 \\
+\ 4{:}35 \\
\hline
8{:}51{:}35
\end{array}
$$

Using back time, how much time will remain when the feature ends?

$$
\begin{array}{r}
11{:}30 \\
-4{:}35 \\
\hline
6{:}55
\end{array}
$$

Once Sarah knows the impact of this change, then she can make adjustments to the length of any of the remaining segments that are not already on tape. Since this error has resulted in an additional 18 seconds being unfilled, she decides to add it to the closing segment with Bill and Kathy. Christine will relay that fact to them during the playback of the school feature.

Intercom Etiquette   As the description of "Sunrise Edition" illustrates, most of the communication on the studio intercom is one way, from the director to the production crew. It is strictly business and comments directed back to the control room are only those essential to make the production run smoothly.

A couple of cautions are in order here. Avoid profanity. It contributes absolutely nothing to the communication process necessary to do the job. And it is offensive to many people.

Be careful about making jokes both before and during a production over the intercom. Remember, the on-camera performers cannot hear the intercom; they may associate your laughter with something they did or said and may become self-conscious for no reason. This is especially true with studio guests, who are generally already nervous.

SUMMARY

This chapter introduced you to the integration and coordination of equipment and personnel that results in studio production.

The "Sunrise Edition" example was used to describe and illustrate how the personnel and equipment function together as a production machine. The procedures used at KXYZ-TV are fairly typical, but every production organization will have some methods and terminology that are uniquely tailored to the nature of the productions they do or the facilities with which they work. Larger stations will probably have more people involved and their roles may become more specialized.

As should be apparent from the example, careful planning and preparation are crucial to the smooth execution of the studio production. Even with fairly simple productions, the process is complex and the demands of the clock create considerable pressure for everyone. When all crew members know their assignments and directions are clearly communicated, the production elements blend smoothly and efficiently.

Your first studio productions are unlikely to run so well. Do not become frustrated or disappointed. When the procedures, terminology, and pressures are all new to you, that is to be expected. If the production process is rough, then the resulting program will probably be rough as well. The important point is that after each production, you take time to evaluate *both* the process and the results so that you can learn from your mistakes and build upon your successes.

REVIEW QUESTIONS

1.   What are some of the primary advantages of television studio production?
2.   Why are group dynamics a factor in television studio production?
3.   Compare and contrast the roles of the producer and director in a television studio production.
4.   List and briefly explain three different timing methods commonly used in television studio production.
5.   You are directing a newscast. The show has a standard 40-second closing that includes advertising announcements and must be run in its entirety. Total program time is 29:15 minutes. The last program segment before the close is normally a recap of the day's headlines and is allotted 45 seconds. The producer tells you in the middle of the show that a last minute story will be inserted just before the headlines if it's ready before the show ends. It will run 1:25 minutes. Using running time, when should that story begin?

PART THREE

Putting the Machine to Work

The first two parts of this book introduced you to the ways various pieces of television production equipment work and how to operate them. In part 2, you were given two examples of how the equipment could be combined into systems for two distinct methods of production, and you learned about the role played by various personnel in the production process.

As was outlined in chapter 1, the essence of television production is not how the equipment works or what the individual tools can do, but rather how those tools can be used to create effective communication of stories, events, ideas, and personalities.

Now you will be introduced to ways of planning, preparing, executing, and evaluating basic production projects. Rather than simply working the television production machine, you will learn about how to put it to work.

There a four distinct stages in the life of any television production project:

1. Research and planning
2. Preparation
3. Execution
4. Evaluation

You have already learned about many of the tools and techniques used during the execution stage. Now you will be introduced to the basic procedures used by producers in the other stages as well as an expansion of the role of directors and editors during the execution stage.

Throughout the book, reference has been made to the importance of effective and thorough planning as a key to the ultimate success of television productions. Chapter 10 deals with that process and the pivotal role of the program producer.

Chapter 11 focuses on the selection process and the role of directors and editors, who implement the production plan and coordinate the components of the production machine necessary to prepare and assemble the production elements into a finished form.

An appropriate analogy to your development as a television production person is the experience of learning to drive an automobile. First you learn how the automobile works and how to operate it. You learn the rules of the road and gain some experience operating the machine in familiar surroundings. You also learn to read a map and how to plan a trip. Then you decide where you want to go. Once the plan is established, your task becomes one of guiding the machine along the chosen route to its destination. Along the way you have to make many smaller decisions and deal with many variables that could not have been anticipated. With a few setbacks, perhaps a few wrong turns or delays, you probably complete the journey. Each succeeding trip becomes easier as you gain experience and learn the various techniques that allow you to take advantage of shortcuts and more efficiently use the automobile.

Producing, directing, and editing are tasks quite similar to planning and driving the trip. You have learned how the various components of the television production machine work and understand their capabilities. The job now is to formulate plans and use the tools in imaginative and productive ways to reach your production goal.

This section concludes with a brief discussion of the evaluation process you should use at the conclusion of all production projects. Evaluation is often overlooked. Feedback is frequently difficult to obtain, partly because production team members are usually tired of the project and anxious to move on to something new. However, both the process and the product must be honestly evaluated if you are to learn from your experience.

CHAPTER 10

Production Planning and Producing

THE ROLE OF THE PRODUCER

Usually it is the producer who starts with an idea or an assignment that will develop into a program intended to communicate a message to an audience. Producers use the television production machine to gather, create, and assemble appropriate production elements into a comprehensive form that will convey the message most effectively. These elements are combined into a product with a new meaning.

The producer, often generator of the idea, keeps an eye on the "big picture."

Often, producers fill other roles on the production team during the preparation and execution of the project: they may write, research, direct, or edit. The producers' primary role, however, is to assume *overall responsibility* for the project from beginning to end. While they may become involved in very specific details, they must also retain a "big picture" of the project with an eye to such factors as major production goals, time schedules, and budgets.

The producer plays a key role in all stages of the production process, although during the execution stage a great deal of responsibility may be delegated to other members of the production team, particularly the director and/or editor. Chapter 11 has more to say about the roles these and other production team members play during the actual program assembly.

Producers must understand the capability of the production machine and the people who operate it. That does not mean that a producer must be highly skilled at every production task. For example, a producer need not be a highly skilled **videographer** to know the kinds of images that will most effectively communicate the program message. Perhaps one of the most important qualities that a good producer must possess is an understanding of personal limitations and a willingness and ability to take advantage of the skills, talents, and ideas of other production personnel.

239

Good producers are good communicators. They are able to get across program goals and production concepts to others. They're also good listeners who are open to ideas from others and receptive to alternatives that may develop during the production process.

Producers are list makers. They're organizers who can keep a project moving forward on several different levels simultaneously.

Producers can never lose sight of the fact that their work will ultimately be judged by the reaction of the audience. In addition to knowing the objective of a project and the capabilities and limitations of the production machine, the producer must understand the audience. One of the major pitfalls to avoid is making a program for oneself or for other production people. A program that is beautifully crafted with elaborate production technique and detail that has no meaning for the audience is a failure.

THE PROCESS

Research and Planning

A television program begins with an idea or a concept; a message to be communicated. Sometimes it is the producer's idea. More often it originates with someone else who contacts the producer for help in developing the idea into a television program. Many production projects are assigned to the producer by the management of the employing production organization. Regardless of its origin, the first step in the production process is to analyze the idea to determine whether or not it has the potential to become an effective television presentation. Too often, alternatives to television production are not adequately considered. The assumption is made that "we'll make a TV show," even though in many cases there are more effective ways of developing and communicating a message through other media. This is a formula for disaster.

Analysis of potential and feasibility comes first.

Preliminary Questions to Be Answered

The initial research and planning stage of the production process is by far the most important. The program must be clearly defined at this stage. The producer must be able to answer these questions before the project can move forward:

1. Message: What is the program supposed to say?
2. Audience: Whom is the program talking to?
3. Medium: Is television an appropriate method to use?

Many inexperienced producers probably fail to give these questions sufficient thought. They tend to find rather general answers quickly and move on.

Define the Message Consider this example. You've been assigned to produce a beer commercial. The goal is to sell beer. The production, therefore, is supposed to say "buy beer." Seems simple enough. But what kind of beer? OK. "Buy Acme Beer." Why? "It's on sale." "It tastes good." "It's sexy." "Everybody's drinking it." "It's now available at local stores." Now we've got "Buy Acme Beer because . . . etc." You can see how the process can become more and more specific.

A television commercial makes an especially good example of the value of clearly defining the production's message. Most good commercials can be summarized by one sentence or phrase. That happens because the producers defined that sentence or phrase long before production began.

In the 1980s, Miller Lite Beer built an exceptionally successful series of television commercials around the simple theme that their product *tastes great* and is *less filling*. The settings, personalities, and production techniques that were used in the spots covered the spectrum, but the basic message always came through.

Longer programs with more complex ideas and themes may be more difficult to summarize so precisely. But often they can be broken down into workable sections, each with a sharply focused message that can be stated in a short sentence or two.

For your initial production assignments, you may find this process difficult — but it is critical to your success. If you as the producer don't know what you are trying to say, then how will the production team know? Or your viewers? Take the time to think through this question carefully.

Identify the Audience Define the audience. Whom are you talking to? Again, the answer often seems so obvious that you may tend to skip over important considerations. The average television viewer? A general television audience? You must be more specific.

Back to the Acme Beer example. Whom are we selling to? College students? Blue collar workers? Sports fans? The more clearly the audience can be defined, the more sharply the production can be focused on that audience.

Commercials lend themselves to this approach because they usually target specific groups within the larger audience as part of the advertising and marketing strategy. But the need to define the audience exists with any program idea.

Consider the assignment to televise a volleyball match. Since volleyball is not as widely followed as sports like football or baseball, you must define your target audience. Whom are we trying to reach and what do they know about the sport? The method of covering the game will be significantly different if the audience is made up of diehard former players than if it is primarily more traditional sports fans who have just been watching a football game in the previous time slot.

Consider the Medium　Once the message and the audience have been defined, the next step is to realistically assess your ability to do the project on television.

You have already made the most important assessment if you moved on to this step; you have decided that television is an appropriate medium through which to communicate the message. But are you capable of doing the job on television?

Three areas need to be considered to answer the question:

1. Resources
2. Time
3. Personal capability

Resources: Money, Talent, Facilities　Most professional producers would tell you that the only really important resource is money. With adequate budget for a project, all of the other resources can be acquired. That's probably true.

But for your first productions, you're unlikely to be dealing with significant budgets, in many cases probably none at all. You must evaluate the resources that are readily available to you. What production facilities are in place? How frequently will they be available for your use? What other production personnel will be available to assist you? Do you have adequate supplies in terms of videotape, sets, props, and so on? What about transportation? Can you realistically plan to work at some distant field location? Who will appear in this program? Do you need on-camera hosts? What about experts? People to perform? Do you need someone to help organize and write the script for the production? Who will direct? or edit?

The list of questions could go on and on. It would be unique for every production. And as the planning process moves forward, the questions become more specific to the project at hand. The point is, it's the producer's job to ask, and then to answer, these questions as the production plan takes shape.

Estimate Time　A realistic assessment of the time available along with the estimated time required for a project is essential. Making that estimate will be difficult until you have had some experience with the total production process. You would be wise to take all your initial estimates and multiply by two as a starting point. Television production is no different from many other complex activities: the work seems to expand to fill all the available time. Things always seem to take longer than expected.

Remember, you must deal not only with your own time. You must work also with facilities that are being shared with others and must consider the time schedules of those who are going to be working with you. Several techniques for planning and organizing production schedules and timetables are introduced later in this chapter.

Know Your Personal Capability　Knowing your own capabilities may be the most difficult assessment to make. Your personality will have a lot to do with how you handle this decision. Some people are risk takers and will always attempt projects that stretch their abilities. Other, more conservative individuals will choose less challenging projects in which they can polish their skills with less risk.

Whichever description fits you, pick a project with which you feel comfortable and one about which you can be enthusiastic. Recognize the areas of the project where you may need help and get it. All projects will include some crises or roadblocks, problems that must be solved. As a producer, solving those problems is one of your primary jobs.

Once you have made an assessment of the project in these areas, you should be able to make a good decision as to whether or not to proceed. If the answer is no, then the idea or assignment must be revised and modified into something more realistic or abandoned. If the answer is yes, your next task is to develop a more detailed production plan.

Formulate a Production Plan — At this point, you are making a commitment to do the project. That doesn't mean that decisions made thus far are "cast in stone" or that new information might not change your decision. But the affirmative assessment should give you a measure of confidence that the project is feasible.

In formulating a production plan you will be faced with more specific problems and decisions. Among the areas to consider are:

1. Selecting the production approach
2. Committing the content to paper
3. Selecting the production method
4. Developing timetables and production schedules
5. Holding production meetings

Select the Approach — What kind of program will most effectively communicate the message? Rarely will the answer be clear cut. Generally there are options. Some common television program approaches include:

Documentary — an in-depth report on an event or issue of public importance; dramatically analyzes the topic in a factual manner.

Demonstration — instructs the viewer by showing how something is done (cooking shows, home repairs, exercise routines)

Discussion — people talking to each other in front of the television cameras

Dramatization — story development through fictionalized re-enactment (daytime soap operas, television miniseries)

Performance — television coverage of sports, fine arts, or other events.

Format is the basic program structure. — The way a program is organized is called a **format.** The format provides a convenient structure upon which to build the various production elements into a cohesive unit. Talk shows, musical variety shows, and newsmagazine shows are all common formats seen regularly on broadcast and cable television. These programs follow a tried-and-true formula with a predictable blend of ingredients. Many popular formats — late night talk shows, for example — combine several different program approaches into one program.

You will find yourself using these formats frequently. They are common because they work well in many situations. But do not choose them just because they are familiar and easy to copy. Convention should not dictate your approach to any project. The nature of the topic should be used as a basis for evolving a combination of production elements and techniques appropriate to that topic and the intended audience.

*Enhancements derived from careful use of the production machine are **production values**.*

In planning the production approach, try to develop **production values** for the program. Even though you are new to the television production process, you have already learned about some simple production techniques that can enhance your production. Also, you have seen thousands of productions that used techniques you may want to adopt and copy.

This is part of the challenge of production work: to identify production elements that can increase the effectiveness of the program and then work through the challenge of making them a part of the final program. Just remember, the technique, whether it be special effects, unusual transitional devices, or unique use of a camera or a microphone, must be used because it enhances the overall production, not just because it has some intrinsic attraction.

The message, not technique, should be evident.

Whatever the approach and the production values selected, the objective is to communicate the message with that approach, not to call attention to the production technique itself.

A simple example illustrates this point. Consider that your task is to televise an interview between a well-known network anchorman and the President of the United States. The program will review the President's last year in office and this is an exclusive for your network. This will be a live broadcast from your network studio in Los Angeles.

You have chosen a simple set with two comfortable chairs and a limbo lighting technique to focus the attention of the audience on these two respected men. The anchorman will ask tough questions; the President is known for his candor.

The studio is equipped with six cameras and an extremely complex video switcher with all of the latest digital special effects. But you don't need a lot of equipment. To use it would be inappropriate for the intimate, straightforward approach to this topic that you have selected. All that is needed here are good close-ups, minimal switching to follow the conversation, and occasional reaction shots. To clutter such a program with superfluous production would be inconsistent with the dignity of the situation and probably detract from the flow of information.

Commit the Content to Paper

Even though television is a visual medium, it still relies upon the written word. Throughout the process, you will need to commit things to paper. This needs to happen in two areas: the program content itself and the various planning and preparation documents. This material provides the guidance essential to a successful production. Ideas, techniques, schedules, and budgets that are on paper are more easily communicated and have a way of pinning down something so that decisions are reached. It does not mean that things can't be changed, but it does give some substance to the plans and the content.

The content of the program is usually laid out in a written description that can take several forms:

1. Treatment
2. Outline
3. Script
4. Rundown sheet

Treatments and outlines are very general in the way they describe the program's content: scripts and rundown sheets are very specific. Often, as the planning proceeds, a treatment will be developed into a full script for a program, or an outline will be filled in and detailed to become a rundown sheet.

Any of these forms can be used, depending upon the needs of the project and the approach being used. Obviously, for the presidential interview mentioned above, a script would not be needed. But a general outline of the areas to be covered, with specific questions written out in advance, would probably be appropriate. During the actual broadcast, a rundown sheet would be needed to guide the production team through the various program segments. Specific shot specifications would probably not be needed, but detailed information on graphics, commercial breaks, and openings and closings would be.

Inexperienced producers are usually surprised by how much of their work can be done in an office with a telephone and a typewriter or word processor. As production people, we all love the editing room and the studio. But for things to go well in the production environment, you must do your preproduction work effectively. That means organizing the production plan on paper with written schedules, budgets, "to do" lists, and notes from meetings and phone calls.

Select the Production Method   Assuming that the facilities for either method are available, you have the choice of doing the production in a studio or on location. Further, you may have the option to do it in real time or to work in segments and assemble the finished product through postproduction.

There are so many variables in each production situation that guidelines for making this decision are impossible. As pointed out earlier, the studio affords much control over all aspects of a production. It is generally less expensive and less time consuming. Field production is more realistic and generally provides greater immediacy but is more difficult to work with because of the lack of control.

You will probably have an opportunity to experiment with both methods in your production training. And many times the best approach may turn out to be a mixture of studio and field, real time and postproduction. As you will recall from chapter 9, "Sunrise Edition" was a blend of studio and field production and included elements of discussion, demonstration, and performance.

*Develop Timetables
and Production
Schedules*

Your production project will almost certainly include a deadline by which the finished program must be completed. So as soon as you commit to do the project, you have a fixed amount of time during which the process must be completed.

*A **timetable** gives broad benchmarks; a **production schedule** pinpoints activities.*

Develop a **timetable** for the project. Work backwards from the deadline data and establish benchmarks: dates by which various phases of the project must be completed. This may be calibrated in weeks, days, or even hours. Many producers use a calendar or similar structure as a means of laying out the production plan on paper. You may develop your own methods. In this regard, television production is no different from any other complex activity. You have developed methods of organizing your activities with regard to your education. Production planning requires the same organization.

A **production schedule** is a more specific outline of the times when various activities must take place during the execution stage of the production. You will find that even with simple productions, coordination will be greatly enhanced and efficiency increased if all production team members know the production schedule in advance. Without the guidance and structure such a schedule provides, production activity can languish and precious time can be squandered on inactivity or less important aspects of the project, to the detriment of the overall program.

As you will recall from the commercial production project outlined in chapter 8, the producer apportioned the one day available for the work. He established benchmarks throughout the day by which certain activities had to be completed and then organized the work to fit within that framework.

As the producer, you should develop these time frames. Furthermore, it's your responsibility to make sure that all production personnel adhere to the planned schedule, and of course that includes you.

*Hold Effective
Production Meetings*

Producers cannot operate in a vacuum. Before any of your preliminary plans are formalized, you should discuss them with the essential production team members. The director, the writer, the editor, the on-camera talent, and others need an opportunity to react and contribute to the plan. Typically, you will talk to many of these people individually as necessary during the early planning. But before the plan can be set in motion, most producers like to bring the essential production team members together in a production meeting to review it. That meeting is often the first of many that will take place as the project moves forward.

Effective production meetings provide an atmosphere of openness and common purpose. They identify problem areas and successes. They promote communication between team members, which is essential to the success of the project. Time schedules are always reviewed. And if pertinent so are budgets.

Although the producer still has overall responsibility for the project, plans developed through effective communication and meetings with others have a better chance for success because they foster the sense of participation so essential in a group endeavor like television production.

Preparation

The second stage of the production process is preparation. Using the production plan as a guide, the producer makes necessary preparations to put the production machine into motion. The complexity and variety of activities required in this stage of production are far too numerous to detail in this book. But there are some general areas into which they can be grouped:

1. Specific research/content development
2. Settings and locations
3. Production facilities
4. Production personnel
5. Talent rehearsals
6. Preproduction
7. Materials acquisition
8. Communication

Specific Research/
Content Development

Preliminary research led to the initial project idea. Once a commitment was made to do the project, research activity intensified. During the preparation stage, research becomes very specific. This is the stage where the treatment is developed into a full script, where the outline is filled in to create a fully formatted program. It's where the facts are organized, where the storyline is embellished, where the various program elements are detailed and the interrelationships established.

On your first productions, you will probably handle your own research and development. Major production organizations often have entire departments dedicated to research and content development. Regardless of who does the work, it produces the substance of the production. This information provides the details about the topic and the essential facts of the message that provide viewers with insight, entertainment, and involvement.

Research frequently uncovers surprises. As Frederick Shook points out in his book *Television Field Production and Reporting,* surprises are a trademark of effective productions:

> Surprises help viewers feel something about the story, and they help lure uninterested viewers to the screen. Surprises can be compelling visuals, wild sound, short soundbites, or poetic script. Always, surprises are moments of drama or feeling that help renew the contract with viewers and lure them back to the screen.[1]

The program idea is fleshed out by research and development.

Producers must constantly monitor research activity because new material will be steadily accumulating while some material will be eliminated. Research and development takes place in the library where books and periodicals can provide background information. It's done over the phone talking to experts in a given field or individuals who are involved with issues or events. It's done in script conferences where creative minds flesh out the situations and details of a story to be dramatized. It's done in audition rooms where potential performers are considered. It's done in viewing and listening rooms where archival materials on tapes and films can be evaluated. Effective producers are always open to new options that develop as preparation moves forward, but they never put themselves in the position of counting on such an option to develop. They always have a plan with at least one approach that is bulletproof.

Effective research is an extremely time consuming and yet rewarding enterprise. Because of the resulting abundance of new ideas and alternatives, it is critical that the producer remain closely involved in research and that flexibility be retained to capitalize on opportunities uncovered through the research and development process.

Of course, limits must be placed on research and development. That is why the clear statement of program goals and the adherence to a production timetable received such heavy emphasis earlier in this chapter. Just as with production personnel, researchers must occasionally be reminded that the goal of their activity is to develop a script or program rundown, not simply to dig ever more deeply into the topic.

Settings and Locations

As you made your decision on production method, you probably made a decision as to the environment in which the production would take place. Now you must either find that location or create that setting in which to execute the project. The director may become involved at this point, since the selection affects the way in which the production will be staged. As with most other production considerations, your goal is to create an environment consistent with the program content and conducive to the communication of the program's message.

*The TV screen is a moveable **window** or frame that includes and excludes.*

Beginning producers often misunderstand the nature of the television screen. It is a *window* through which the audience can see many views, many angles, and many different settings in very close proximity and rapid sequence. That window can move around and through the scene. It is not like a proscenium arch theater where the audience is separated from the stage and sees the action from a single vantage point. You need be concerned only that the settings necessary for the desired camera shots are available. There may be portions of the setting or location that are undesirable when viewed in person. But so long as the shots selected by the director or editor can convey the desired setting while concealing inappropriate sections, the setting or location may work quite well. For example, you need not create an entire beach in your studio for a swimsuit commercial. Only enough sand and palm leaves to fill in the television frame is required. Add a little surf sound effect, and the setting is there.

Production Facilities

As mentioned earlier, you will probably be using production facilities that are shared with other production projects. As soon as the production plan is formulated, take inventory of your anticipated needs and the facilities available. Using your timetable as a guide, *reserve them for your use* if possible.

As the program content and the production details are worked out, make sure that you keep the facilities' capabilities in mind.

Select Production Personnel

On even the simplest production, you're probably going to need help. What production jobs do you enjoy most? Which ones do you do well? Who else can assist you and enhance the outcome? You can always use the input of a good writer, for example, though these talented people are often hard to find.

Smart producers surround themselves with capable assistants and delegate tasks in areas where talented or skilled people are available. Most successful productions involve synthesis and the creative energy of several people. Your role as a producer is to encourage and channel that process toward the production goals established at the outset.

Talent Rehearsals

Among the most important decisions that you will make about any production is the selection of the people who will appear in the program. There simply is no substitute for talented performers who have the charisma to attract and hold your viewer's interest.

The producer communicates intent to the talent.

Once these people are selected, the producer will work extensively with them in meetings and rehearsals to assure that production goals are clearly understood, that audiences are properly defined, and that the message and the method of communication is clearly understood. As the research and development activity proceeds, on-camera talent will become involved in the specific sounds and actions that will make up the program.

In a news documentary, for example, as the line of inquiry is developed, on-camera anchors and reporters will become actively involved in the development of themes, lines of questioning, and specific areas of exploration. In a dramatic program, actors will be involved in detailed character development and may make contributions to the specific wording of the dialogue.

As preparation progresses, rehearsals will be held — first formal talent rehearsals and then full production rehearsals, which involve all the production facilities and personnel.

Preproduction

Producers often decide to do production work on some segments of the project in advance of the final assembly process. Images and sounds can be recorded and edited on magnetic tape for later insertion into the final program. Graphics can be developed and stored in character generator memory or on disks so they will be ready in advance.

For example, commercials to be included in a live program can be assembled and edited together onto a single videotape to make playback more convenient during the broadcast. Appearances by guests who are difficult to schedule can be taped at convenient times. Images and sounds from archival sources can be isolated and assembled in a more convenient storage system where appropriate.

This kind of preproduction work is often done for the producer by **production assistants** who are given a variety of assignments.

Materials Acquisition   The material used in many productions is not newly gathered or created; it is acquired and reworked to blend into the overall production plan. Sounds and images of all kinds have already been created and stored using the various storage and retrieval systems discussed in chapter 6. A major part of the preparation process on many projects is the locating and acquisition of these materials.

Unlike written materials that are catalogued and easily accessed through traditional libraries, audio and video are not so well catalogued and easy to find. Although many separate catalogues and individual libraries exist, they are not cross referenced and cannot be located through any centralized list.

Audio and video materials often have reuse limitations that require permissions and payments. Strict copyright restrictions usually apply when these materials are to be included in a new production that will be stored on tape, duplicated, or released in real time to an audience. The intricacy of obtaining copyrights and clearances is beyond the scope of this introductory text. But you should be aware that this is an area that requires additional study lest you find yourself confronted with a charge of unlawful use of another's work.

Maintain   The producer must assure effective communication among those working on
Communication   the production project. It's often said that the producer's job is to know everything. That may be true. But it's also critical that the producer make sure that direct communication between other members of the production team takes place as well.

Producers sometimes forget that other team members also need a broad view of the project, that they should see the big picture so that they understand how their efforts fit into the overall project.

With all of these activities going on simultaneously, it should be easy to see that coordination of even the simplest production is a challenging task. A producer must be well organized if the project is to succeed. Discipline is essential if decisions are to be made in a timely fashion and problems are to be addressed. During the preparation stage, the producer is the key to success or failure.

Execution

Much of the producer's job has been done when a project arrives at the execution stage of production. If the planning and preparation have been done well, the execution should run smoothly.

During this stage, the producer often turns over the actual operation of the production machine to a director or an editor. The role that those people play in the project is detailed in the next chapter. That does not mean that the producer gives up control of the overall project or becomes uninvolved. But it does sometimes mean that — as difficult as it may be — the producer must step back to allow other creative people room to do their part in the production.

During the execution stage, the producer must be sensitive to the morale and attitudes of the production team. Sometimes overall production goals must be restated. Enthusiasm may need rekindling. The producer may need to encourage and support others faced with difficult assignments or tough decisions.

Evaluation

You will find that it is difficult to be objective about the overall success or failure of your first production while the process is ongoing, even if you have no other production task to perform than simply watching it come together.

But the ability to make a preliminary evaluation of the results during the execution stage is another mark of a good producer. There are times when things are going so well that minor production problems should be overlooked in the interest of the overall results.

There are also times when things are going so poorly that production should stop for an analysis or discussion of problems before a lot of time is wasted and the entire project suffers. Directors, editors, performers, and others often are unable to see this happening and it's up to the *producer* to step forward and intervene if necessary.

Chapter 12 discusses a more thorough evaluation stage that follows the execution of a production project. The process and the product deserve close scrutiny so that successes and failures can be identified and analyzed.

The producer took on responsibility for the project at the outset and must complete that process by making sure that evaluation takes place. The results may be gratifying or they may be painful. But a realistic assessment of whether or not the original production goals were achieved is imperative to improving your producing skills and developing a more effective approach for the next project.

SUMMARY

Producing is a challenging and rewarding endeavor. The producer is a manager confronted with all of the attendant problems that are part of the overall direction of any activity, including coordination and communication with many people, limitations on resources, demanding time schedules, and unanticipated problems to solve.

Managing television production may be more difficult than most management jobs because it involves a creative activity. It requires the blending of the skills and talents of creative people, who often have strong opinions and a deep personal commitment to their work.

After listening to a heated argument over changes in the set lighting between a professional producer and a lighting director in an adjacent studio one night, a production student asked, "Why are they yelling at each other? It's only a minor change." The instructor was quick to respond curtly, "They get mad because they care!"

The producer is the person responsible for turning an idea or an assignment into a finished television product. The producer guides that program concept through the four stages of television production: research and planning, preparation, execution, and evaluation. Good producers are well-organized individuals who can communicate effectively, who can coordinate the activities of others and motivate them to do their part well. The producer must always keep the overall production goals in mind and channel and focus the production activity to that end.

NOTES

1. Frederick Shook, *Television Field Production and Reporting* (White Plains, N.Y., Longman, 1989), p. 8.

REVIEW QUESTIONS

1. What are the four stages of the television production process? Briefly describe the activities that occur during each stage.
2. How do producers *use* the production machine?
3. What three questions must the producer be able to answer at the beginning of a production project?
4. Answer those three questions for a project that you may be doing in the near future.
5. What three areas must be considered in evaluating your capability to do a specific television project? Briefly explain the significance of each.
6. List five considerations in formulating a production plan.
7. Describe three television program approaches and how they are commonly used.
8. What is a program format?
9. What are production values?
10. Give an example of how production values might be inconsistent with a program's content.
11. Describe the various forms in which program content can be organized on paper.
12. Briefly outline the advantages and disadvantages of studio and field production.
13. How do you chose the production method that is most appropriate for your project?
14. What is the difference between a production timetable and a production schedule?
15. Why are production meetings important?
16. List at least four general areas of preparation that should be covered prior to the execution stage of production. Explain what happens in each.
17. Typically, what is the producer's role during the execution stage of a production being directed by someone else?
18. Why is producing a television program a uniquely difficult management task?
19. Briefly describe the characteristics of an effective television producer.

CHAPTER 11

Directing and Editing

This chapter introduces you to the process of directing and editing a television production. In doing so, it focuses on the execution phase of a project beginning with the selection process that takes place as a television program is put together.

THE SELECTION PROCESS

The selection process begins when the producer commits to develop an assignment or idea into a television production. Various production approaches and production elements and techniques are considered. Some are adopted; some are rejected. As the research and planning moves forward, the selection process becomes more specific.

As you saw, options are discovered during the preparation stage. Decisions are made as to which concepts and themes will be included, which will not. Production personnel are selected and the director and/or editor becomes involved in the decision-making process. Performers, guests, and on-camera talent options are considered. Settings and locations are evaluated. During preproduction, alternatives are prepared.

As the project enters the execution stage, the producer hands control to the director or editor.

The execution stage of the television production process is where *final* decisions and selections are made. As the project moves into production, the materials and personnel have been gathered and the rough shape of the production has been decided. At this point, producers usually turn over control to the director or editor, who will make the final decisions during the construction of the program. Your responsibility in one of these roles is to mold the various production elements into the finished product.

The Role of the Director or Editor

As a director or editor, you will make the final decisions about which images and sounds will be used. For example, an editor will normally have several alternative shots and perhaps several different takes of the same shot to choose among. The final selection is made in the editing room, where the shot can be finally evaluated in the context of the images that precede and follow it as well as the sounds that will accompany it.

*Final selection decisions include **sequence** and **connections** between images and sounds.*

You will also determine the *order* in which these images and sounds will appear. And you will decide how the various production elements will be *connected* by such techniques as instantaneous cut transitions, video dissolves, audio cross fades, and fades to black. These decisions establish the relationships between the production elements that give new meaning to the resulting sequence of images and sounds.

In most situations, the producer's plan will guide your decisions while you execute the production. But few scripts or program rundowns are so detailed that instructions are provided for every aspect of the program. Rather, directors and editors interpret and apply the plan while following their own creative instincts. From that standpoint, supervision of the final program assembly procedure can be an extremely creative and imaginative endeavor.

If pickup devices are being used, for example, you will determine the way in which they gather pictures and sounds. Camera operators can be instructed how to compose shots; audio operators can place and adjust microphones as desired.

As director or editor, you will control how production elements are *combined*. Using special effects, images can be superimposed, graphics can be keyed over, split screens can be used. Sounds can be mixed from several sources to create a unique sound environment appropriate to the particular production needs, all at your discretion.

In the hands of a director or editor, the isolated images and sounds can take on a new meaning. Frederick Shook talks about the process in his book *Television Field Production and Reporting*:

> Television is much like music. Its meaning is not established until it plays out through time according to predetermined rhythms and moods. Television is not meant to survive as a still photograph (or isolated sound), or even as a series of unrelated scenes in which message, context, and meaning speak for themselves. Just as a single note of music has virtually no meaning, so a single television scene is virtually mute. Only when the scene is placed next to others, and the complete work is absorbed, does it assume larger meaning.[1]

Directors and editors use the tools of the television production machine to *implement their decisions* and assemble the images and sounds into a completed work that has meaning. They determine how it will play out through time.

As a director, you also have a unique leadership role to play in the production process. This leadership responsibility is analogous to that of the ship's captain, who must direct the crew in order to be able to control the ship and guide it along its chosen course to a destination. During that process, everyone's fate is in the captain's hands.

Characteristics of Directors and Editors   Directors and editors come in all sizes, shapes, and descriptions. Not everyone, however, is cut out to handle this demanding and challenging job. A few traits that characterize those who do these jobs are:

1. Imagination
2. Pragmatism
3. Decisiveness
4. Leadership
5. Patience
6. Charisma

Directors and editors must be **imaginative**. They must see and hear options. Given some intitial input, these people immediately begin to see possibilities, ways that the concept or theme can be developed and presented. They have the ability to visualize how things may look before the actual images have been created or combined.

Alfred Hitchcock, one of the true masters of motion picture production (his film classics include *Psycho, North by Northwest, The Birds,* and many others), had the ability to visualize an entire film before it was actually produced. He reportedly considered the mechanical process of actually staging and filming the production to be somewhat of an anticlimax.

Solutions must be practical.   **Pragmatism** is high on the list of qualities needed by directors and editors. A pragmatist is a realist. That does not preclude high expectations or lofty goals. But it does mean that all productions must fit within some constraints. The director or editor must do the best job *possible* with the time and resources available. You will often be faced with situations that require a practical solution, even though a better solution might be possible given more time, more facilities, or more money.

Television production can be a trying experience for a perfectionist. Postproduction techniques have introduced a great deal of precision into the process, but it is still fraught with compromise and the need for pragmatic solutions to problems.

Once a project reaches the execution stage, some very **practical decisions** are often required. Directing and editing involves choices from among realistic alternatives. You must evaluate the options within the context of the available time and resources, make a choice, and move forward with the project. This is often quite difficult for the new director or editor.

The quality of **leadership** is more applicable to directing, where the activities of several other production team members must be coordinated, although some editing situations require leadership as well.

During the program assembly stage, you will be in charge. Others will look to you for decisions and guidance. True professionals lead by example and earn respect by being well prepared to do their part.

Leadership does not mean dictatorship. If you have been chosen to direct or edit a production, your authority is already established. Exercise it gently. There will be times when firmness is necessary. But remember, you need the help of other people to complete a project. You won't get much cooperation if you antagonize everyone.

Skillful leaders encourage participation.

Your goal should be to encourage participation by other production team members. Give them some "ownership" in the project, too. Respect the contribution that others can make and they will probably respect your role.

The production process is not necessarily a democratic one. You are the one who will make decisions. But whenever possible, listen to suggestions from others. You may be surprised to find that they have some good ideas that can enhance the final product. Your goal should be to take advantage of such input in order to produce the best program possible. Unfortunately, directors and editors sometimes reject good ideas simply because someone else thought of them.

Cultivate **patience.** The production machine has been placed under your control. You have a job to do and a schedule to meet. That creates considerable pressure on you. It's easy to become impatient with delays and problems, whether they are caused by equipment, people, or the production design itself.

Your patience will almost surely be tested from time to time. But hasty decisions made out of frustration are often bad decisions. Outbursts at a production colleague can impede future communication and erode motivation. Frustration or anger vented on the television production equipment is clearly unacceptable.

The television production process is a complex one that is always filled with potential problems. Expect them. Deal with them. You were chosen to direct or edit the production because of your ability to cope with these situations and to keep the production activity moving forward.

Last on the list but not least: **charisma.** The job of supervising the production team is a lot easier if people like and respect you. You have authority by virtue of your position, but you will be more successful when you create a friendly, open, and fair environment. Television production can be fun and your leadership position makes you one of the principal factors in the development of that kind of atmosphere.

Role Differences

While directors and editors both make final selection decisions and share many similar traits, there are some important differences in the role that they play and the circumstances under which they work.

For example, as a director you will often become heavily involved in handling rehearsals and preproduction work during the preparation stage of a production.

If you're an editor, on the other hand, you generally begin your work when all of the required images and sounds have been gathered, created, or acquired. Your job begins with a review of the production plan and that material.

As a director you are likely to use all of the production tools described in this book. Not all will be used on every production you do, but eventually you will need them all.

As an editor, you work primarily with the editing system; you are unlikely to be involved with gathering images and sounds in the field. That work will have been done already. You will select from the results that have been stored on videotape.

These two jobs entail different circumstances, as well. Directors must interact with many other people and must lead and supervise their activities. Directors must be quick-thinking individuals who can make good decisions on the spot. Directing a real-time production with several different audio and video sources and a cast of performers creates a high-pressure situation.

Editors usually have less pressure and the opportunity to work more independently. The postproduction process can be more precise and deliberate. Options can be considered. Alternatives can be previewed and studied. Their work requires less spontaneity.

Keep in mind that you should not be overly concerned with the title that is given to the person who supervises the television production process. Techniques and skills needed depend upon the production system and the approach being used. The judgment and talent necessary to choose and assemble production elements in an imaginative and effective fashion depend most of all on the person's individual ability and understanding of production goals and audience reactions.

Measuring Success   Your success as a director or editor will be measured in two distinct areas: (1) the quality of the finished product, and (2) the manner in which you handled the production process.

You may find that your limited experience with the production tools gets in the way of implementing some of your intentions during your first few attempts at directing or editing. Not only have you taken on a new, broader responsibility for directing or editing the production, but you are also still relatively unfamiliar with the individual tools, procedures, and techniques required to do the job. It's a challenging situation that involves the use and coordination of a complex system. You may feel like the apprentice juggler who has difficulty keeping all the balls in the air at one time!

Your skill and imagination are evident in the decisions that are made about the precise way in which the production elements will be composed, combined, and presented. You will develop a style that will distinguish your work.

Another measure of your ability is the manner in which the production process is managed. You often rely to a considerable degree upon the talents of others to assist you in your job. You will work with the same people frequently. Having a reputation for professionalism and technical competence will prove to be a real asset in achieving consistently good results.

DIRECTING

Types of Directing

When you direct a television production you may face two separate tasks:

1. Talent direction
2. Production direction

Talent Direction   Whenever you direct a production using pickup devices to capture the actions of on-camera talent, it will be your responsibility to supervise and guide those performers. Planning and rehearsing their actions will usually be done first by itself, often away from the studio or field location, before the additional complexity of cameras and microphones is added.

Directing the   When the time comes to put the production machine into motion, your job
Production Team   is to direct the actions of the other production team members such as camera operators, technical director, and audio operator. If the production involves on-camera talent, you will direct them as well. This process is called **staging** the production: guiding and positioning the performers and production tools as necessary to obtain the desired effect.

With single-camera production, which usually is a matter of gathering materials to be assembled later in postproduction, directing may involve little more than conferring with a camera operator, working with the on-camera talent, cueing action, and making sure that you capture the images and sounds required by the production plan. In some ways, your most important function in this situation will be to catch minor errors and to encourage the talent and production crew to give their best efforts — to be a keen observer.

More complex production, involving multiple cameras, videotape playbacks, and lots of graphics and sound sources, is sometimes called **control room directing.** It is more demanding. For example, directing coverage of a sporting event would involve coordinating a large production crew and announcers, interacting with the game officials and the event's management personnel, and following the game (usually with the assistance of the producer) to show the action and to develop a storyline as the game unfolds.

During your first attempts at control room directing, you will probably be so busy that at the conclusion of the production you will have little idea of how the production looks and sounds. Just following the script, giving the cues, and trying to see and hear the various video and audio sources as you select them will totally occupy your attention.

As you gain experience, however, these procedures will become more natural. You will be able to direct the talent and the production team while at the same time evaluating the production as it is being assembled. This is a valuable skill to develop. Much time can be saved in rehearsals and video-taping sessions if you can recognize problems and stop the production to address them rather than continuing as difficulties compound. Also, when programs are being videotaped, if you must always go back and watch a complete replay of the material just completed before deciding whether or not to do another take, you have effectively doubled the total time required to do the production. Experienced directors note potential problem areas as they happen during a videotaping session and then go back to check those portions with tape playback rather than simply watching everything again.

Directing Procedures

As you can begin to appreciate, directing, especially control room directing, is a demanding task. But there are some things that you can do to handle this complex job better.

Observe and Listen   Directors are often so busy talking and directing that they fail to see and hear things that are crucial to their success. They overlook valuable ideas from performers and production team members. Especially during set-up and rehearsal, don't become so absorbed by your way of doing something that you miss a good suggestion.

Be sensitive to the attitudes of your co-workers. Not everyone shares your enthusiasm or motivation to succeed. Find ways to involve others and to let them share in the creation of this project.

Know when to let go.   Recognize when you have reached the point of diminishing returns. In most every production situation there is a point where the best possible results have been obtained. It may be recognizing that something has been rehearsed enough and is ready for production or that an adequate number of takes have been recorded and you should move on to some other activity. You must have a feel for when you've gotten the best combined effort from the group.

This moment of maximum effort can happen, for example, when you have spent considerable time before the production rehearsing the on-camera talent. When their performance is honed, you move to the studio to capture it with the production tools. Now your attention is focused on ironing out the production problems, getting cameras moved as necessary, mixing the sound, and rolling in the pretaped segments. That may take several production rehearsals. And during each one, your talent performs flawlessly.

Now, just when production has its act together, the on-camera talent begins to make mistakes; the delivery lacks vitality. Your talent has peaked before you ever rolled the tape to record or put the program on the air. The talent is overrehearsed; the material has gone stale.

*The Director's
Triangle*   The job of the control room director is to constantly anticipate what happens next and prepare the necessary people and equipment to do it. In doing so, a technique called the director's triangle can help you organize the way you

shift and focus both your attention and the verbal cues required. Figure 11.1 illustrates this triangle.

When you are ready to begin the production you enter the triangle at the reference corner. Your attention is directed to the rundown sheet or the script. It tells you what is supposed to happen. You scoop up as much information as possible. What is the next video source? Audio? What talent cues are necessary? What time cues?

You then immediately move to the preparation part of the triangle. Visually, you look at preview and source monitors through the control room glass, over your shoulder at the audio or videotape operator, or at the clock. Verbally, you give preparatory cues: "Ready camera two, ready spin cart, standby to cue Kathy."

At the appropriate time, you move on to the execution corner of the triangle. You do whatever was prepared in the preceding action. "Take camera two, spin cart, cue Kathy." As you give these verbal cues, you glance at source monitors and then look to the program monitor and listen to the program audio to confirm that your directions have been carried out.

It's at this point in the process that you may have some problems. You can't relax. Ask yourself immediately what happens next and move on around the triangle for another circuit. A quick check of the script (reference); up to the source monitors giving more ready cues (preparation); execute those actions (execution); then around you go again. Inexperienced directors tend to spend too much time watching and listening to the results of their last execute commands rather than moving on immediately to reference and then preparation. Experienced directors spend most of their time in the preparation sector of the triangle.

In some directing situations, for instance, covering live news or sports

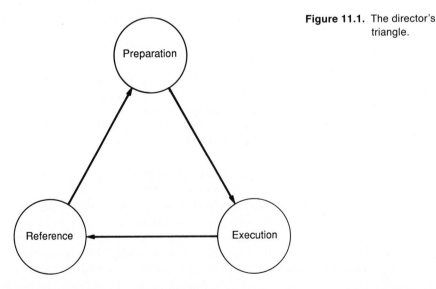

Figure 11.1. The director's triangle.

events that have no script, there really is no reference corner. Your knowledge of the production machine and preplanning for this specific event take its place. You move back and forth between preparation and execution. In this case, the preparation stage consists of anticipating what is likely to happen next and using the production tools available to provide yourself with as many options as possible to capture that anticipated action.

For example, you are directing coverage of a college basketball game. You have a camera located high in the stands at midcourt that you are using to follow the game action on a medium shot. You also have cameras at floor level on both ends of the court. The layout of this situation is shown in Figure 11.2.

The visiting team has the ball on the right end of the court. You're on camera two. Suddenly, the home team steals the ball and starts a fast break moving right to left. As an experienced sports director, you know the images you need to show this play. You want a dramatic low angle from camera one with the players coming right at the camera. A quick glance at the source monitor: "Camera one, follow the ball to the basket, ready one, take one." If the home team scores, the fans will go wild. You need a crowd reaction shot. "Camera three, pan left and give me a medium crowd shot." The shot is ready should the home team score. "Ready slow-mo A if you've got it, camera two, ready with the hero shot if he scores." Camera two will know to zoom in for a close-up of the player who makes the basket if he scores. A glance at the program monitor just as the good guys score on camera one. "Ready three (fans on their feet cheering), take three. Ready two (hero shot), take two. Got it on A?" Slow-mo A has it. "Roll A (replay of camera

Figure 11.2. Camera placement for basketball game.

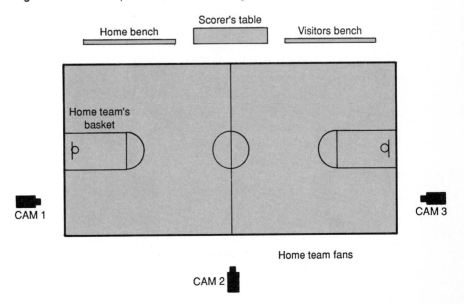

one's shot of the scoring play), take A. Camera two, back to the ball. Ready two (medium shot of visitors bringing the ball up court again), take two."

The images selected told the story of the steal and the crowd's reaction and identified the hero. The director was able to have them available when needed because he anticipated what was likely to happen and prepared options to cover it. Had the home team failed to score, he probably would have simply cut back to camera two on the medium shot and continued the regular routine of following the ball up and down the court.

Directing multicamera coverage of a live event like the one just described is exhilarating to say the least. And believe it or not, an experienced director working with a capable production team can handle the hectic pace with relative calm and may even be able to watch and enjoy the event while directing its coverage.

Handling a Script

The director's ability to spend minimum time in the reference corner of the triangle is directly related to the way the script was prepared and the way it is handled in the control room.

Annotating your script makes for fluid directing.

You should spend considerable time prior to the start of a production going over the script and making **notations** on it to highlight important sections. Write in cues at the point where they will be needed. That doesn't mean you should write down everything that you need to say. One of the worst things you can do is try to direct a program with your head buried in a script. But mark where each camera should be selected, where VTR inserts must be rolled and inserted, or where audio cues are needed. Make note of any important production consideration — just don't get carried away. Figure 11.3 shows an example of how a page of script might be marked by a director. Practice the verbal cues that you will need to give as that point in the production comes up.

Apply the same what-happens-next approach to handling the script. You need to be able to see not only the page you're on currently but also the one that follows. Again, so that you can work ahead, anticipate and prepare for the next action. Place the script before you in a stack. Remove the first page and start a second stack to the left of the first. Now the page that you're on is to the left, and the one that will follow it to the right. As each page on the left hand stack is completed, cover it with the one that is on top of the right hand stack. Just move it across. The page you're on is now at the top of the left hand stack and you have uncovered the one that will follow on the right hand stack.

Verbal Dexterity

Good directors have the ability to talk fast. A lot of information must be conveyed rapidly. That doesn't mean that you must shout. But you must be efficient in your choice of word cues.

Consider this comparison. "Ready to open Kathy's microphone, ready to cue Kathy, ready to fade up to camera one." The same message: "Ready Kathy's mike and cue, ready fade one."

SUNRISE EDITION
Opening

	Roll VT-A		
Standard VTR Opening	*VT-A*	(SOT Up Full)	*SOT*
Runs :30			

Dissolve Cam 2 ——————

WS Kathy & Bill

(SOT under, then out)
(Bill:) GOOD MORNING: WELCOME TO "SUNRISE EDITION" FOR THURSDAY THE NINETEENTH. I'M BILL ROSE.

Mics Cue

MCU Kathy *Cam 1*

(Kathy:) AND I'M KATHY WEBER. WE'VE GOT AN INTERESTING LINE-UP FOR YOU THIS MORNING.

MCU Bill *Cam 3 / W/CG*

(Bill:) THAT'S RIGHT. HALLOWEEN IS JUST AROUND THE CORNER AND WE HAVE A SPECIAL STUDIO GUEST WITH SOME NEW IDEAS ON DECORATING FOR THE HOLIDAY.

CU Kathy *Cam 1 / W/CG*

(Kathy) AND SPEAKING OF HOLIDAYS, PREPARATION IS ALREADY UNDERWAY FOR THE ANNUAL THANKSGIVING DAY PARADE. MARK SMITH HAS A SPECIAL REPORT.

CU Bill *Cam 3*

(Bill:) THIS WEEK'S FEATURED SCHOOL IS CENTRAL HIGH. . . WITH A UNIQUE TUTORING PROGRAM ORGANIZED AND STAFFED BY SOME OUTSTANDING STUDENT/ATHLETES. THIS STORY MAY CHANGE YOUR MIND ABOUT SOME OF THE PREVAILING STEREOTYPES!

Two Shot – Kathy & Bill *Cam 2*

(Kathy:) ALL OF THAT PLUS PAUL HERNANDEZ WITH NEWS. SPORTS AND WEATHER. . . COMING UP IN THE NEXT HALF HOUR.

Dolly back to WS *Cam 2*

(Bumper Music up under)
(Bill:) STAY WITH US.

Spin

Key – Pumpkin Carving Next *CG*
Fade
Black

(Music up full, then out)

Fade

Figure 11.3. Television directors usually mark scripts so that the precise location and timing of cues and transitions are easy to see. This technique allows the director to spend more time looking at the control room monitors and less time looking at the script.

The production team will tend to take on the same demeanor as a director. If you sound hurried and flustered, the production crew will tend to become rattled. If you are confident and smooth, generally the crew will perform better.

To re-emphasize a point made earlier, don't ever say anything on the intercom while directing that you would be ashamed for the audience to hear. Avoid profanity. It certainly doesn't contribute in any way to the efficiency that you need, but it can be damaging to production team morale and there's always the possibility that a microphone just might pick up something from one of the headsets in the studio.

Discipline   Don't waste time on apologies or criticism for mistakes made during the production. Correct mistakes or, better yet, try to anticipate problems and keep mistakes from ever getting on the air or on the tape. After the production is completed, then take the time to analyze problems that occurred and take appropriate action so that those situations can be avoided on future productions.

An example. You are directing a studio interview program. Camera three was directed to get an over-the-shoulder reaction shot of your reporter during the interview. Then, just when she nods her head in reaction to something the guest has said, you take camera three and find that the shot is out of focus and framed incorrectly. "*#^*#! Camera three, you +#⁻|*! Take two."

Compare. Same situation. "Ready three." You look at the source monitor first, see the problem. "No . . . let's stay on two. Three, pan left and check your focus!" You keep a potential mistake off the air. And the firm tone lets camera three's operator know a mistake was made. After the production, take the offender aside for a quick word about the camera operator's responsibility to frame and focus without being told. The operator should appreciate not being embarrassed and will probably be extra careful to do well next time out.

Storyboards and   In preparation for a directing assignment, you may find **storyboards** and/or
Floor Plans   **floor plans** helpful in visualizing the production.

A storyboard is a sequence of simple drawings that show the primary images that will be included in a production. If a storyboard is available for your project, you will definitely want to become familiar with it. In most production situations, the storyboard serves as a guide or starting point for creating and assembling images to communicate the desired message. You may find that it provides a springboard to other options and combinations that may be equally or more effective. Rarely will a producer insist that you follow the storyboard precisely. It is a plan that can sometimes facilitate the creative process and help you convert ideas on paper into a polished production. Descriptions of sounds and the script for any spoken narration or dialogue are usually provided adjacent to each drawing. An example of a simple storyboard is shown in Figure 11.4.

CAMERA: Linda Behind Car Door - MS

AUDIO: "You can drive away in the open air too!"

CAMERA: Key Logo

AUDIO: Music Up Full

CAMERA: C U Linda

AUDIO: "5 different models are in stock right now."

CAMERA: WS - Dealership

AUDIO: Music Up Full

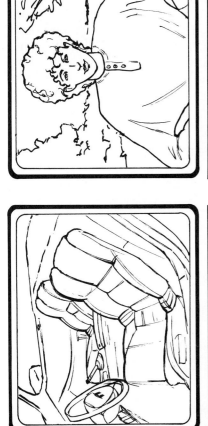

CAMERA: C U Car Interior

AUDIO: Music Under "So put the top down."

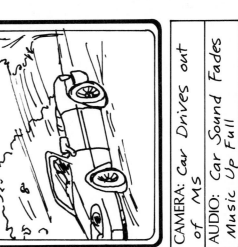

CAMERA: Car Drives out of MS

AUDIO: Car Sound Fades Music Up Full

Figure 11.4. This storyboard shows some of the images that were planned for the Linda's Auto Sports World commercial described in chapter 8.

A floor plan is a diagram that shows the position of set pieces and locations of production equipment. The lighting design may also be included. Two simple floor plans, omitting lighting diagrams, are shown in Figures 11.5 and 11.6.

Floor plans are especially useful with multicamera shoots because they allow you to visualize where cameras can be positioned. Once you draw in any given camera position, you can then visualize what the composition will look like since the floor plan will include the set pieces and the lighting design. This is a good way to get the creative process started and to anticipate problem areas. Often, you may see ways to make minor changes in the set, the lighting, or your shooting plan that will enhance the look of the production. Remember, the floor plan is a guide that can be modified until the set-up yields the results required.

Most directors approach an assignment with at least one planned approach that experience tells them will work. It may not be very original, but it will suffice. But good directors also search constantly for alternatives, for new and better ways to use the production machine.

For example, you have been assigned to direct the taping of a panel discussion involving a host and two guests. The producer gives you the floor plan shown in Figure 11.5. You have three cameras to cover the discussion.

The floor plan will work. You have used those same camera positions several times before. But you often have to cut away to a wide shot just to get camera two or three onto a shot of A or B. And many times when A and

Figure 11.5. Panel discussion floor plan (lighting diagram omitted).

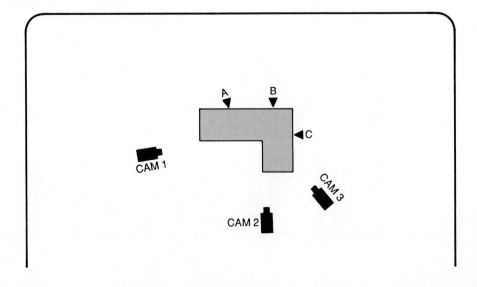

B talk to each other you end up with very unattractive profile shots of both of them.

What if you shot this discussion in the round? Move the cameras all the way around the set. It might look something like the floor plan in Figure 11.6. This alternative offers some interesting possibilities. By leaving the openings between the backdrops, you can shoot each participant head on and you have interesting over-the-shoulder shots on all three. The only drawback is that no camera has a shot in which all three faces are visible. That is a problem, but then, how often do you really need that shot? Probably just at the very beginning of the show. As a director, you might decide that you're willing to give up that shot in exchange for the much better angles that will be available on all cameras throughout most of the production.

Be Sensitive to Pacing   As you develop your directing skills, you will be able to manipulate the production machine at a much faster pace than at first. You will be able to prepare and execute a variety of camera shots, videotape inserts, special effects, and other techniques in rapid succession. But the pace at which production elements are presented should be appropriate to the natural pacing of the material being presented.

The basketball example given earlier illustrates the point. The pace of the game is constantly changing. During the steal and fast break, the pace was quick and required lots of rapid images. Imagine that after losing the

Figure 11.6. Alternate panel discussion floor plan (lighting diagram omitted).

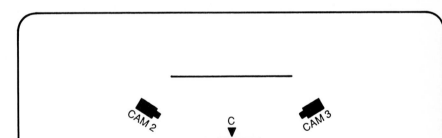

ball on the previous possession, the visiting team walks the ball up the court and goes into a delay offense. To continue a rapid-fire sequence of camera shots would be inconsistent with the tempo and story of the game. The wise director would slow down.

Overproduction, that is, excessive technique, won't add interest.

You will probably direct some boring shows. A simple panel discussion on an uninteresting topic is not going to be very exciting. You will be tempted to try to generate some action with a flurry of production techniques: frequent camera changes, zooms, pans, dollies. Resist the temptation. If the program is boring, do something about the content. If that is not possible, overproduction will become apparent quickly, and the program will still be boring.

Develop Your Own Style

Most of this section has been aimed toward introducing the skills required to direct your first productions. But there is more to the job than simply talking fast and mechanically moving through the various production elements. Good directors have a recognizable style. Whether it's the way they position cameras, the types of transitions they use, or the way they interact with the on-camera talent and the production team, something will set their work apart. As your skills develop you will discover certain techniques and procedures that you favor and begin to develop your own style.

EDITING

As an editor you must have a clear understanding of the goals of the production and the plan that has been formulated to achieve those goals. Since you will be working primarily with images and sounds that have already been gathered or created, your job is to make decisions on final selections, ordering, or sequencing.

Editing may include creating new images.

That doesn't always preclude the opportunity to create new images and sounds. Many sophisticated postproduction facilities include pickup devices and synthesizers and generators. Also, you will often have the option to request additional materials from the producer, who in turn will send production crews back out to obtain them.

As an editor you will often work with little or no assistance. Your job is to operate the postproduction facility as necessary to assemble the materials provided according to the production plan. This is not assembly line work, however; you will exercise considerable creative control. Skilled editors earn the confidence of producers and are expected to come up with options and new ideas during the editing process.

Sometimes the producer and the editor are the same person. In the shooting and editing of a car commercial described in chapter 8, the editor assumed several other production roles, including producer and camera operator/director. That kind of duplication of roles can make the editing job easier, since you already know which elements are required and know what has already been captured on videotape. You can make plans and do certain things during the field production activity with the editing session needs in mind. Since you will be the one to edit the material later, you try to make sure that all of the essential images and sounds are gathered.

Editing Procedures

You might want to review the presentation of editing system operations provided in chapter 7 before proceeding.

Although the process you will use to edit a project will always be tailored to the unique needs of that project, the following basic procedures are usually a part of the editing assignment:

1. Logging and previewing all videotape
2. Formulating a plan
3. Editing a rough cut
4. Revising the plan/acquiring additional images and sounds
5. Editing the final version

Logging and Previewing Videotape   To edit a production, you must know what production elements are available. The production plan specifies an image and/or sound. You need to know where that material is and how it looks or sounds. Someone (often the editor) must review and **log** all the raw tape to create a list of production elements that correlates to the final script or rundown sheet. For any given part of the production, you can then consult the production outline, script, or rundown sheet, along with the videotape logging notes, and from that information select the appropriate source for the next edit.

Logging the videotapes is a tedious task that requires methodically looking through them and making notes of where on each tape specific information will be found. Methods of marking or coding times are discussed on page 193.

Since logging tape is a time-consuming process, if possible it should not be done in an editing room. Most production facilities have small viewing rooms for this purpose so that the editing facility can remain available for actual editing work.

Often, you will choose to view large portions of the logged tape, assuming you did not do the initial logging, to have a better impression of what is on videotape.

Formulating a Plan   With the logging notes completed, your next task is to sit down with the script and your notes and analyze how to do the job outlined with the materials available. Few final decisions can be made at this time, but you may begin formulating a general approach that can get the editing process started. A common technique is to break the production down into smaller, more manageable segments and then deal with each individually, working your way back and forth between the planning and rough-cut editing stages segment by segment.

Editing a Rough Cut   With an editing plan formed and final script and logging notes in hand, you will move the project to an editing room to do a rough cut.

In many production facilities, rough-cut editing, like logging, is done in modestly equiped editing rooms intended for off-line editing, as explained in chapter 7. These rooms may not have special effects capability, graphics, or special sound mixing equipment. They may have only one source VTR. Their function is to provide the minimal facilities necessary for you to make editing decisions, explore options, and create a rough cut.

In some situations, the off-line editing is done using duplicates or copies of the original raw tapes. This is done to preserve the quality of the original material. It may also be done to provide copies in convenient videotape format for the rough-cut process. For example, your original tapes may have been shot using 3/4-inch U-matic format, which have been copied onto 1/2-inch VHS (Video Home System) so that you can log them using your home VCR and do the rough cut in a less-expensive VHS off-line editing room.

This rough cut version is analogous to a rough draft of a written document. It is a trial that allows you to see and hear how your plan will work. As you gain experience, your rough cuts will become more polished because you will learn the capabilities of the equipment and what techniques work in certain situations. This rough cut will probably be shown to the producer as well as to the writer and other production team members to obtain feedback and gather suggestions for improvement. You need to be critical of this version.

Frequently, at this stage — if not already during logging — you will discover that **additional images and sounds** are needed. Critical material may have proven to be of poor quality and require redoing. Perhaps there are gaps in the material or transitional elements needed to maintain the continuity of the message. These may have been overlooked or they may have become necessary because of the way you have decided to edit the material.

If the production schedule was properly planned and followed, there should be some allowance for the possibility that additional production may be needed after the rough cut is prepared. Sometimes all the basics are present but the need for additional images and sounds to strengthen and enhance certain sections may also have been uncovered in the rough cut. The opportunity to see a rough cut and then make changes, additions, and deletions is one of the primary advantages to the postproduction approach.

*The **rough cut** will uncover opportunities for adding and cutting.*

Keep an open mind and be willing to scrap the rough cut entirely in favor of a totally different approach. You may decide to make two or more versions, assuming the production schedule and facility availability permit you the time. This allows you to compare and decide which approach works best. The ultimate test of your approach is how it looks and sounds on videotape and the reactions that it provokes from viewers.

Revising the Plan/
Acquiring Additional
Images and Sounds

The information obtained from the off-line editing process will be used to finalize the editing plan and create an editing list of images and sounds that still need to be gathered.

Editing the Final Version

Once changes to the rough cut have been worked out and additional images and sounds created or acquired, the final edit list can be prepared. Depending on the type of facility to be used for the final edit, this edit list may consist of notes on specific tapes and takes that will be used as a guide, or it may be a listing of precise time code numbers that can be programmed into a computerized postproduction system.

On-line editing should be thought out and efficient.

The editing of the final version is, as you will recall from chapter 7, often referred to as **on-line editing**. You will probably be using the best postproduction room available. On-line editing uses the original raw tapes to create an **edit master** that will be the final edited version of the program. During the on-line editing process graphics are added, special effects are created and recorded, and sounds and pictures are mixed and assembled in their final sequence.

Depending once again on the type of facility being used, you as editor may be working alone during this time or you may be supervising others who will operate the equipment. The goal is always to have editing plans finalized so that this process can be done efficiently (this on-line editing facility is likely to be more heavily scheduled than others and probably costs a lot more per hour if you're paying for it). But sometimes changes still need to be made. Within the time and resources available, you as editor should pursue the best results possible. If the changes are relatively minor and can be accomplished efficiently, make them.

If major changes seem warranted, you would probably be wise to stop the editing session and return to an off-line situation to make another rough cut with the changes before committing yourself on the final edited version of the production. Furthermore, major changes likely will require consultation with the producer.

Decision Making

One of the problems with this process is that it can go on forever. After making some changes, a second rough cut can be made. Then more changes and another rough cut. Few productions ever reach perfection; most could always be improved given enough time and resources. So the revision process must have some limits. Usually the production schedule and looming deadlines provide those limits. Your job as editor is to make the production the best it can be within those limitations.

As you can see, editors sometimes have the luxury of time to ponder alternatives that a director in a studio production simply does not have. The danger posed by that luxury is that editors sometimes don't give adequate thought to a project before they enter the editing room. The editing then can take tremendous amounts of time and become extremely expensive. You should strive for efficiency in your work.

Of course there are some situations, notably broadcast news editing, that require the same kind of quick decisions of the editor as are required of the control room director. In most news operations time is at a premium and you will have to work efficiently to meet deadlines.

For many of your projects, you will probably edit your own material. You will execute your own plans. In this way, you will learn the possibilities and limitations of the videotape editing process. Because of the control the editing system provides, you will probably find it difficult to make decisions on some occasions. I have seen students spend hours agonizing over one edit decision. An editor needs to learn to be decisive. Have a plan, explore some options, make a decision, and move on to the next edit.

Because there is always the opportunity to go back and make changes, editors and producers often tend to second guess decisions long after a production has been completed. That's why clearly defined goals are so important. There may be other ways to edit the material, but if the decisions that were made in the editing room accomplish the communication goal, then there is no need to second guess them.

It's important to remember that the editing process combines the production elements one at a time, whereas the audience will see them as a unit. It's difficult to have a feel for the pacing and "flow" of a sequence while you are editing it. The tightly spaced edits may seem very precise, but when viewed together at normal speed they may seem very choppy and lacking in continuity. Most editors periodically back up the tape they are editing and watch it to try to sense this factor.

There are few rules in editing. The great degree of control that is possible means that manipulation in both its best and worst sense are possible. Editors and producers assume a heavy ethical responsibility when editing. Distortion and misrepresentation are ever-present dangers. And while most television viewers are aware of the editing process, they nonetheless assume that the edited materials they see represent reality. But, as you will learn, the editing process can condense and enhance reality, and it can also distort it.

SUMMARY

Regardless of which role you play, director or editor, the responsibilities are similar. You will determine which elements are included in the final production. You will select them, determine the order and fashion in which they will be presented, decide how they will be connected, and supervise the production process that executes those decisions. Your job is to use the production machine to accomplish set goals. You will determine how the finished product looks and how its sounds.

NOTES

1.   Frederick Shook, *Video Field Production and Reporting* (White Plains, N.Y., Longman, 1989), p. xxvii.

REVIEW QUESTIONS

1. What is the role of the director or editor in the television production process?
2. How does a director or editor use the producer's production plan?
3. What does the director/editor try to do as the individual images and sounds are assembled during the execution stage of production?
4. List at least four traits that characterize directors and editors. Briefly explain why each trait is important.
5. Which of these traits do you think is most important? Why?
6. Discuss the differences in the roles of directors and editors.
7. How is your success as a director or editor measured?
8. Briefly describe the two types of directing.
9. What is control room directing?
10. How do you know when you have reached the point of diminishing returns?
11. What is the director's triangle?
12. What is the purpose of a storyboard? a floor plan?
13. Outline the basic procedures used in the videotape editing process.
14. What is the distinction between off-line and on-line editing?
15. Why is thorough logging of videotapes crucial to effective editing?

CHAPTER 12

Program Evaluation

In this book, considerable emphasis has been placed on the fundamental issue: Television productions must ultimately be judged by the response they create in those who view them. How does the final version look to the audience? Did the viewers receive a message? Was it the one that was intended? If the goals and reactions that were identified in the initial planning of the project have been realized, then by most measures, the production has been a success.

But as a practitioner of this craft, production people need to place equal emphasis on an evaluation of the production process that created the final version. Was the process handled properly? Was the result the best it could have been? Can you take pride in the effort put into the project and the results that have been attained?

Message impact and efficiency of production process should each be evaluated.

These two separate standards must be applied independently. The result can sometimes be quite good, even when the process was not. Or conversely, you may be quite pleased with the way you used the production machine, but the audience may totally miss what you were trying to say. True satisfaction will result when a production succeeds by both standards.

The general approach to television production in this book has been a practical one; television is a tool for communicating messages to others. Throughout, you have been encouraged to use your imagination and talent to accomplish that task in a creative fashion.

Some will contend that an equally persuasive argument can be made for television as an artistic medium in which the television production itself is the focus of the process. In that context, in the same way that many artists create works to please no one but themselves, television artists are free to take the artistic approach to their work. However, it is fair to say that most introductory production courses take a practical approach similar to the one presented here. So the reactions of others and the critical evaluation process proposed in this chapter *are* an important measure of the success or failure of your projects.

Break down a production into small units for meaningful evaluation.

The evaluation process must dig beyond the fundamentals. If your work is to improve, you must try to break it down into manageable segments and consider each separately. *Which* portions of the production or process went well and which didn't? If you are to improve your ability to use the production machine to communicate ideas and stories, to cover events and meet personalities, you must learn from both successes and failures. You will find the learning process easier when it focuses on *specifics* and *discrete units* of the task.

As a student of production, it is especially important that you analyze the part that you played in any production. Sometimes that will be a major leadership role; sometimes it will be a minor role. Whichever it is, try to find out how you did your part. How could you do it better? Seek feedback. Observe how your classmates do the various jobs. Adopt the approaches you like; reject others. Create your own blend of techniques and procedures, your own style.

This chapter provides guidelines that can be used in evaluating the work of the production machine and the results it obtains. But its most important message for you is, in whatever manner seems most suitable, to complete the evaluation process.

THE ELEMENTS OF EVALUATION

Sources of Feedback

The greatest enemy of the evaluation process is silence. Regretably, there is often little or no feedback.

As a professional, you will rarely have any direct contact with the final audience for your work. In professional production situations, results are implied indirectly, for instance, through tape sales, **Nielsen ratings**, or comments from the client or your boss.

As a student of production, though, you will likely receive very direct feedback in the form of evaluations and grades from your instructor. Many who teach television production grade the process and the product separately.

You will probably receive additional feedback from your classmates. Some courses require that students evaluate the work of their classmates as well as their own work. This may be done during group viewing of productions or through anonymous written comments.

Consider and Grow

Not everyone will like your work. Any creative endeavor requires that you put some of yourself into the product. When that product meets with disapproval, it can hurt. To borrow a line from Mario Puzzo's novel *The God-*

father, "It's nothing personal; it's just business." Take the criticism in stride. Try to learn from it. If you feel that your work was appropriate in spite of others' reactions, that's all right too. People may disagree.

Grow through trying.

One of the wonderful things about television production is that there are very few rules. There seldom is only one correct way of doing something. There may be a commonly accepted way (remember the anecdote about the titles on the music videos in chapter 5?), but nothing says that you can't do it some other way. So go ahead. Television production needs more of that. Much of what you see today on major television distribution outlets is patterned after techniques developed in the motion picture business during the 1920s and 1930s. Those approaches have survived because they work. But you can build new ways on them.

Trust Your Instincts

Television production students of the 1990s have an acute visual sense. You have already stored up a phenomenal variety of visual and aural impressions. You have access to a marvelous array of production tools that give you the opportunity to create powerful and exciting new programs.

Evaluate Your Own Work

Try to distance yourself from the completed program.

Many find that it is difficult or impossible to view their own work critically just after it is completed. Often a cooling off period is necessary to allow you to distance yourself from the pressure of the actual production process.

It may be useful for you to write an evaluation of yourself. Some individuals find the process of putting these thoughts on paper helps them to organize and formalize specific pluses and minuses. You might find the production rundown sheet or script helpful as an outline or structure upon which to base your evaluation.

Try to prepare your thoughts based first on your recollection of the process and the results. Try to picture in your mind how you handled the production assignment. Let these written comments cool for a day or two. Then read them and watch a playback of the production. You will probably be pleasantly surprised. Often, production students view their work in this way and find that it is considerably better than they had remembered.

Consider the comments you have received from your instructor and your classmates. Ask them for additional input. And listen to what they say. Too often, people are so busy formulating a response or a defense to criticism that they miss most of the other side of the conversation. Rather than defending what *you* did, find out why others reacted as *they* did. You might find some valuable ideas on how to improve your work in this way.

The evaluation process will help you learn how to focus your efforts in ways that get results. But don't sell yourself short. Don't abandon a good idea just because of some negative feedback. Make certain changes and try it again. Television production is a creative endeavor. You have the *capacity* to create innovative projects. As you hone your understanding of the production process and your skill with the production machine, you will rapidly develop the *ability* as well.

Watch the Work of Others

Learn through observing.

If you were to conduct a survey of some of the most successful people in television production, they would probably tell you that at some time in their early career, each was a "studio rat," one of those people who is always around the television production facility when something is going on. It's a marvelous way to learn about the process — through observation.

That doesn't mean that you should become a nuisance or interfere. You won't last long around the studio or editing room if you make a habit of being in the way or telling others how they should be doing their jobs. But when you can observe quietly, there is much to be learned from the way others run the production machine.

You should now have enough basic knowledge of the tools and techniques of television production to be a critical observer of the process. You should also have much greater insight into the methods that created the final results you see in various forms of television production. You will find yourself analyzing programs that you may have previously watched purely for enjoyment or information. Production students often complain that the introduction to production has destroyed their ability to watch television casually. You will find yourself seeing many routine techniques in a new light; you now know how they are done and can often infer why they were used. You will also frequently find yourself puzzling over how a particular effect was accomplished or why a certain approach was taken. That's critical analysis. It's an excellent way to learn more about television production.

SOME STEPS TO GETTING BETTER

Inevitably, the evaluation process will result in the identification of some areas that need improvement. I've never met anyone who has done a "perfect" production. It's what we all strive for, but will never achieve.

So how do you respond to the critiques of your first few production efforts?

Analyze Results

It is important that you try to discover *why* your work succeeded or failed. Often, the feedback will point out where the problems occurred, but sometimes the reasons for the problems will be more difficult to identify.

If you had difficulties with the equipment, for example, consult technicians and others to uncover the cause of the problem and to find ways of avoiding its duplication in future productions.

Positive feedback may be vague and generalized. If you've done your job well, the techniques will not be obvious. So the viewer will have more difficulty pointing out exactly why the production was good.

Practice Skills

Your ability to get the most out of the various production tools is sometimes tied to your physical ability to operate the equipment. If you have difficulty zooming a camera smoothly, or mixing audio sources, or loading and cueing tapes quickly and precisely, find a way to use the equipment for practice.

Frequently, there will be opportunities to do this during down times between studio productions or editing sessions. Sometimes, right in the middle of a session there will be a lull while changes are made to the script or talent takes a break between scenes. If you're part of that team and won't be needed for a few minutes, do some additional practicing on a particular skill.

Give Yourself a Second Chance

Whenever feasible, plan your production schedule in a way that will provide you with an opportunity to discover problems and redo the work as necessary to get it right before the production reaches its final assembly stage.

For example, on your first field shooting assignments you are likely to encounter problems with correct exposure and white balance. Try to allow for the possibility and schedule the initial shoot far enough in advance of the editing session or deadline to permit a second shooting session to get it right.

Learn the Terminology of Production

Your ability to communicate during all stages of the production process will be greatly enhanced if you learn to use terminology that accurately conveys your ideas and needs. As mentioned earlier, every production situation has its own unique terminology for certain procedures, techniques, and effects. Until everyone on the production team understands what is to be accomplished and what actions are required, your chances of success are limited.

Experiment

As a student of production, you have the opportunity to try out new ideas and to sample novel ways of using the tools of production and untested methods of using the production machine. Take advantage of that opportunity.

Should you find yourself working professionally in the television production field at some time in the future, you may not have the freedom or flexibility to do much of that. But even then, you owe it to yourself and your continued creative development to find ways to reach beyond the routine and conventional approaches.

Listen and Observe

Tune in to what goes on around you. You will be spending considerable amounts of time in the production environment. Observe how different production teams work. Try to analyze the process of production.

View the production results. It is especially valuable to see the work created by others when you also have been able to observe the production process that led up to that result. Knowing the facilities and people involved, the same ones that you will probably be working with, allows a much more insightful evaluation of the production.

You should especially focus on the interaction among team members during the production process. Why do some groups consistently come up with good results? How do they organize their efforts? What kinds of communication exist during the production process? What motivates them?

The answers are often elusive. But you will benefit from the effort you put into trying to understand the successes and failures of any production project, whether it is your own or that of a colleague.

A PROFESSIONAL ATTITUDE

Another area that deserves scrutiny is your personal reaction to the television production process itself. Do you enjoy working with the production machine? Do you find it challenging? Frustrating? Exciting? Boring? Probably all of those feelings will be experienced at one time or another.

There is nothing wrong with having a little fun in television production. Sometimes production people take themselves too seriously.

On the other hand, there is nothing wrong with taking your work in this field seriously. And while a thorough discussion is beyond the scope of this text, you must have a profound respect for the power of television and the responsibilities that you assume when you use the production machine.

You have been introduced to the operation and use of a production system that can literally change people's lives. You can take them places they've never been, show them events from afar, tell them stories from the past or from the future, or introduce them to people they would never meet in person.

The television production system has many limitations and shortcomings. Your skill in using the system will be measured to some degree by your ability to work within those restrictions; to provide your audience with visual and aural impressions that allow them to experience the stories, ideas, events, and personalities to the fullest extent possible.

The television production machine has the capacity to create erroneous impression, to misrepresent reality, too. The danger in that and the potential for abuse should be obvious to you. Your goal should be honesty and a commitment to use television for the good of the society and the world in which we live.

Don't ever underestimate the power of television. What you do with these tools and techniques will draw attention. It can have a profound impact on others.

You have been introduced to a powerful craft. Your ability to make responsible decisions rests with your personal ethical standards and basic values.

Use the television production machine wisely.

REVIEW QUESTIONS

1. What is the fundamental issue in television production?
2. What other evaluation should be made of a production project?
3. How can you obtain feedback on your television production work?
4. List and explain at least four steps that you can take to improve your production work.
5. Discuss some of the dangers posed by the capacity of the television production machine to misrepresent reality.
6. How can you use the television production machine wisely?

GLOSSARY

The terms and explanations presented here represent generally accepted usage. As noted in the book, terminology can vary. You will no doubt learn terms and phrases that are unique to the production environment in which you work.

A/B rolling. An editing technique using two source tapes so that dissolves, fades, and other special effects can be done by transitioning from one to the other during the assembly of the edit master.

AC power supply. An electrical converter used to power portable television equipment from standard household electrical circuits in lieu of using battery power.

Actualities. Prerecorded excerpts of sounds and/or pictures from a real event that have been selected for use in a later audio or video report telling the story of that event.

Additive color. The method used by the color television system to capture and reproduce a full range of color by separating and recombining the three primary colors of light (red, blue, and green).

Addresses. Time code or control track identification numbers that mark the beginning and ending points of videotape segments to be edited.

Amplify. To electronically boost the strength of a video or audio signal.

Anchor. The host or primary talent on a newscast. The anchor usually works from a studio location, presenting some news stories and introducing others.

Animation. The creation of a series of still images that will produce the impression of movement when viewed in rapid succession.

Annunciator lights. Lights whose illumination indicates certain equipment functions or modes are engaged or selected. For example, when the record mode is selected on most video tape recorders, a red annunciator light comes on to alert the operator to that fact.

Aperture. The opening in the iris of a lens that regulates the amount of light passing through the lens.

Arc.   A basic camera movement in which the camera is moved on a curving path around an object while maintaining a consistent distance from it. The result is a gradual change in perspective on the object. This move also gradually reveals objects in the foreground and background as the relative positions of various elements in the scene and the camera change.

Aspect ratio.   The ratio of the height of the television screen to its width: three units high by four units wide.

Assemble edit.   A common editing mode used to build a sequential series of images and sounds on videotape. Each succeeding scene is added to the end of the one that precedes it. The video tape recorder builds a control track during this process.

Audio console or mixer.   The piece of equipment used to mix, combine, and blend the various audio sources in the production system. Includes potentiometers (pots) and signal monitoring to permit the adjustment of signal strengths on two or more separate channels. May also include equalization and speaker systems.

Audio fade.   To gradually open or close the potentiometer of audio sources.

Audio feedback.   A high-pitched squealing sound that results when the output from an audio source is routed back to the input of the same source, creating a looping of the signal.

Audio mix.   The new sound that results when two or more audio sources are combined with an audio console or mixer.

Audio operator.   The person responsible for the gathering, retrieval, mixing, and recording of sounds during a television production.

Audio pads.   Attenuators used to lower the signal strength of some audio sources to match other sources in a system.

Audio patch bay.   A system of cables and plug-in receptacles that facilitates the reconfiguration of an audio system. Using the audio patch bay, an operator can reroute various sources to different audio channels or record equipment.

Audio synthesizer.   A generator that creates electronic audio signals directly from the inputs of the user. When reproduced by a speaker, audible sounds result.

Audio tape recorder (ATR).   A machine that stores audio signals on magnetic tape. Also, sometimes used to refer specifically to the piece of equipment that uses an open reel of magnetic tape to record and play back sound.

Audition.   To observe the performance of individuals being considered for an appearance in a production. Also, to utilize a nonprogram channel of an audio console to preview an audio source before it is heard on the program channel. Often used to cue up and test sound sources.

Background light.   A light (usually a floodlight) used to illuminate the background of a scene. Background lights are used to maintain proper contrast ratios with the foreground illumination.

Back light.   A light (usually a spotlight) that is placed above and behind the person or object being illuminated to provide additional modeling and to add to the illusion of depth.

Back timed.   A timing method that calculates time remaining in a program segment or the program itself.

Bank.   A row of buttons for selecting different sources on a video switcher. *See* Buses.

Barn doors.   A hinged accessory fitted to the front of a spotlight to control the distribution of the light. The shutters can be positioned to block light from reaching selected areas.

Battens.   Individual sections of pipe or track suspended from the ceiling of a television studio to form a grid or framework onto which various lighting instruments can be attached.

Beam splitter.   A component of the internal optical system of a color television camera that separates the incoming light into the three primary colors.

Beep tones.   Short bursts of a reference tone that are synchronized with the numerical countdown placed before the beginning of the program or segment and used as an aid in cueing videotape playback sources.

Betacam.   A professional-quality 1/2-inch videotape format developed by the Sony Corporation.

Betamax.   A 1/2-inch videotape format developed by the Sony Corporation for use in home video systems.

Binocular.   As viewed with two eyes, giving slightly different perspectives, aiding depth perception.

Black.   The video signal that results in a blank screen. Black is commonly used at the beginning and ending of television programs. A fade in and out of black usually denotes the passage of time.

Booms.   Support structures to which microphones can be attached. Booms use extension arms to permit the placement of a microphone near the sound source while keeping all or most of the support structure and cables out of camera view.

Bulk eraser.   A powerful electromagnet used to neutralize the charges stored on the iron oxide particles of a magnetic tape in preparation for reuse. When this process is completed, the tape has been bulk erased.

Bumper.   A short video and/or audio transition used between program segments. These frequently contain short review or preview excerpts from the main program employed to maintain viewer interest. Commonly used in commercial television before and after commercial breaks.

Buses.   Groupings of input channels on a video switcher that share a common output.

Camcorder.   A video camera and video tape recorder that are combined into a single unit.

Camera body.   The main housing of a television camera containing or supporting the image sensor, viewfinder, optical system, and associated electronic systems.

Camera control unit (CCU).   A control panel used to adjust technical camera functions from a location away from the camera itself.

Camera crane.   A specialized camera mount that allows horizontal and vertical movement of the camera and its operator through a range of several feet. The camera and operator are positioned on a platform attached to the end of a sturdy boom.

Camera left or right.   Left or right as seen through the camera.

Camera mount.   A structure such as a tripod, studio pedestal, or camera crane used to support the television camera.

Camera perspective.   The point of view the camera takes in relationship to the scene that is being captured.

Capacitor.   A device capable of storing an electric charge.

Cardioid.   A type of unidirectional microphone pickup pattern characterized by its heart shape radiating out from the receiving element.

Cartridge.   A self-contained unit of magnetic tape that forms a continuous loop inside a housing designed to load directly into compatible audio record and playback equipment. Also, the unit containing the stylus that is attached to the tone arm of a turntable used to reproduce sounds from records.

Cartridge machine.   A recorder/playback unit compatible with the use of magnetic tape cartridges.

Cassette.   A self-contained unit of magnetic tape that includes feed and take-up reels as well as the tape itself in a housing designed to load directly into compatible audio or video record and playback equipment.

Character generator.   The unit that converts operator input into electronic signals that in turn create graphic symbols directly on the television screen.

Chip (or CCD) camera.   A television camera that uses a charge-coupled device image sensor.

Chip chart.   A specialized gray scale presented on a flat rectangular surface in television aspect ratio that is used to adjust the contrast range of a color video camera. The chart contains solid blocks of black, gray, and white with specific reflectance values that will produce a standardized stairstep waveform display when reproduced by a properly adjusted camera.

Close-up.   A commonly used camera shot; allows considerable detail to be visible and isolates visual elements within a scene.

Color background.   The video signal that results in the display of a full screen of solid color. Most are adjustable for color/tint, saturation/color intensity, and video gain/brightness.

Color bars.   A standard video test signal used to calibrate a variety of equipment and monitoring systems.

Color palette.   The range of colors available for use in a video generator.

Color temperature.   A unit of measurement used to describe the relative color characteristics or quality of a light source. Light with a low color temperature has a reddish cast; that with a higher color temperature is bluish. Color temperature is expressed in degrees Kelvin.

Compact disc.   A small plastic disc containing digital audio signals that can be retrieved by a playback unit that scans the disc with a laser beam. Compact discs provide extremely high quality storage and retrieval.

Composition.   The arrangement of the various picture elements within the television frame.

Condenser microphone.   A sound pickup device. Using a diaphragm attached to a capacitor with moveable plates, it converts sound waves into electrical signals. Condenser microphones produce excellent sound quality. An external power supply is required to induce the audio signal.

Confidence head.   A playback head mounted immediately behind the record head in some videotape machines. It allows the operator to see an immediate playback of material as it is being recorded.

Contrast ratio.   The ratio between the brightest and the darkest elements within a scene. Most television cameras can reproduce limited contrast ratios.

Controller.   A component of the videotape editing system through which functions are selected and the operation of the system is governed.

Control room.   The area of the television production facility from which the entire system can be controlled. Camera controls, video switchers, sync generators, and videotape machines are among equipment normally located in this area.

Control room directing.   A production method in which a director operates the television production system and supervises the production team from the studio control room.

Control track.   The reference signal recorded on videotapes as a means of regulating tape speed and synchronizing all other tape functions during playback and editing.

Countdown tape.   A videotape that contains a graphic sequence of numbers descending from 9 to 2. The countdown is often edited onto the front of videotape programs to facilitate cueing.

Crawl.   A continuous single-line display of graphic information that moves horizontally across the screen from right to left.

Credit roll.   A continuous display of graphic titles that scrolls up from the bottom of the television screen. Frequently used to acknowledge the contributions made by those involved in a production and presented near the beginning or end of the production.

Cross fade.   The audio transitional technique of slowly reducing the volume of one audio source while simultaneously increasing that of another so that they overlap as one smoothly replaces the other. Also, the cue used to request that action.

Cue card.   A large piece of paper or cardboard on which words to be spoken on-camera are written. Usually displayed near the camera lens to provide prompting.

Cue tones.   Signals recorded on an audio tape cartridge to automatically stop the machine at a position marked by the tone.

Cue up.   The process of positioning a retrieval source to a preselected position.

Cuts.   Instantaneous transitions from one image or sound to another. Also called takes.

Cuts-only editor.   A simple editing system with one source VTR and one record VTR; can perform take transitions only between individual shots, scenes, or sounds.

Decibels (dB).   A unit for measuring the relative loudness of sounds. The scale on most VU meters is calibrated in both decibels and percentage of modulation.

Decoded.   The process of reading and translating an electrical signal back into pictures and sounds.

Depth of field.   That portion of the field of view of a lens that is in focus. Lenses with a large depth of field show most elements in a scene to be in focus while lenses with a shallow depth of field focus those elements only within a very narrow range of distances from the lens.

Diachroic mirror array.   A type of beam splitter. An internal optical element in some color television cameras that separates the incoming light into its three primary colors.

Diaphragm.   The component of a microphone element that moves in response to the force exerted upon it by sound waves. Also, another term for the iris of a lens that regulates the amount of light passing through the lens.

Diffused light.   Light that comes from many different angles, for example, sunlight diffused by an overcast sky or artificial light diffused by a scrim. Diffused light results in soft-edged shadows and low contrast between lighted and unlighted areas of a scene.

Digital video effects (DVE).   A sophisticated video special effects method that permits manipulation of video images in a variety of dimensions. Many of these effects create a three-dimensional illusion on the television screen.

Dimmer system.   An array of rheostats that can be connected to various circuits in a lighting system to adjust voltage to individual lighting units. Light intensity can be controlled through use of a dimmer system, and lighting effects involving gradual changes, such as fading up lights, are possible using such a system.

Direct light.   Light from a source of illumination that produces roughly parallel beams of light — for example, the sun. Direct light creates sharp-edged shadows and high contrast between the lighted and unlighted areas of a scene.

Director.   The person responsible for supervising and executing the production process. The director decides which images and sound will be used and how they will be used in the construction of a television program.

Disk drive.   A mechanical transport system that allows the use of moveable magnetic storage disks in computers and generators.

Disk storage.   A means of storing digital information on flexible magnetic disks. Graphics generators, for example, use disk storage for operating systems and input commands that can later be used to recall specific configurations.

Dissolve.   A special video effect in which one image slowly disappears as another appears so that the two images overlap, with each being transparent during the period of overlap.

Distortion.   The result of overmodulating a signal. Audio signals that are distorted become indistinct, fuzzy, and difficult to decipher.

Distribution system.   That portion of the total television system through which the results of the television production process are delivered to an audience. Common methods of distribution include broadcasting, cablecasting, satellite transmission, and mass duplication and delivery of videotape.

Dolly.   A basic camera movement in which the camera mount is moved toward or away from the object in the scene. A dolly can be used to reposition the camera between shots in a multiple camera production, or it may be used as part of a shot to make the principle object in the scene gradually appear larger or smaller. As the camera moves during the dolly, the relative position of the various other elements in the scene changes. This can often result in a very dramatic effect. Also, the set of wheels sometimes attached to a tripod.

Downstream keyer (DSK).   A section of some video switchers with limited special effects capability. Typically, DSKs can fade the switcher's program output in and out of black and can key selected video sources over the switcher's program line.

Dynamic microphone.   A sound pickup device that uses a diaphragm connected to a coil of wire surrounded by a magnetic field to convert sound waves into electrical signals. Dynamic microphones produce good-quality sound and are quite durable.

Edit.   To decide which materials will be included and which will be excluded; a selection process. Also, the process of assembling selected images and sounds using a videotape editing system.

Edit-in/edit-out.   The selected point at which an edit will begin/end.

Edit master.   The newly created videotape that results from the editing process.

Editing systems.   Videotape systems used to selectively and precisely duplicate images and sounds from one videotape to another, thereby creating a new combination of images and sounds.

Eject. The process used by many video and audio cassette machines to release the tape container and allow its removal.

Electromagnetic spectrum. A range of electrical and magnetic waves that radiate from a variety of sources like the sun, radioactive ores, or electric lights.

Electronic edits. Selected transfers of images and sounds from one videotape to another. This process permits the arrangement of those images and sounds into a new sequence.

Electronic field production (EFP). The method of using portable television cameras and recorders to gather images and sounds on location.

Electronic news gathering (ENG). The application of the electronic field production method specifically to the process of gathering images and sounds for news programs.

Element. The component of a microphone that converts sound waves into electrical signals.

Elipsoidal spotlight. A spotlight that uses two facing planoconvex lenses to focus the light output and create precise directional lighting.

Encoding. The process of converting light and sound into an electronic signal that can be processed and manipulated by the television production system.

Engineer. A technician responsible for the installation, maintenance, and technical operation of television equipment.

Equalizer. An audio processing unit that can boost or suppress selected frequencies to alter the sound quality. Equalizers are often used to "sweeten" sound.

Erase head. A component in a magnetic recorder that neutralizes the charge stored on the tape in preparation for reuse.

Exposure. Introducing light onto the light-sensitive surface of a television camera.

Extreme close-up. One of four basic shots used in television production. Isolates and places emphasis on detailed elements within a larger scene.

F-stop. A series of numerical designations assigned to the various aperture settings of a lens. Low f-stop numbers correspond to large aperture openings; high f-stop numbers to small ones.

Fader bar. The control lever on a video switcher used to execute various special effects including fades, dissolves, and wipes.

Fade out. To gradually reduce the level of an audio source to zero. Also, the cue used to request that action.

Fade under. To gradually reduce the level of an audio source to a volume that places it in the background relative to some other more dominant sound. Also, the cue used to request that action.

Fade up. To gradually increase the level of an audio source from zero to a predetermined setting. Also, the cue used to request that action.

Fast forward. An operating mode used to advance video- and audiotapes rapidly.

Field of view. The area from which a given lens gathers light. Wide-angle lenses have a large field of view; telephoto lenses have a more narrow field of view.

Field production. The process of doing television production in nonstudio locations.

File tapes. Archival images and sounds from a previous production, sometimes reused to illustrate background information contained in a television news story.

Fill light. One of the three lights used in a basic three-point or triangle lighting arrangement. The function of the fill light is to reduce contrast ratio by filling in the shadow areas of a scene without totally eliminating the shadow.

Film. An optical/chemical storage and retrieval system. In the television production situation, usually refers to 16 millimeter motion picture film.

Film multiplexer. A special optical system that provides a method of projecting one or more film and/or slide projectors into a video camera so that the optical image from the projector can be easily converted to a video signal.

Filter. An external or internal optical element used in some television cameras to control the quantity and the quality of the light passing through the lens to the image sensor.

Fish pole. A hand-held microphone extension boom used frequently in field production work.

Fish eye. A camera lens with a very short focal length and an extremely wide angle of view. The convex surface of the front element in the fish eye lens takes in light from such a broad field of view that it distorts the image by making objects near the edge appear to be larger than those in the center. This can enhance the illusion of depth in the resulting image.

Flat artwork. Drawings, paintings, graphic designs, and similar works created on paper, art board, or other flat surfaces. A camera is required to integrate flat artwork into the television system.

Floor director. A production assistant who functions as the eyes, ears, and body of the director in the studio. The floor director gives cues and directions to the studio talent and crew and serves as a communications link back to the director in the control room.

Floor monitor. A television monitor placed in the studio to allow the studio crew and talent to see various special effects and preview and program outputs from the video switcher.

Floor plan. A diagram showing the overhead view of a setting, the position of set pieces, and locations of production equipment.

Fluid head. A special type of pan/tilt head that uses a heavy fluid surrounding the internal moving parts to dampen and smooth out the movements of the camera.

Focal length. The characteristic of a lens that determines its field of view. Short focal lengths correspond to a wide angle of view; long focal lengths to a narrow angle of view.

Focus ring. An external control that allows an operator to adjust the relative position of lens elements to shift the focal plane nearer or farther from the front element of the lens.

Foldback monitoring. A system used to allow performers to hear the various other audio sources and/or program audio mix during a production.

Font styles. Design characteristics of graphic symbols and type. Most character generators offer a variety of styles with and without serifs, in standard or bold face, block or script lettering, and so on.

Footcandle. A unit for measuring the intensity of a light source. One footcandle equals the quantity of light emitted by a standard candle at a distance of one foot.

Frame. The basic video unit in the television system. One complete scan of the image sensor, which lasts 1/30 second. Also, the area within which visual elements are arranged as seen through the television camera.

Framing. Moving and adjusting the camera in order to arrange the visual elements as seen through the camera.

Frequency response. The capacity of an audio component to preserve and/or reproduce the full range of frequencies present in the original sound.

Fresnel spotlight. A multipurpose spotlight that allows adjustment of the distance between the lamp/reflector unit and the lens so as to adjust the quantity and quality of the light emitted.

Gain control. A device or control that regulates the amplification of a video or audio signal.

Gels. Transparent sheets of synthetic material tinted in a variety of colors. Gels can be placed in the beam of light produced by a lighting instrument to create colored light.

Generators. Specialized television production tools designed to produce a signal directly from the inputs of the user.

Gen lock. A method of referencing more than one piece of television equipment to a synchronizing generator so that their frame rates and scanning sequence will be synchronized.

Get on the headsets. A common request for a production team member to put on the intercom headset and get ready to receive further cues and instructions.

Graphics generator. *See* Character generator.

Graphics pad. A flat drawing surface on which artists can create free-hand graphics directly into the television system. The contact of the drawing instrument with the pad results in a video signal and an image on a television monitor.

Grid system. An array of battens suspended from the ceiling of a studio to provide a convenient means of positioning various lighting instruments. Most grid systems include electrical connection for the lights. Sometimes entire grids or individual battens can be adjusted to varying heights above the studio floor.

Group dynamics. The forces caused by human interaction that affect the productivity of a group.

Hand held. Equipment that is actually supported by its operator. Cameras and microphones are often used in this fashion for flexibility and convenience.

Hand microphone. A sound pickup device designed to be held by the user while gathering sound.

Head. *See* Confidence head, Erase head, Playback head, Record head.

Headphones. Individual earphones mounted on a headband so that the wearer can hear the sounds reproduced without distraction or interference from extraneous noises. The earphones are normally mounted inside small muffs padded to fit comfortably over the user's ears. Audio operators often use headphones during production.

Headsets. Individual microphone and earphone components attached to a headband or other appliance worn on the user's head. Headsets are connected to an intercommunications system permitting production team members separated by a considerable distance to talk with each other.

Headwheel. The rotating assembly upon which the video record and playback heads of some videotape machines are mounted.

Helical scan. A generic term applied to a group of videotape machines whose video heads create a diagonal track across the videotape as it moves through the machine. Also called slant track.

Hypercardioid.   A precise directional microphone with a narrow cardioid pickup pattern.

High-definition television (HDTV).   An upgraded television system that uses more individual lines in each frame to provide better resolution and more sharply detailed images.

Input.   All television production tools used to mix and switch or to store images and sounds; also, the capacity to receive audio and video signals from other equipment. Those signals will be received by the input of the mixer, switcher, or recorder, and then processed and stored or routed on through the system as part of a new audio or video signal.

Input gain.   The relative strength of the video or audio signal being delivered to the receiving section of a record machine. The input gain generally can be adjusted to fit within the equipment's requirement so that the proper signal strength will be stored.

Insert edit.   In videotape editing, the process of selectively placing new pictures or sounds into the middle of a sequence while preserving the materials before and after the point where the new materials have been inserted.

Instant replay.   A production technique that uses videotape recording followed by immediate playback to give viewers another look at images just seen. Often these replays are done in slow motion.

Intercom system.   A two-way communications system used to allow production team members to talk with each other while isolating the resulting sound from the actual program sound.

Interruptible foldback monitor (IFB).   A system of delivering back to performers, usually via headphones, program audio sources and mixes that can be interrupted with intercom messages for cueing purposes.

Interruptible program line (IPL).   *See* Interruptible foldback monitor.

Iris.   The internal lens mechanism that opens and closes to regulate the amount of light passing through the lens. Also known as a diaphragm.

Iron oxide particles.   The part of a magnetic tape upon which video and audio signals are stored. The individual particles are charged positively or negatively during recording into a pattern that can later be used to re-create the original signal when the tape is played back.

Kelvin scale.   A range of color temperatures used to describe the relative color value of light sources.

Key.   A video special effect that combines two images, with one appearing to overlay the other. Both images are solid and the keyed image replaces the background images through a process of brightness or color discrimination. Most commonly used with graphic titles that are keyed over the images they describe.

Key light.   One of the three lights used in the basic three-point lighting method. The key light functions as the primary light source and provides the majority of the frontal illumination on the subject.

Kinescope.   A storage process used in the early days of television to capture the electronic images and sounds from the television screen onto 16-millimeter motion picture film.

Leader.   The portion of a videotape that contains test signals, slates, countdowns, and any other images and sounds intended to be used by playback personnel to prepare the actual program content for showing to an audience. Precedes the beginning of the actual program material. Also, blank 16-millimeter film, video-, and audiotape used to thread the open-reel supply into the appropriate recording or playback equipment.

Lens tissue. A special material (often made of rice paper) available in small sheets used in cleaning the exposed glass surfaces of a lens. When used properly, lens tissue will not scratch the glass surface.

Level. The strength of an audio or video signal. Adjusting gain is synonymous with adjusting level.

Light meter. A device used to measure the intensity of a light source. Usually calibrated in footcandles.

Limbo lighting. A technique of lighting a scene in such a way that the background seems to disappear. This can be achieved with a totally black background or with a uniformly illuminated background with no corners or shadows.

Lip sync. Synchronization of a performer's lips with the appropriate voice sounds. Lip sync can be lost in the videotape editing process where sound and picture can be shifted independently. Also, a technique through which performers move their mouth to synchronize with prerecorded sounds to give the impression that they are actually creating the sounds. Singers often lip sync to music that has been previously recorded in a sound studio.

Live. Television productions assembled and distributed simultaneously so that the audience sees the results of the production process as it is being executed.

Live on tape. The production method of videotaping a program in a continuous fashion with no editing. When this approach is used, videotape serves as a means of storing and retrieving the production but the program is unchanged from the way it appeared when originally performed.

Load. The process of placing tapes, disks, films, records, and CDs into the appropriate equipment so that they will be accessible and useable during a television production.

Locked down. Securing a camera by tightening the pan and tilt brakes on the camera head so it will not move.

Logging tapes. The process of viewing videotapes to make notes about the content and location of material on the tape. Images and sounds can thus be considered for use in a future production.

Look space. The picture composition technique used when the person in the shot is looking toward the edge of the frame. Rather than placing the person in the horizontal center of the frame, a slightly off-center position is used, opposite the direction the subject is facing. This creates a slightly larger space in front of the person and provides a comfortable space to look into.

Lower third titles. Graphic identifications added in the bottom portion of the television frame. Commonly used in news broadcasts, for example, to give the name and title or affiliation of the newsmaker being seen and heard.

Magnetic recording and playback. A method of storing and retrieving electronic video and/or audio signals through creation and review of a pattern of positive and negative charges on flexible magnetic tape.

Master control. The area from which a television distribution system is operated. The place where the selection is made of the video and audio sources to be routed to the transmission facility (satellite uplink, television transmitter, cable channel).

Medium shot.   One of the basic shots used in television production to bring the viewer closer to a scene. It develops context and builds interest by revealing detail not visible in a wide shot.

Menu.   A list of possible actions available to the operator of a computer or generator.

Microphone adaptors.   Specialized cables and/or connectors that permit the interconnection of audio equipment using different styles of connectors. Microphone adaptors promote system integration.

MII.   A broadcast-quality 1/2-inch videotape format developed by the Panasonic Corporation.

Mike line.   The cable that connects the microphone to the other components of the audio system.

Minilights.   Portable miniature spotlights and floodlights, or combination spot and flood units that are smaller, lighter, and require less power than their studio counterparts.

Mix/effect (M/E) buses.   Sections of a video switcher that perform special effects such as fades, dissolves, wipes, and keys. Sophisticated video switchers may have several M/E buses, giving them the capability to do multiple special effects in combination or rapid succession.

Mixer.   *See* Audio console or mixer.

Mixing.   The process of selecting, combining, and blending two or more audio signals into a single signal.

Mobile satellite uplink.   A portable electronic system used to transmit signals directly to an orbiting satellite for distribution to other locations.

Monitoring system.   Electronic components used to allow production personnel and television technicians to see the television pictures and sounds, or a representation of the electronic video and audio signals that produce them.

Monophonic.   An audio system consisting of a single channel of sound.

Multicamera.   A television production technique that uses two or more cameras to capture images from a given scene. These separate cameras can each be recorded for later editing or they can be edited instantaneously through the use of a video switcher.

Musical variety show.   A common television entertainment program format. Usually consists of a variety of singing, instrumental, dance, and other performance acts. These programs often have a host to provide continuity between acts and to introduce performers. Comedy acts and short skits may also be included.

Music bed.   Music mixed at low volume with other sounds (usually voices) that are louder. The effect is of music in the background or under the primary sounds contributing to the sound environment being created.

Music videos.   Short miniproductions built around a musical selection. Can involve images and sounds including music, dance, and dramatic vignettes. Pioneered by the cable service Music Television (MTV) in the United States during the 1980s.

Muting.   A method of wiring audio systems so that speakers are turned off automatically whenever a microphone in close proximity is turned on. Muting prevents the audio feedback that results when a microphone's output is reproduced by the speaker and returns to the mike's receiving element.

Natural sound.   The sounds that normally accompany the images being seen and that would be audible if the viewer were actually in the location from which the camera is gathering pictures.

Neutral density filter. A filter used in a camera optical system to reduce the amount of light reaching the image sensor. Used when extremely bright light exceeds the capacity of the lens iris.

Newscast. A common television format used to present a large variety of short stories (from a few seconds to a couple of minutes in length) about news events.

Newsmagazine show. A common television informational program format used to present several unrelated stories about newsworthy topics. These reports typically involve more detail and time (from three to ten minutes or more) than the shorter stories common on a television newscast.

Nielsen ratings. Quantitative measurements of the television audience for a television program. The A.C. Nielsen Company is one of the leading audience research organizations.

Noise. A grainy or snowy picture quality resulting from an increase in the image sensor's electronic sensitivity.

Objective perspective. A common point of view for the television camera, which makes the camera an observer of the actions and events unfolding before it.

Off-line editing. A procedure that utilizes simple viewing and editing equipment and working copies of tapes to make preliminary edit decisions before moving to the final editing process.

Omnidirectional microphone. A sound pickup device with a receiving element that is equally sensitive in all directions.

On-line editing. A procedure that utilizes the complete editing system and the original raw tapes to assemble the final version of a television program after preliminary decisions have been made using the off-line editing system.

Open/close mikes. The cue given to turn on or off microphones that have been preset to the desired level so that the transition is instantaneous.

Open reel. A magnetic recording system that does not use cassettes or cartridges. The magnetic tape is supplied from a reel or spool that must be loaded onto the machine so that the tape can be threaded through the transport to a take-up reel. At the conclusion of the recording or playback, the tape must be rewound back onto the supply reel. Open-reel systems are available for both audio and video recording and playback. Also, sometimes used to refer to the unit of tape itself as well as the equipment used in the system.

Optical elements. The various glass components used to obtain the desired field of view and focusing characteristics of a lens.

Optical system. One of the three basic parts of the video camera. The optical system gathers light from the scene in front of the camera and focuses it on the camera's image sensor.

Oscillator. An electronic generator that produces signals of a specified frequency, amplitude, and other measures. Audio tone oscillators, for example, are commonly used to generate reference tones.

Oscilloscope. A specialized waveform monitor that graphically displays a variety of electronic signals.

Output. The signal that results from the operation of a piece of television equipment or system.

Overmodulation. Amplifying a video or audio signal beyond the prescribed intensity so that the resulting image or sound is distorted.

Pages. Individual screens of graphic information created and stored by an electronic character generator.

Paint box. An electronic character generator that converts visual inputs to digital signals that can then be manipulated to modify the appearance of the original images. A paint box also creates graphic images from the free-hand inputs of an operator on a graphics tablet.

Panning. Horizontal movement of the camera as it pivots around the center of the camera head.

Pan/tilt head. A component of the camera mount that permits smooth movement of the camera in both a horizontal and a vertical plane. The pan/tilt head is located between the camera body and other parts — the tripod, studio pedestal, camera crane.

Pedestal. A vertical movement of the camera mount that changes the height of the camera in relation to the elements of a scene.

Percentage of modulation. A relative measure of audio signal strength. Most VU meters are calibrated in both percentage of modulation and decibels. When the signal reaches 100 percent modulation it is at the maximum allowable volume beyond which distortion will occur.

Perform. Initiates recording of an editing sequence programmed into an electronic controller system. This creates a duplicate of a prescribed section of videotape onto an edit master tape.

Persistence of vision. A characteristic of human vision that causes visual impressions to be retained briefly by the retina of the eye after the image is removed. When one image is quickly replaced by another, similar one, the brain connects the two and perceives the slight change of position of picture elements as continuous motion.

Pickup pattern. The area around the receiving element of a microphone in which it is most sensitive. Sounds received from within the pickup pattern will have presence or an "on mike" quality.

Pixels. Individual light-sensitive segments or cells of a charge-coupled device image sensor. Variations of electrical charge produced by the pixels in response to varying light intensity creates the mosaic pattern which forms the television image.

Playback head. The specialized magnetic head on audio- and videotape machines that reads the patterns stored on the magnetic tape and converts them to the corresponding electrical signals.

Postproduction/editing. The production technique that uses videotape editing as a means of selecting and assembling individual shots, sounds, or scenes into a new sequence stored on an edited master tape.

Potentiometer, or pot. A variable amplifier used to adjust audio signal strength, and consequently volume, in an audio console or mixer.

Preamplifier. An amplifier that boosts signal strength to a level that will permit its distribution through a larger video or audio system. Preamplifiers assure that the signal will be at a useable level when it reaches the main amplifying unit.

Preroll. The process of putting an audio- or videotape source in motion a few seconds prior to its starting point to allow the equipment time to stabilize and process the input or output signal.

Presence.   The sound quality of being "on mike," of being close or realistic. Sounds received by a microphone from within its pickup pattern have greater presence than those gathered from beyond it.

Preview.   To look at a video image prior to selecting that image for showing to the audience. Control room directors preview each shot, special effect, and graphic before selecting its source on the video switcher. Also, the control input that allows the operator of the videotape editing system to see how a programmed editing sequence will look prior to actually executing the edits.

Preview monitor.   A video screen used to display an image before it is selected on the final program output. Preview monitors are usually connected to a separate preview bus in the video switcher that makes possible selecting all video sources for previewing.

Prism.   A type of beam splitter. Part of the internal optical system of a color television camera that separates the incoming light into its primary components.

Producer.   The person who determines how the television production system will be used. The producer takes an idea or an assignment and develops it into a program that will communicate a message to an audience.

Production.   The process of gathering, creating, and assembling sights and sounds using television equipment.

Production assistants.   Members of the production team who are not assigned to operate any specific equipment but rather are assigned to a variety of tasks as requested by the producer, director, or other production team member.

Production machine.   The conglomerate array of tools, techniques, and personnel that creates a television product.

Production manager.   The person who supervises the production staff and coordinates the use of television production facilities.

Production values.   Results obtained with the production machine that enhance the presentation of materials on television by capitalizing on the capabilities of the equipment and the special techniques available during the production process.

Program format.   The organizational structure of a television production. The approach taken to a topic or the way in which it is put together. Common formats include musical variety shows, newsmagazine shows, news documentary, and drama.

Program monitor.   The video screen that shows the image currently selected on the program output of the video switcher.

Program output.   The video or audio signal resulting from the switching or mixing process.

Properties, or props.   Functional items required as part of a scene being staged. Usually portable and not attached to the set in which the scene is being staged. Examples are telephones, books, tableware, plants, firearms, and other items the performers need in order to accomplish the action required by the scene.

Proscenium arch.   The traditional plane through which an audience views a stage performance. The proscenium arch and the curtain separate the audience from the action on the stage.

Punch up.   The act of selecting a source on the video switcher by depressing the appropriate button.

Quadruplex.   The original videotape format that uses four separate video heads rotating in a vertical plane to record and play back images on two-inch-wide tape. The standard for broadcast television throughout the 1960s and 1970s.

Raw tape.   Unedited images and/or sounds stored on the original audio- or video-tapes used to gather them.

Receptive perspective.   A common camera point of view in which the camera receives material. Performers talk directly to the camera as if it were the audience. Television newscasts are a good example of receptive perspective; the news anchor talks directly to the viewer through the camera.

Rechargeable battery pack.   A removeable power supply that can be replenished after the electrical energy previously stored has been depleted.

Record head.   The part of a video or audio tape recorder that magnetizes the particles on the magnetic tape to create a pattern that stores the electrical signal received at its input.

Record tab.   A removeable button or flange on an audio or video cassette that must be in place before the compatible record equipment can make a recording upon the tape. Removal of the record tab prevents inadvertent recording over signals already on the tape.

Recue.   To cue again. To reposition a storage or retrieval system to a previously designated location.

Reel-to-reel.   Tape that is transferred from a "feed reel" to a "take-up reel" as it is used by recording or playback equipment. Often called open-reel tape. Machines that use this type of tape are sometimes called reel-to-reel machines. (*See* Audio tape recorder.)

Reference tones.   Electronically generated signals that produce a continuous sound or tone at selected frequencies within the audible range of human hearing, which is roughly 15 cycles per second to about 18,000 cycles per second.

Reflectance.   The capacity of a material to reflect incident light. A surface with low reflectance absorbs much of the light falling upon it; one with high reflectance absorbs very little light.

Reflected light.   That portion of the incident light falling upon a surface or object that is not absorbed. For example, when light strikes a highly reflective surface such as a mirror, most of the light is reflected back toward the viewer or the camera. On the other hand, when light strikes a dark-colored, textured surface such as a wool blanket, very little light is reflected.

Reflectors.   Shiny, nonabsorbing surfaces used to redirect incident light. Most studio lighting instruments have a reflector as one of their components. Large, flat moveable reflectors, sometimes called shiny boards, are often used in field production to redirect naturally occurring light.

Remote production.   Field production done with a complex system similar to that found in a television studio. Work done at a location removed from the studio or primary production facility that requires the use of a full-capability system.

Resident memory.   Capacity of some equipment to store digital information internally rather than on portable magnetic disks or tapes.

Return video.   The video playback signal from a portable recorder as seen through the viewfinder of the portable video camera. Most portable units have a switchable viewfinder to allow the operator to see return video so that recordings can be checked in the field. Also, in studio cameras, output that can be selected from the video switcher to permit camera operators to see special effects, tape playback, and other video elements.

Rewind.   To back up a cassette or reel of tape or film to its starting point or beginning.

Ribbon.   The moveable component in the receiving element of many high-quality microphones that vibrates in response to the impact of sound waves upon it.

Ribbon microphone.   A sound pickup device that uses a thin metal ribbon suspended in a magnetic field to convert sound waves into electrical signals. Ribbon microphones are extremely sensitive, produce excellent sound quality, and are quite fragile.

Riding gain.   The process of monitoring and adjusting signal intensity during a production.

Roll.   A continuous display of graphic information in which the symbols scroll up from the bottom of the screen in a continuous motion. Also, the verbal cue given to start an audio- or videotape. For example, "Roll VTR A."

Rolling the tape.   The act of starting a storage or retrieval source that uses a moveable magnetic tape.

Rundown sheet.   A listing of production elements (times, cues, sources) used as a guide in organizing and executing a television production.

Safety chains.   Cables or chains looped around the lighting grid and the individual lighting instruments as an independent means of preventing the instrument from falling, should its primary support fail.

Satellite.   A man-made space vehicle that orbits the earth for the purpose of relaying television signals from one portion of the planet to another.

Scanner.   The component of some video tape recorders and players to which the video heads are attached.

Scoops.   Commonly used floodlights that feature a lamp and reflector to create a broad beam of diffused light.

Scrims.   Materials placed in front of a lighting source to diffuse the light emitted.

Search.   *See* Shuttle.

Set dressing.   Adding props and other items (plants, paintings, lamps, furniture) to a set to enhance its appearance.

Set lights.   Individual lights used to illuminate selected portions of the setting. Can be used to create mood, call attention to set pieces or props, add to the illusion of depth, and control contrast ratios.

Shiny board.   *See* Reflectors.

Shotgun microphone.   A unidirectional sound pickup device with a hypercardioid pickup pattern. Shotgun microphones are used to isolate sound sources in a noisy environment and to capture sounds occurring a considerable distance from the receiving element.

Shots.   Individual views or vistas of a given scene. A shot is the basic unit of video grammar in the same way that the word is the basic unit of verbal language.

Shuttle.   A videotape operating mode that moves the tape through a broad range of nonstandard speeds forward and backward while permitting the operator to see and hear the images and sounds. The shuttle mode facilitates cueing.

Single camera.   Using only one camera. Much television production is done using one camera to shoot a scene from several different angles. These different images are stored on videotape and can later be edited together to create the impression that several different cameras were observing the scene simultaneously.

Slant track. *See* Helical scan.

Slates. Images and/or sounds recorded at the beginning of tapes to identify what the tape contains. Useful in cueing and locating materials on unfamiliar tapes.

Slides. Individual still images stored on 35-millimeter film.

Slow-motion playback. Playing a videotape at slower than normal speed so that the action depicted moves at less than normal speed.

Sound bites. Portions of video and/or audio actualities selected for inclusion in a television production.

Sound perspective. The spatial relationship of sound sources. For example, the sound volume of an approaching railroad train increases as it gets closer to the listener.

Sound sweetening. The process of enhancing sound quality by boosting or diminishing certain frequencies during recording or reproduction.

Sound tape. The cue given to an audio operator when the audio from a videotape playback is to be brought up on the audio console.

Sound waves. The vibration of molecules in the air in response to the physical movement of some object at a frequency within the audible range.

Source monitors. Video screens in the television production control room or editing room that continuously display the image from individual video sources.

Special effects. A wide variety of methods and techniques used to mix, blend, and reshape images and sounds.

Special effects systems. A broad range of television production equipment that can be used to mix, blend, and reshape images and sounds electronically.

Spin. *See* Roll.

Splicing. The process of physically cutting, separating, and reattaching pieces of audio- or videotape as a means of editing the materials they contain.

Split screen. A video special effect in which more than one video source is displayed simultaneously in the same frame with only a portion of each being visible. For example, a vertical split screen would show the left half of one image and the right half of another with a vertical edge marking the division between them.

Squawk box. A loudspeaker public address system often found in television studios and control rooms.

Staging. The process of building or assembling a set and moving performers and cameras within that environment to create the visual impression desired.

Standby. A commonly used cue meaning "get ready." The standby cue is usually accompanied by specific instructions. For example, "Stand by to open microphones."

Station break. The time interval between the end of one television program on a television station or network and the beginning of the next, during which commercials are shown and station identifications are made.

Steady-cam body mount. A specialized camera support worn by the camera operator. This mount features rotating gyros to stabilize the movement of the camera itself and to isolate it from the movements of the operator. Makes very smooth camera movements possible while retaining extreme portability.

Stereo. An audio system that uses independent left and right channels to simulate a binaural sound perspective.

Still frame. Repeated display of a single frame of video from a retrieval source to give the appearance of no motion. Often done by stopping the movement of a videotape so that the playback heads continue to scan the same tracks over and over.

Storyboard. A sequence of simple drawings that show the primary images to be included in a production. Storyboards typically also contain a description of the audio that will accompany the images.

Strike the set. The process of disassembling the materials used in a television set, removing them from the production location, and storing them.

String the mikes. The process of positioning microphones and cables and connecting them to the rest of the audio system. This process usually includes a preliminary test to make sure that the equipment works.

Striped filter. A type of beam splitter used in some color television cameras to separate the incoming light into its primary components. Commonly found in cameras having a single image sensor.

Studio crane. *See* Camera crane.

Studio production. A television program assembly procedure that is done in a room or rooms specially designed for that process. Studio production offers considerable control over all elements of the production process.

Subjective perspective. A common camera point of view in which the camera becomes a participant in the activity taking place. The viewer sees the action through the eyes of someone who is involved in the scene; others talk and react to the camera as if it were another person in the scene.

Super. A video special effect in which two or more images are superimposed or overlapped so that each is visible but transparent.

Switcher. The title sometimes given to the operator of the video switcher. *See* Video switcher.

Sync generator. The electronic unit that produces a synchronizing signal that can be supplied to other video equipment. The system allows scanning and frame rates to coincide. Essential if various video sources are to be switched through a video switcher.

Take. Instantaneous transition from one image or sound to another. The same as a cut. Also, one version of a portion of a television production. It is common, for example, for a reporter to do several takes of an on-camera introduction to a news story during field production so that the best one can be chosen later by the editor. Having several takes of a production element provides editing options.

Take-up reel. The place where tape and film is gathered after passing through the recording or playback equipment in a reel-to-reel system.

Take VTR. The cue given to the switcher and/or the audio operator when the output from a VTR is to be selected on the video switcher and/or the audio console. A single cue is often given when video and sound are to be selected simultaneously. When sound only is required, some directors say "sound tape."

Talent. Term used to refer to actors and performers in a television production.

Talk show. A common television program format featuring a host and one or more guests who talk about a variety of topics. These programs can be informational or entertainment oriented.

Talking-head show. A television program, with little or no production value, that consists of the pictures and sounds of people talking. Unless the topic or the people are especially interesting, talking-head shows can be very boring.

Tape counter. A simple meter that measures the footage of tape as it moves through the machine. A crude cueing device that is activated by a simple roller in contact with the moving tape.

Tape path. The routing of the magnetic tape over, around, and through the various components of equipment designed to use that style of tape.

Tape release. Another term to describe the eject function of a cassette-type audio or video machine.

Tape transport. The mechanical components of an audio- or videotape player or recorder that handle and move the tape through the machine and in some cases load and eject it.

Target. The light-sensitive surface of a camera pickup tube that is scanned by an electron beam converting varying light intensities into variations in voltage.

Technical director. The production person who operates the video switcher. Sometimes called the switcher.

Telephoto. A camera lens with a long focal length and a narrow field of view. Telephoto lenses project the light from a limited field of view onto the surface of the camera's image sensor, which results in a magnified image of that portion of the scene.

Teleprompter. A prompting device that displays scripts, cue words, outlines, and other material adjacent to or directly over the lens (made possible through the use of a one-way mirror) of a television camera. Most are moveable so that a number of pages can be displayed consecutively. The teleprompter makes it possible for an on-camera performer to read from visual aids while appearing to look directly at the camera.

Telestrator. A video special-effects system that utilizes a graphics tablet to permit free-hand drawing over images from another video source. Frequently used in sports telecasts by analysts to highlight and illustrate certain aspects of sports action during a videotape replay.

Television director. The person in charge of the execution stage of production. The director uses the resources of the television production system to create the television presentation as spelled out in the production plan.

Television monitor. The screen used to display a video signal. The monitor does not have a channel selector to tune in normal broadcast stations. It must be connected by cable to a video output.

Test signal generator. A generic term describing a number of different pieces of equipment that generate various audio and video test signals.

Test signals. Electronically generated video and audio signals that provide a standardized reference for checking equipment performance and making adjustments.

Time base corrector (TBC). A video processor that stabilizes videotape playback by adjusting for tape speed variation. Most TBCs include amplifiers to adjust signal strength and make minor color adjustments.

Time code. A special signal recorded on tapes that assigns a different numerical address to each frame of video. Time code allows very precise editing through its capability to locate a specific frame.

Toggle switch. A spring-loaded two-position electrical switch.

Track. The path of a magnetic recording or playback head over the surface of the magnetic tape. That section of the tape used by a specific head to store or retrieve electronic video and audio signals.

Track dollies. A camera mount that is moved along sturdy tracks to provide extremely smooth camera movement. Because of the time and effort required to position the tracks for each shot, these units are not used extensively in any but the most elaborate television production situations.

Tracking control. The operating control used to align a videotape playback machine to the control track placed on the tape when it was recorded so that playback functions will be properly synchronized.

Transducer. A device used to convert one form of energy into another. The receiving element of a microphone is a transducer that converts physical sound waves into electrical signals.

Tripod. A three-legged camera support used to provide a portable and yet stable base for the camera. Some tripods have detachable wheels or dollies that increase their mobility.

Truck. A basic camera movement in which the camera mount is moved laterally in relation to the elements in the scene.

Turntable. The piece of equipment used to retrieve audio signals stored on records.

Twist lock. Electrical connectors designed to resist separation once they have been mated and twisted into a locking position.

U-matic. A 3/4-inch videotape format commonly used in professional video production.

Umbrella. A reflector accessory for some lighting instruments that can be detached and folded like an umbrella for storage. When attached to the instrument, it serves to diffuse and soften the illumination provided by the unit.

Under. The audio mixing technique of playing some audio sources at lower volumes than others so they provide a background for the louder sounds. *See* Music bed.

Unidirectional microphone. A sound pickup device with a receiving element that is most sensitive in one direction.

Vectorscope. A waveform monitor used to display specific parameters of the color components in the video signal.

VHS. A consumer-grade 1/2-inch videotape format (video home systems).

Video. The electrical signal that represents the visual portion of the television signal.

Video boost. The process of increasing the voltage supplied to the image sensor in order to increase its sensitivity. Boosting video permits gathering images in lower lighting conditions, but also introduces additional "noise" into the resulting video.

Video control position. The place from which a production team member can adjust the technical parameters of the video equipment in use.

Video output. The electrical signal that results from the processing of visual images and video signals by various pieces of television video equipment.

Video switcher. The television production tool that selects, mixes, and blends the various video sources in the production system.

Videotape cartridge player. A specialized machine used by broadcast stations to play individual cartridges of two-inch-wide videotape. The machine is capable of playing several different short cartridges in rapid succession and was used extensively during the 1970s to play commercials and other tapes of short duration.

Videotaped.   The result of storing images and sounds on moveable magnetic tape.

Videotape formats.   Distinctive methods and designs that result in noncompatible videotaping procedures and equipment. Tapes recorded on one format will not play back, or even load onto, machines of a different format. Formats are usually delineated by the width and packaging of the videotape stock that they require.

Video tape recorder (VTR).   A generic label that can be applied to a broad range of equipment capable of storing both video and audio signals on magnetic videotape.

Volume unit (VU) meter.   The most common signal monitoring equipment found in television audio systems.

Walk-through.   A preliminary rehearsal technique in which performers move through their intended actions slowly so that production team members can become familiar with the way a scene will be staged.

Waveform monitors.   Signal monitoring equipment that produces a graphic display of an electronic signal.

White balance.   The process of adjusting the camera's color circuits to properly reproduce color in the existing lighting conditions. Changes in color temperature make this process necessary.

Wide angle.   A camera lens with a short focal length and a wide angle of view. Wide-angle lenses gather light from a large portion of the scene in front of the camera.

Wide shot.   One of the basic camera shots; provides a broad perspective of a scene. Often used as an established shot to give the viewer an overall impression before showing portions of the scene in more detail.

Wind screen.   A porous sleeve or cover that is attached to a microphone to reduce the flow of air against the receiving element, which could result in undesirable sounds.

Wipe.   A video special effect during which one image is gradually replaced by another. Both images are solid and the transition area between them is usually defined by a border in some geometric shape.

Wireless headsets.   Individual components of an intercom system that require no cable interconnection between users.

Wireless microphone.   A special transmitter/receiver system that can be used between a microphone and the rest of the audio system, thereby eliminating the need for microphone cables.

Work tapes.   Videotape copies of the images and sounds stored on original recordings used during logging, viewing, and off-line editing. Using work tapes protects the original tapes from damage and wear.

Zooming.   The process of moving the controls to alter the focal length of a variable focal length lens.

Zoom lens.   A variable focal length lens. Internal optical elements can be moved with an external control to alter the focal length of the lens.

BIBLIOGRAPHY

Alten, Stanley R. *Audio in Media*. Belmont, Calif.: Wadsworth, 1986.

Breyer, Richard, and Moller, Peter. *Making Television Programs*. White Plains, N.Y.: Longman, 1984.

Browne, Stephen E. *Videotape Editing: A Postproduction Primer*. Boston and London: Focal Press, 1989.

Burrows, Thomas D.; Woods, Donald N.; and Gross, Lynne Schafer. *Television Production: Disciplines and Techniques*. Dubuque, Iowa: W. C. Brown Co., 1989.

Mathias, Harry, and Patterson, Richard. *Electronic Cinematography*. Belmont, Calif.: Wadsworth, 1985.

Millerson, Gerald. *The Technique of Lighting for Television and Motion Pictures*. New York: Hastings House, 1972.

Shook, Frederick. *Television Field Production and Reporting*. White Plains, N.Y.: Longman, 1989.

Verna, Tony. *Live TV: An Inside Look at Directing and Producing*. Boston and London: Focal Press, 1987.

Zettl, Herbert. *Television Production Handbook*. Belmont, Calif.: Wadsworth, 1984.

Index

A/B rolling, 195
Abstract settings, 102
Accident prevention, 91–92
Actualities, 124
Additive color system, 23
Anchorman, 228–229
Angle, 63, 66, 68
Annunciator lights, 194
Aperture, 29, 30
Arc, 51, 52
Artificial light sources, 85
Aspect ratio, 25, 26
Assemble editing, 192, 196–197
Assistant director, 225
Audience identification, 241
Audio, 6, 7. *See also* Sound
Audio cassette machines, 157
Audio feedback, 119
Audio generator, 13
Audio mixers, 14
    application of, 169, 171–172
    components of, 167–169
    functions of, 172–173
    operation of, 173–175
Audio operator, 122–123, 166–167
Audio pads, 169
Audio patch bay, 173
Audio production equipment, 156–157
Audio synthesizers, 136
Audiotape recorder (ATR), 156–157

Background light, 94, 98
Back light, 94, 96, 97
Back time, 225, 235
Barn doors, 88
Batteries, 38, 39
Beam splitter, 25, 27, 33

Beep tones, 214
Binocular view, 25
Black, 176, 178
Booms, 121
Breyer, Richard, 16
Brightness, 137, 139
Bulk erase, 157
Bumper, 231–232
Buses, 178, 179

Camera body, 25, 27
Camera control unit (CCU), 41, 42
Camera cranes, 39
Camera mount, 39–41
Camera operator, 51, 53
Capacitor, 110–112
Cardioid, 113, 114
Cartridge machine, 157
Cassettes, 157
Centering, 59, 60
Character generator, 13, 126, 127
Charge-coupled device (CCD), 33–35
Chip camera, 33
Chip chart, 22, 23
Close-up shot, 55–58
Color background, 176, 178
Color bars, 137–141
Color rendition, 23
Color saturation, 137, 139
Color temperature, 81
Commercial break, 232
Compact discs (CDs), 158
Composition, 46, 59–68
Condenser microphones, 110–113
Confidence head, 153
Content development, 247–248
Contrast, 22, 137, 139
Contrast ratio, 80

Control room, 10–11
Control room directing, 258, 259.
    See also Directing
Control track, 150, 153, 160, 196, 198
Controller, 192–193
Copyrights, 250
Countdown tape, 214
Crawl, 132, 134
Credit roll, 130, 131, 133
Crew call list, 221, 222
Cue cards, 209, 229
Cues, 174–175, 225–227, 232
Cuts, 178, 187
Cuts-only editors, 195

Demonstration program, 243
Depth illusion, 72, 74
Depth of field, 30–32, 78, 79
Diaphragm, 29
Diffused light, 83–85
Digital video effects (DVE), 135
Directing
    decision making in, 271–272
    procedures for, 259–271
    production, 258–259
    talent, 258
Direct light, 83
Direction of movement, 63, 67
Director, 220–221, 254–258
Director's triangle, 259–262
Discussion program, 243
Dissolve, 179–181, 186–188
Distortion, 5–6
Distribution system, 1–2
Documentary, 243
Dolly, 51, 52
Downstream keyer (DSK), 181, 183, 185

Dramatization, 243
Dynamic microphones, 110, 112

Editing. *See also* Directing
  decision making in, 271–272
  postproduction, 10
  procedures, 215–216, 269–272
  process of, 189
Editing systems, 14, 15
  advanced, 194–195
  components of, 189–194
  methods and procedures of, 195–
    199
Editor, 254–258. *See also* Director
Electrical power, 38, 87–91
Electromagnetic spectrum, 80
Electronic field production (EFP)
  description of, 205–207
  postproduction, 213–217
  process, 207–212
Elipsoidal spotlight, 90, 91
Engineer, 225, 228
Equalizer, 117
Erase head, 148
Evaluation, 251, 274–280
Exposure, 44
Extreme close-up, 55, 57, 58
Eyes in the upper third, 59, 61–63

Fade, 187
Fader bar, 179
Field production, 7, 9, 205. *See also*
    Electronic field production
Field recording, 145–146
Field of view, 27, 29
File tapes, 198–199
Fill light, 94, 96
Film, 162
Film multiplexer, 161, 162
Filters, 30
Financial resources, 242
Fisheye lens, 27
Fishpoles, 116, 117, 121–122
Floor director, 221, 225
Floor monitor, 220
Floor plans, 264, 266–267
Fluid head, 210
Focal length, 27
Focus ring, 30, 44–46
Font styles, 132
Footcandles, 75
Foreground, 63, 66
Format, 243–244
Frame, 22
Framing, 46
Fresnel spotlight, 89–90
F-stop, 29

Generators, 13
  advanced video, 135–136
  audio, 136
  explanation of, 126–128

graphics systems and, 131–132
  monitoring systems and, 127, 136–
    137
  test signals and, 137–142
Gen-lock, 178
Graphic crawl, 132, 134
Graphics
  considerations in creating, 133–135
  developments in, 128–129
  functions of, 129–131
  generators, 131–133 (*see also*
    Generators)
  role of, 128
Graphics pad, 128

Hand microphone, 116, 121
Headphones, 119
Headroom, 59, 60, 62, 63
Heat, 92
Helical scan machines, 151
High definition television system
    (HDTV), 5, 25
Housing, 87–88
Hypercardioid microphones, 113,
    114

Illumination, 72
Image sensor, 33–35
Incident light, 75, 77–78
Input gain, 122, 148
Insert editing, 192, 198–199
Instant replay, 3
Intercom systems, 42, 235
Iris, 29

Kelvin scale, 81
Key, 181, 184–186, 188
Key light, 93–95
Kinescope process, 8, 10

Lamp, 87
Lavalier microphones, 115–116, 120–
    121
Leader, 213
Lens, 25, 27–30
Light
  diffused, 83–85
  direct, 83–84
  functions of, 71–75
  properties of, 75–85
  sources of, 85–87
Lighting equipment, 87–91
Lighting techniques, 93–97
Light meter, 75, 77
Limbo effect, 101
Lip sync, 108
Live on tape production, 8
Live production, 8
Location selection, 248
Locking down, 212
Logging tapes, 269
Look space, 63–65

Magnetic recording and playback, 3,
    4, 7, 145
  equipment, 148
  operating mode and procedures
    for, 153–156
  retrieval process, 152–153
  storage process, 148–152
Master control room, 222
Master tape, 189
Medium shot, 54–56
Message identification, 241
Microphones, 107
  categories of, 109–113
  criteria for selecting, 119–120
  description of, 109
  monitoring system for, 119
  placement of, 120–122
  signal processing for, 117–118
  types of, 114–117
  using for natural sound, 123–124
Minilights, 88
Mix/effects bus, 179
Mixing, 166–175
Moller, Peter, 16
Monitoring systems, 127, 136–137
Multicamera production, 10
Music Television (MTV), 130
Music videos, 108

Natural light sources, 85
Natural sound, 123–124
Neutral-density filters, 30

Objective perspective, 54
Off-line editing, 193, 270
Omnidirectional microphones, 113–
    115
On-line editing, 193, 271
Open-reel audio recorder, 149, 150,
    156–157
Optical system, 25, 27–33
Oscillator, 139
Oscilloscope, 136
Overmodulation, 142

Pacing, 267–268
Paint box, 135
Pan, 15, 46
Pedestal, 47, 50
Performance program, 243
Perspective, 53–54
Pickup devices, 12–13
Pickup patterns, 112–113
Picture and sound monitoring, 136
Pixels, 35
Playback heads, 149, 150, 152–153
Portable light kits, 88
Postproduction, 10, 213–217
Potentiometer (pot), 122, 169, 170
Power sources, 38, 87–88, 91–92
Preamplifier, 117

Preproduction, 207–208, 249
Preroll, 151–152, 160
Presence, 112
Press conference lighting, 97, 99–100
Producer, 2, 219–220, 239–251
Production
    categories of, 7–11
    development of, 3
    field, 205–217, 245
    scheduling, 246
    studio, 7, 8, 219–235, 245
    tools of, 2, 12–15
Production assistants, 249
Production machine
    direction of, 258–259
    explanation of, 2, 16–17
Production manager, 221
Production plan, 243–245
Production process
    description of, 11–16
    evaluation of, 251
    preparation for, 247–251
    research and planning for, 240–247
Program output, 183
Props, 103

Quadruplex videotape recording,
    151, 159

Raw tape, 206
Realistic settings, 101–102
Receiver, 6
Receptive perspective, 54
Record heads, 148–150
Recue, 157
Reference tones, 137, 139, 141–142
Reflected light, 75, 78
Reflector, 88, 211
Remote production, 205–206
Research, 240, 247–248
Resolution, 23–25
Retrieval process, 13–14, 152–153.
    See also Storage and retrieval
    systems
Ribbon microphones, 109–111
Riding gain, 172
Rough cut, 270, 271
Rule of thirds, 59, 61
Rundown sheet, 221, 224
Running time, 224, 225, 235

Scoop, 90
Scrims, 88
Scripts
    commercial, 207, 208
    handling, 262, 263
Segment time, 222–223
Selective focus, 32, 63
Set dressing, 103
Set light, 94

Setting
    functions of, 101
    influence of lighting on, 73, 75, 76
    selection of, 102–104, 248
    types of, 101–102
Shiny board, 211
Shook, Frederick, 247, 254
Shotgun microphones, 116, 117
Shots, 22
    close-up, 55–57
    extreme close-up, 55, 57, 58
    medium, 54–56
    moving, 57–59
    wide, 54–56
Signal monitoring, 136
Single-camera productions, 10
Slates, 161, 214
Slides, 162
Slow motion, 3, 146, 153, 156
Sound
    process of gathering, 119–123
    system for, 108–119
    using natural, 123–124
    in visual medium, 107–108
Sound bites, 124
Sound effects, 136
Sound sweetening techniques, 109
Sound waves, 108
Special effects systems, 14
Spot reels, 196–197
Squawk box system, 220
Staging, 101, 258
Stereo, 150
Still frame, 153
Storage and retrieval systems, 13–14
    background of, 144–145
    equipment, 156–161
    functions of, 147–148
    role of magnetic recording and
        playback process in, 145, 148–
        156
Story telling, 66, 69
Storyboards, 264, 265
Studio floor plan, 221, 223
Studio lighting systems, 88–89
Studio production, 7, 8
    description of, 219–221
    process of, 221–235
Subjective perspective, 54
Super, 179
Switcher, 188–189
Switching, 175. See also Video
    switchers
Sync generator, 42

Takes, 178, 187
Talent, 249, 258
Tape counter, 154
Tape speed, 150
Target, 34

Technical director, 188–189
Telephoto lens, 27, 28
Teleprompters, 229, 230
Telestrator, 130
Television, 3, 5–7
Test signal generator, 137
Test signals, 137–142
Three-point lighting, 93–94
Tilt, 46, 47
Time calculations, 234–235, 242
Time code, 293
Time-base corrector (TBC), 153
Timetable, 246
Tint, 137, 139
Track dollies, 39
Tripod, 39, 40
Truck, 51
Tubes, 35–36
Turntables, 157–158

U-matic tape format, 151, 152, 159
Umbrellas, 88
Unidirectional microphones, 113, 114

Vectorscope, 136
Verna, Tony, 17
Video, 6, 7
Video cameras
    components of, 25–42
    electronic process of, 21–25
    operation of, 43–53
    telling story with, 66, 69
    use of, 53–68
Video display adjustment, 137–139
Video switchers, 14
    components of, 176–185
    function of, 176
    methods and procedures for using,
        183, 186–189
Videotape, 145–146
Videotape cartridge player, 230
Videotape formats, 146, 158–160
Viewfinder, 35–38
Volume unit (VU) meter, 118, 139,
    141, 142, 169

Walk-through, 211
Waveform monitors, 136–139
White balance, 30, 44, 81–82
Wide-angle lens, 27, 28
Wide shot, 54–56
Wipe, 181–183, 186, 188
Wireless microphone, 120
Work tapes, 193

Zoom, 15, 47–49
Zoom lens, 29